FIGARO'S
FLEET

FIGARO'S FLEET

RAYMOND REAGAN BUTLER

NONSUCH

Published by Nonsuch Publishing in 2008

Nonsuch Publishing is an imprint of The History Press Limited

Cirencester Road, Chalford, Stroud, Gloucestershire, GL6 8PE
www.thehistorypress.co.uk

Copyright © Raymond Reagan Butler, 2008

The right of Raymond Reagan Butler to be identified as the Author of this Work has been
asserted in accordance with the Copyrights, Designs & Patents Act 1988.

British Library Cataloguing in Publication Data:
A catalogue record for this book is available from the British Library

ISBN 978 1 84588 636 3

Typesetting and origination by The History Press
Printed and bound in Great Britain

Contents

Acknowledgements

In England, I am indebted to the staff of the British Library, the British Museum, the Leamington Spa public library and Dr Nicolas Hiley. At The History Press, I would like to thank my editor Jo Howe and Simon Hamlet for their help at all times. In Paris, my thanks go to the staff of the Archives National, the Bibliotheque National, and the Carnavelet museum. On a personal note, I owe a debt to Colette Gernet, Louis Mireaux, Emile Troyat and Louise Levron.

My greatest debt, of course, is to the 'hero' of my book, P.A. Caron de Beaumarchais, whose spirited and flamboyant letters are its backbone.

I

The King's Spy

In 1770, King Louis XV's censor had banned Beaumarchais's comedy *The Barber of Seville* from being staged in Paris for two years, since its inflammatory potential was easily recognized.[1] However the text had been all the more talked about because of it, with censorship increasing aristocratic curiosity and private readings in fashionable salons becoming all the rage. Afterwards, as the creator of the irrepressible barber 'Figaro,' Beaumarchais came to be known as that character's 'father;' but he had in himself so much of the spirit of that astute and able rogue, that many would have thought of him by that name, as I do myself—hence the title of my book.

The shadowy individuals who directed Beaumarchais's secret life as an undercover agent may also have thought of him as this character; for 'Figaro' seems the perfect codename for a spy—although I doubt if it was ever used as his alias, being, perhaps, too obvious. But the author was so much his own creation in real life—the perfect 'servant' who nevertheless cleverly spends his energy in undermining the existing state of society—that I always think of him as the moving spirit behind the events this book recounts.

There was, of course, a gap in their ages; for Figaro remains forever young while, at the beginning of this adventure in 1775—the year that Beaumarchais arrived in London—he was forty-two years old. He was a stout, coarsely handsome man, grey-haired but merry-eyed, a man with the face of one that had lived and prospered by his fertile wits. For, throughout the previous twenty years, he had played an astonishing number of roles beyond the spheres of politics, espionage and the theatre. Trained to be a watchmaker like his father, he had invented a new escapement that allowed for greater accuracy and a smaller size in pocket watches. When a rival watchmaker, Lapaute, claimed the credit for its invention, the injured Beaumarchais taught himself law in order to argue his own defence, brilliantly winning his case and afterwards being totally vindicated by the Academy of Science, who had earlier granted him a patent. With an ear for music and for composition, he had turned himself into a professional music-master, with such success that he had been hired to teach the disagreeable daughters of King Louis XV, no less, to play the violin.

Always a wit, he started writing sketches in 1758 for the amusement of high society; but to enter their circles on his own terms he had purchased the 'ennobling' honorary title of 'Secretary to the King.'[2] Two years later he had managed to procure the even more imposing style of 'Lieutenant-General of the King's Hunt,' which—until as late as 1785—would allow him to judge any misdemeanours connected with that office, but which, more importantly, would allow him to enter the lower reaches of the court hierarchy.

The '*Sieur*' de Beaumarchais was, of course, equally his own creation as far as names went, since he had simply added the style of his first wife's property to that of his pedestrian surname. Such an elegant addition looked as impressive on a theatre programme as it did on a business contract, and would his name have rung with quite the same resonance had he remained plain Pierre Augustin Caron?

Beaumarchais had also shown a remarkable talent for business, becoming a jack of all trades—with even stronger shades of 'Figaro' here—to a grandee-banker, who despite his high-born connections, was a man of dubious character. But exactly how the tyro financier had managed to extract 50,000 *ecus* from the old miser before he died in such mysterious circumstances in 1770 was a question that would afterwards intrigue le Tout Paris, when the banker's young, aristocratic heir later challenged the old man's settlement on Beaumarchais in open court.

The marriage to his first wife, Marie-Catherine Aubertin, was also a matter of some conjecture in high society. There was a strong rumour that he had stolen land from her along with its title, and there was even a possibility that he had poisoned her, after having secured her estate.[3] These charges remained unproved, of course, but still, 'no smoke without fire …'

The man was an undoubted force and was certainly to be reckoned with. After making—and losing—at least two fortunes before he was forty years old, he had been grudgingly accepted at court as an aristocrat of the 'mercantile order.' But with a highly developed flair for intrigue, Beaumarchais had also proved himself to be an accomplished cloak-and-dagger man. For what else was he doing in Spain between April 1764 and March 1765 if not spying? What point was there in travelling to that benighted country if not to obtain the secrets of the 'enlightened' despot Carlos III?[4] Their family compacts made Carlos an ally of sorts to the French king, but an eye had to be kept upon a monarch so staunchly anti-clerical, and who was intent upon pushing through the most radical reforms—not only throughout his empire, but also in Spain. Such 'improvements' would sweep away the most ancient privileges of his nobles. Naturally, his fellow European rulers viewed him with suspicion, for what would become of them if his example spread? As the social observer, Beaumarchais was swift to point this out in the monograph on Spain that he afterwards submitted to the Duc de Choiseul,[5] then foreign minister. It was a strange contribution from a man who later adopted the same brand of radicalism that had motivated the innovative Spanish monarch.

At that time, it has to be admitted, Beaumarchais was intent upon social advancement, to which he devoted much of his prodigious energy; although the self-styled aristocrat could behave very foolishly at times. After the successful productions of his sentimental drama *Eugenie* in 1767 and the even more maudlin *Les Deux Amies* in 1770, he had ventured his reputation on the revolutionary play, *The Barber of Seville*—a total fiasco as an opera, though played with some success later as a comedy. By the mere act of writing it, the author seemed to be cutting away the rungs of the social ladder he was trying to ascend, even as he climbed it! Yet the theatrical diversion had, perversely, amused his aristocratic victims, and so they continued to indulge him.

But, in the real world, he should never have quarrelled with a genuine nobleman over the sexual favours of an actress. What choice had she, other than to accept the support of an authentic blueblood, whatever her feelings for Beaumarchais as a lover? His rival in the affair, the Duc de Chaulnes,[6] had been jailed in the castle of Vincennes for creating a public affray, which was grim enough; but Beaumarchais had known the inside of the Fort l'Eveque— the 'actors' prison—which was far worse.

He had been fully aware of the particular danger in challenging a genuine nobleman, for he had explored the subject of social inequalities in many essays and sketches. In the near-feudal society in which he moved, even a brilliant man like himself would never, at any time, be more than a favoured pet, indulged by his betters. The best he could hope for was to act as a useful factotum to an aristocratic patron, good for carrying out any mission, however demeaning or underhand the task turned out to be. Despite the fact that a servant could prove himself to be the moral and intellectual superior of his master, he would always be socially inferior to him, and therefore forever at a disadvantage.

He certainly understood that state of affairs better than most and, as a secret agent, he had always been aware of how much he needed to 'watch his back' and be alert to danger at the French and Spanish courts. More so at Versailles perhaps, for although the courtiers flattered him, without *exactly* mocking him for his social pretensions, in their eyes he would never be more acceptable to them than as a man of unique resources, to be made use of. He would be humbled whenever he overstepped the boundaries, even as they patted him on the back for his achievements.

This was certainly true of the relationship between Beaumarchais the spy and his aristocratic controller, Antoine de Sartine[7]—the most feared of King Louis XV's servants—being his most efficient and ruthless Lieutenant of Police; the last in a long line. Unique, too, among his kind in that he had set up a specialized organization within his own force; an undercover operation designed to keep important courtiers and the King's closest ministers—and even the monarch himself—under close surveillance. He had quickly set Beaumarchais to work for him, realizing his talent for such work.

But Beaumarchais, always trying to play his own cards and very soon proving himself a top player in the espionage game, had handled the tricky situation with finesse. At the same time that he had served under the dreaded Minister of Police, he had also begun to act covertly, under Louis XV's personal direction, in what was known as 'the King's Secret'—the questionable activities of which were concealed from the monarch's official intelligence services. It was an organization originally formed by King Louis to spy upon his own ministers, even as they plotted in his name, but which had developed into a labyrinthine network of separate yet interrelated units by the end of his reign, with each unit being—for the most part—ignorant of the others' business.

In the final years of Louis XV's long reign, the 'Secret' had developed into an interminable game of political hide and seek; involving the King, his ministers, and above all his ambassadors, whom Louis always sought to keep in ignorance of his true plans. Yet the 'Secret' had, in reality, been little more than a diversion for him, for he played political games largely to keep boredom at bay, suffering greatly from the tedium of kingship. Spying had been little more for him than an amusing exercise in diplomatic malice, but Beaumarchais had played a considerable part in the game.

During the time he had languished in jail, with regard to the affair of the actress, the lawsuit involving the eminent banker Paris-Duverny[8] and his heir had been reopened. Goezman,[9] the judge in the case, had quickly settled it in favour of the banker's nephew, the Comte de La Blache,[10] and as a result of this Beaumarchais's property had been seized as partial repayment to the successful litigant. But worse was to follow when, freed from Fort l'Eveque, he was almost immediately charged with attempting to corrupt the course of justice, since the judge's wife had accepted gifts from him, which could be seen as a bribe. In truth it had been necessary for Beaumarchais to use her as a go-between in order to be granted a vital audience with her husband.

To the astonishment of friends and enemies alike, since he was only following a well-worn precedent, the judge then sued him for attempted bribery, despite the fact that his wife had been equally culpable. This was clearly seen as a further attempt to embarrass a man who had on occasion embarrassed the administration and, since Goezman was an appointee of an unpopular ministry, the case took on a political dimension. It was seen as a challenge to the incumbent chief minister, Maupeou,[11] Goezman's patron. Again, the case went against Beaumarchais and, on 27 February 1774, he was found guilty, officially 'blamed,' and sentenced to a 'civil death.'

As a 'non-person' Beaumarchais had left for England in April 1774, in order to escape a return to an even grimmer prison than the one from which he had recently been released. In London, seizing an opportunity he thought would help him to be rehabilitated by the King, he had offered to suppress a libel printed there against the last mistress of Louis XV, the ex-prostitute Madame Du Barry.[12] Despite succeeding brilliantly in this, a personal triumph that would have automatically reinstated him at the Court of Versailles, he had ultimately failed because—unknown to him at the time—Louis XV had died of the smallpox within a month of his spy's arrival in London. His successor was not interested in an ex-whore's reputation.

But Beaumarchais, always quick to grasp the nettle of opportunity, had swiftly written a political paper calculated to engage the new king's attention. This radical analysis, 'Ideas on the Recall of the *Parlements*,'[13] was submitted to King Louis XVI, who—despite being notoriously slow on the uptake— seems to have immediately recognized the monograph's significance. It certainly helped to reinstate Beaumarchais in the new king's estimation, and even though he was still seen as an 'unwelcome person' at the French court, it was accepted that he would still have his 'uses' away from it; if only, for the time being, as a spy.

The young king, though, had little taste for espionage. Morally uncomplicated for a Bourbon prince, he had responded both sensibly and promptly once he had fully explored the structure of his grandfather's undercover network. With no liking for subterfuge, he had quickly seen that such covert practices served no useful purpose, and might even jeopardize his new administration. So he had set about disbanding the 'Secret' while at the same time shutting down the old regime's police department, a focal point of corruption in itself. Antoine de Sartine had speedily been deprived of the extraordinary power he had wielded as Controller of Police, and he had then been fobbed off with the Ministry of Marine.

Yet Sartine, an astute and guileful politician, kept something of his old authority even when sidelined and, influenced by him, the inexperienced Louis XVI retained a section of his grandfather's 'Secret.' Guided by Sartine, he insisted for the time being upon Beaumarchais continuing some of the secret missions he had carried out so successfully for the old king (which Sartine persuaded Beaumarchais to do as a means of rehabilitating himself at court, despite the fact that he had come to loathe the task). Then, when Beaumarchais agreed—for how could he refuse if he wished to rise in the young king's favour?—Sartine made it plain to his spy that he owed the new king's continuing interest to his good offices alone. In this way, Beaumarchais was successfully turned into Sartine's 'man': his 'factotum,' his 'Figaro.'

But his 'Figaro' was also determined to function independently whenever possible, and he tried to sidetrack his 'benefactor' at every turn. Although when his stratagems failed, as they sometimes did, he would be reduced to making personal appeals to the young king, asking him to recognize his particular merit, along with his previous good service, and to give him an opportunity—of any sort—to work at a higher political level.

Louis XVI, however, ignored these pleas with the dogged intractability that he would show throughout his tragic reign whenever a breakthrough judgement was to be made—although he possibly acted in this instance at the behest of ministers who wished to keep the *arriviste* Beaumarchais out of the more elevated reaches of politics. Yet the essentially conservative Louis's decision may well have been his own, since he must have recognized that one of his best 'secret' advisers was politically too radical for the good of the system that Louis had inherited. As a talented locksmith himself, the King might well have appreciated the genius of Beaumarchais the expert watchmaker, but as a vacillating traditionalist, he could never trust Beaumarchais, the rogue adventurer.

Louis XVI was an absolute monarch and he could recognize subversion when he saw it, as he showed by his reluctance to allow any further productions of *The Barber of Seville*, appreciating the incendiary nature of its wit. To the last, Louis would remain puzzled by the enthusiasm of his courtiers for the play, since its stinging attacks upon the ruling class were comprehended perfectly by them, and yet they stood to applaud its most inflammatory speeches. Even his Queen[14] and his brother, the Comte d'Artois,[15] clamoured to see it!

As such, the young king, with his bovine temperament and leisurely judgement, thought it best to steer clear of Beaumarchais, even though he might well have benefited from listening to a man who had the ear of the public and was blessed with political wisdom.

But nothing could subdue Beaumarchais for long. Bursting with energy—his entire life fuelled by ambitious expectations—he wrote to King Louis XVI concerning the April visit to England, his letter being handed on by Sartine.

It was a typical mixture of his liveliness and swagger, with even a touch of risky condescension; for in order to 'facilitate the burden for the young monarch … should the exercise weary him,' Beaumarchais had simplified the layout of the letter in a way that might have given offence to a more sensitive nature.

He had provided a wide margin on the left side of his letter, which he called 'headings,' and which were enclosed within brackets. To the right was another wide margin, in which he hoped the inexperienced king would make suitable comments. The substance of his report lay between these two borders.

27 April 1775, to King Louis XVI

(My trip from Paris to London.)
> I charted a small boat for myself alone. Although the wind was quite contrary for the crossing, I had myself deposited upon the coast of England, fifteen leagues southwest of Dover. After a painful journey of seventeen hours, I landed in a town named Hastings,[16] from where I headed towards London.

(My search for libels printed there.)
> I.   I receive a threatening letter containing some verses that are insulting to your Majesties.
> II.   I show myself openly in London.
> III. I have an answer to an anonymous letter that I had inserted in the newspapers.
> IV.   My precautions for the future.
> V.   On the way I found that a certain Vignoles,[17] an unfrocked regular canon, publishes in London a scandalous newspaper, the contents of which, received from Paris through the normal mail-service in manuscript form, is returned there, now printed, through the same route.

I have shown the first fifteen pages to M. de Sartine. Astonishingly, one can read here in London everything that is done in Paris against the government, and which often vilely slanders Yourself and the Queen. In my next abstract I will point out the shortest way to destroy this viper's nest, without getting compromised, if Your Majesty so desires.

And he then directly broached a political issue that he hoped would interest the king and his ministers—far too rashly in the circumstances. He had been devoting himself to 'a nobler study, a more satisfying research' which would, he was sure, 'greatly enlighten' the King, when he had finished his fact-finding. He boasted that he had been assisted in his researches by the most important people in England, his 'name alone' having made him welcome within the different political parties. As a result, he had now studied the British establishment at such close quarters he 'could draw for Your

Majesty's eyes a striking, faithful and instructive picture,' having made a particular study of King George III[18] and his 'favourite, Lord Butte'[19] [sic].

Beaumarchais never made clear how closely he had come to the subjects of his study. The membership of the Court of St James was as large as that of Versailles, and was in many ways more formal in manner, with greater restrictions against a casual entry than at the French court, where anybody who was respectably dressed could watch the royal family at dinner. But as some members of the highest British nobility were often unacceptable to King George III and barred from his presence, Beaumarchais could only have gained entrance through being introduced into the palace by someone who was tolerable to the royal household. Yet at that time he seems to have been running in the company of the King's opposition party, towards whose more radical policies he was naturally more sympathetic.

He did not, in this first letter, enlighten the King as to the exact nature of his 'noble study,' seeking to pique his interest, perhaps; but, typically, after having bragged at length about his prowess as King Louis's 'eyes and ears' in London, and after crowing about his phenomenal success in London's high society, he ended this letter with a pathetic plea for the King's protection (although this practice was quite typical at a court notorious for its internecine squabbles). For all its mannered etiquette and the exquisite politeness for which it was famed, Versailles was a social and political minefield:

> Your Majesty will not abandon me, I pray, to the resentment and hatred of those ministers and courtiers who will certainly strive to ruin me, should they hear that something from me has reached Your Majesty without going through their channel.

It would seem that the people he wished to be protected from were his superiors; but so anxious was he on this score that he repeated himself almost word for word in a subsequent paragraph.

Beaumarchais also brought the king's attention to the mysterious Chevalier d'Éon,[20] who had come to his lodgings in some distress, seeking his 'friendship or his trust.'

The eccentric—many would have said 'deranged'—chevalier was also a former secret agent of King Louis XV, whom he had served for many years in that capacity. His first assignment having been at the Court of St Petersburg when he was eighteen—dressed in female clothing to such effect that he had been received by the Empress Elizabeth[21] as a woman. The deception was so convincing that 'Mademoiselle Lia de Beaumont' had even penetrated into the imperial bedchamber as a lady-in-waiting. It might have been Louis XV's idea of a joke to make the effeminate lad adopt a female disguise—in order to best spy upon the Russian court—but the chevalier himself seemed to have been uncertain of his true gender at this stage in his life.

He had, however, from 1762, been living in London as a man and under new orders from Louis XV, having been sent there officially as a temporary *chargé d'affaires* until the arrival of the official French ambassador. Having reverted to his masculine side on his return from Russia, d'Éon had astonishingly been permitted to serve King Louis on the battlefield, where he had proved himself a mettlesome combatant. As the temporary head of the diplomatic mission in London, he had also been under instructions to continue spying for his royal master, and as a result of his undercover work in London, a number of compromising papers had come into his hands; some of which were said to detail a scheme for a French invasion of the English south coast. To the consternation of his superiors, Éon refused to hand the papers over to the accredited ambassador, the Comte de Guérchy[22] when he arrived in London in 1762, claiming they were his personal property. He also refused to obey King Louis's order to revert to wearing female dress and 'to retire from public notice.'

Having spent an inordinate amount of money—through extravagant entertaining in the service of the Crown, he claimed—he had then demanded that all his debts should be settled and his expenses in London charged to the French embassy. When the ambassador refused these demands for payment unless Éon gave up the compromising papers, there ensued a lengthy and devious struggle between the two men.

There were determined efforts to seize Éon in order to capture the critical papers, and he was undeniably pestered and even hounded by security agents acting for the French embassy. The prolonged infighting hugely entertained the London public, since it was regularly reported in the press, and it ended with the chevalier bringing a charge against Guérchy of arranging to have him murdered—presumably as a menace to the diplomatic stability of his country.

As a result of this allegation, and since Éon could—to some extent—support his outlandish claim, the chief French representative at the court of King George III was humiliatingly hauled before an English judge accused of an 'assassination attempt upon the Chevalier d'Éon's person.' After a short trial in which both men fully aired their differences, to the prolonged delight of the public, a London grand jury brought in a 'true bill'[23] in favour of the chevalier in February 1764, and the ensuing scandal was a major embarrassment for both France and Britain.

George III, rather tardily, went to the aid of the French, and—advised by the 'finest legal counsel'—it was maintained that the English courts held no proper jurisdiction in the matter, with the result that King George could grant the French ambassador a *nolle prosequi*[24] decree and the case was quashed. Éon, recognising a legal evasion that left him dangerously exposed to further French attack, and alarmed for his continuing safety, retreated into his quarters in Brewer Street, Soho, where he was said to live in an atmosphere of rough masculinity and even fortification. His walls, it was rumoured, bristled with every type of weapon, both ancient and modern, for his defence.

But this was England, where the underdog was invariably championed and where eccentricity was cherished, and the Chevalier d'Éon was much to the popular taste. As dangerous with a sword as with his tongue and pen, he was treasured by the mob, and even more so after the debacle of the trial. They 'expressed themselves to be violently in his favour' and the vilified French ambassador only narrowly escaped with his life on a number of occasions, when threatened by outraged supporters of his 'victim'. Hostile crowds held up Guérchy's coach, threatening to drag him out and manhandle him and the windows of his official residence were repeatedly smashed, while his walls were daubed with obscene threats. The ambassador was relieved to be called back to France.

The chevalier was also extremely popular, however, because of the mystery of his sex. When the revelation of his 'girlhood' in St Petersburg reached London—with the arrival of a Russian aristocrat who recognized him as the former '*Mlle* Lia de Beaumont'—Londoners, always gambling mad, then commenced to wager enormous amounts of money as to his true gender. Both women and men tried to seduce him in an effort to gain 'inside' knowledge and there were numerous attempts to seize him by force, in order to haul down his breeches and examine the disputed parts. His life in London, by the time that Beaumarchais arrived in 1775, had for over a decade been one of bribery and deceit, and of violence against him. On the streets he walked surrounded by his personal 'bullies,' and he had on any number of occasions fought duels with challengers 'to defend his dignity,' for no one questioned his sex while he could still draw a sword.

But now he approached Beaumarchais for assistance, since he was badly in need of his diplomatic help; although when he broached the matter, Beaumarchais could only assure him that he had no mission concerning him, and was therefore not empowered to deal with his business. (Though what a coup it would be, if he could persuade the chevalier to return the infamous papers!)

In turn, Éon was very put out to find that Beaumarchais had not been charged with his return to France, for he had thought that a new monarch meant a fresh prospect of reconciliation. He dearly wished to see his 'sweet Burgundian lands' again, and to be able to revive his vines. 'I would have been back in my country a long time ago, if matters had been better ordered,' he told Beaumarchais; and the new king would have received all the important papers that were relative to the 'Secret' of his grandfather; the papers that, the chevalier warned, must not remain in England, 'however safely they are housed.'

To back up his claim at their first meeting, Éon showed Beaumarchais some copies of his correspondence with the Comte de Broglie,[25] one of the main secret agents of the late king, which were certainly disturbing. Éon also showed him a few samples of his even more sensitive communications with the Comte de Vergennes,[26] who was now the new king's Foreign Minister. As a special favour, the chevalier requested that Beaumarchais, on his return to Paris, should bypass his superiors and, instead, place these 'inflammatory' letters 'at the feet' of the Prince de Conti,[27] asking that the prince should speak up in his favour—for the prince was not only a Bourbon relation of the King, but also had a family connection with the chevalier.

Beaumarchais saw at once that the letters were spectacularly hazardous to the new French government, should they ever be made public. Vergennes, in particular, for all his polished diplomacy, was possessed of a burning hatred of Britain and, as this shone through his letters, their publication would be a serious embarrassment to the French court. Upon seeing that Beaumarchais was satisfactorily impressed, Éon was not slow to add a touch of blackmail to his demands; although, as he pointed out, his requirements were not excessive. All he wanted—for the moment anyway—was to be paid what was due to him; he had a position to keep up and London was an expensive city. One must eat, and political information was a source of ready money, particularly the sort that he had to offer to the enemy. But, beyond everything, all that the chevalier truly wished for was to be able to return to France, and to take his rightful place at the new court!

Beaumarchais was aware that the few examples Éon had shown him were only a lure; the man must be in possession of even more explosive material, and he must be handled with the greatest delicacy. He tried in vain to explain that Éon could expect no help from the Prince de Conti, who now 'lived in a state of philosophical estrangement from the Adminstration,' but he promised to bring the chevalier's predicament to the attention of his superiors on his return to France. Yet Éon, clinging to the belief that his best chance of amnesty lay through his influential—if unpopular—relations, refused to let Beaumarchais leave London without a package for the prince, 'whose protégé I once was.'

Strangely, despite understanding that if he were to obtain the chevalier's hoard of threatening correspondence it could only enhance his own precarious position, Beaumarchais ended his report to King Louis XVI by stating that:

I.   He did not wish to act as a go-between for the Chevalier d'Éon and the Prince de Conti, 'with the King's permission.'
II.   That Éon would be easy enough to bring back to France.
III. That Éon was undeniably a woman, but with the 'political pretensions of a man.'

Even the observant Beaumarchais had his blind spots, and the chevalier was a genuine enigma; many reporting that after spending hours in his company his gender remained in doubt. Beaumarchais was always aware of himself as a 'rare animal,' and he certainly recognized Éon as being an equally uncommon creature, but he totally failed to understand the very singular nature of the insanely conceited cross-dresser. Though, at that time, he could not have thought the matter of 'his' true sex to be all that important.

He was actually more concerned to arrive back safely in Paris, which he did on 23 April 1775, after a boisterous twenty-four hours on the wind-buffeted 'English Channel,' and after some very rough riding over French roads that could never be compared with the excellent highways of England.

II

'The Enigma of the Age'

By 14 July 1775, Beaumarchais was once again taking the road from Dover to London, using this time to deal expressly with the Chevalier d'Éon (a commission that he could not have anticipated). King Louis XVI had authorized him to accede to everything the prickly knight might demand, with reasonable precautions, if he would agree to give up all the incriminating documents, for which Éon would receive a pension of 12,000 *livres*. But it was to be stressed that, in return, the chevalier must surrender *all* the public documents that covered his political life in London into the custody of Beaumarchais.

In direct confrontation with the volatile chevalier, even the wily 'Figaro' found him difficult to deal with; Éon was consumed with a sense of persecution and the papers were his only leverage against a government that had consistently delayed the payment of an earlier pension. In theory, he had been in receipt of 12,000 *sous francs*[1] for many years, and half his financial troubles had arisen because these had so often been left unpaid. The only way he had ever been able to persuade his masters to honour their debts to him, in fact, was by threatening to reveal their secrets. So if he were now to be paid off without a certain guarantee of further instalments, and was no longer in possession of his bargaining counter, he would require considerably more money paid up front, in a lump sum, as security.

He named his price, and Beaumarchais said at once that his expectations were too high. 'He will have to come down,' he advised the Comte de Vergennes, who had charged him with the mission, 'and by quite a bit for us to arrive at an agreement,'—assuming, with his customary boldness, that he could speak for the minister.

These financial transactions aside, Beaumarchais had to proceed with added delicacy in his dealings with Éon for another reason; he was in constant contact with him, and yet must not appear to have any connection with the man. The English authorities had already noted Beaumarchais's presence in London for the second time in a few months, and he was busily keeping up the fiction that he was there only on private or commercial business. No secret agent had ever made himself so public as had the unstable Éon, and his company must always be avoided by others in the same line, for fear of exposure by association. Yet Beaumarchais was often forced into the chevalier's company, for he had not only been ordered to secure his cache of papers, he had also been charged to stop him duelling in public, by using whatever methods he could. If only to keep the notable swordsman from exterminating his enemies in defence of his 'secret'.

Apropos of which, Beaumarchais was also under orders to force Éon to obey the King's wishes on an even more delicate matter, and one that he knew would seriously tax the chevalier's fragile self-control. For although Vergennes had always addressed Éon as 'Monsieur' throughout his letters, it had been agreed at Versailles that the chevalier was to publicly announce that he was in reality a female, and should return to wearing 'suitable' clothing, as 'she' had at St Petersburg. As Vergennes wrote to Beaumarchais, it would be impossible for *Monsieur* d'Éon to take leave of the King of England, 'the revelation of her sex would not allow it. That would cover both Courts with ridicule.'

The fact that the chevalier had, for many years, been ignoring a previous command to return to wearing skirts was overlooked by the new king's advisers; but in fact it had been a major consideration in his long fight against the government, since—having once experienced it—he had no desire to surrender the heady freedom that came with masculinity. The new king, however—or perhaps more likely his counsellors—was adamant. The chevalier, however determined, could not hold on to his sword and breeches, and he must be persuaded of this 'for the lady's own good.' Beaumarchais, by using his most compelling arguments, Vergennes felt sure, would succeed where others had failed.

Although even Beaumarchais had argued, before setting off to carry out this disagreeable assignment, that what the King's advisers were demanding of the knight was unreasonable, if not unseemly.[2] How could the chevalier who, since his time as a shy young maiden at the Russian court had mutated into a captain of dragoons and a knight of the Royal Order of St Louis, submit his hard-won reputation to such humiliation?

But it was thought at the highest level that Éon should submit to this demand, as Beaumarchais was haughtily instructed—although no adequate reason was advanced for this requested change of gender. It was, perhaps, to more effectively emasculate a formidable adversary. The Comte de Vergennes was in no doubt that his 'Figaro' was the very man to persuade the *chevaliere* to sign the 'transaction,' as it was called; and which was to be signed in duplicate, without seal or witnesses.

'The *Sieur* de Beaumarchais is enlightened and prudent, and you know men,' wrote Vergennes, as adept at laying on flattery as the man he addressed. Forgetting that, in this particular case, Beaumarchais was supposedly dealing with a *woman*.

But the go-between had also been charged with a more sinister instruction, and one that was against his every instinct; for if his 'blandishments' were to fail, the obstinate Éon was to be 'summarily dealt with.' Assassins, it would seem, were once again to be procured and the chevalier done away with. Éon had, after all, proved false to his country, at least in the view of the government he had mocked so successfully. 'It is a very humiliating part to play, that of the exile with a varnish of treason,' Vergennes wrote to Beaumarchais, seeking to allay any qualms about official bloodletting that he may have felt.

Two days after writing to Beaumarchais on the subject of patriotic incorruptibility, the Comte de Vergennes was writing to the new French ambassador at the Court of St James, the Comte de Guines,[3] on a not dissimilar subject. In this letter, Vergennes exhorted the ambassador to convince King George III that the French government would never seek to take advantage of the difficulties Great Britain was then experiencing with her rebellious American colonies, who were daily becoming more encouraged to unite against the mother country. '... We would rather help Britain to solve her problems,'— the Foreign Minister wrote to de Guines, with a goodwill he would later abandon—'for the Spirit of Revolt, wherever it breaks out, will always give a dangerous example.'

Nevertheless, whilst earnestly assuring the British government of his country's non-involvement in their American unrest, the ambassador was told to monitor the progress of the growing revolution, as it was being reported in London; and if possible, at the highest level. Guines was particularly 'to take notice of the influence which Lord Chatham[4] will be able to gain over the King of England' as a direct result of the increasingly catastrophic developments in America. It was known in France that King George III, alarmed by the increasing friction between his government and the thirteen American colonies, and aware that his own obdurate policies were in some part responsible for this state of affairs, had reluctantly requested Chatham to return to government. Chatham was the most feared of all British ministers by the French, since he had been almost solely responsible for their crushing defeats in India and Canada during the Seven Years War.[5]

At the same time that Vergennes instructed his ambassador to reassure King George III of France's permanent neutrality in his American affairs, he was also suggesting that the Chevalier d'Éon—still in masculine guise—'might perhaps be able to procure some interesting information in this respect. That is, if you feel that you can indirectly get in touch with him.' As Vergennes correctly pointed out, Éon had acquired many highly-placed friends among the Opposition, 'which is not the worst channel through which to obtain information.'

There were, significantly, no instructions for the secret agent Beaumarchais to pursue this same line, at least by his unaided efforts. His operators thought, perhaps, that the place-seeker was still not entirely to be trusted: despite the fact that he was 'doing his chores well' (and not only in his own estimation). For by 14 July he had succeeded in getting all of Éon's papers into his hands; or at least those papers necessary for the French government to recover its peace of mind. They would, Beaumarchais assured his employers, be bound in an iron coffer, 'of which I will give the King the key.'[6]

Meanwhile, apart from this triumph, Beaumarchais was greatly enjoying his time in London. Apparently the reason for his reappearance in the capital so soon after his last visit, he wrote, was the 'great puzzle game' in high society. Despite his efforts to disassociate himself from the chevalier, he had been in the man/woman's company often enough to arouse suspicion. Was it, some people wondered maliciously, a very French 'affair of the heart'? But Beaumarchais managed to persuade important people, by extravagant flattery, that he was there simply because of his enthusiasm for the English way of life. '… Oh, this England, how I admire it! Such different matters, attitudes, even the method of constructing a house—different, different!'[7]

On the other hand, he knew that the British authorities still regarded him with suspicion, in which he also took a risky pleasure. 'I am charged with [carrying out] four missions at once,' he bragged—which may have been true, since he had informed his employers about many intrigues involving other London-based French exiles from the last King Louis's displeasure. Though whether it was true or not, his main concern for the moment was in getting Éon to comply with the orders from his government.

But the chevalier continued to object to the proposed change of gender, since it would mean that his public life would effectively be over. The most preferable of the London clubs, exclusively male, would certainly be closed to him, as would be the arena of 'Angelo's Fencing Academy'[8] (also open only to men), in which he had proved a star attraction. While, on the question of fashion, it was certainly the worst time to be dressed as a woman, with their towering wigs, wired skirts, ruffles, ruching and ornamentation of every kind. Queen Marie-Antoinette, by now the acknowledged arbiter of prevailing fashion, had much to answer for. The 'lady-knight' would look like a frigate 'dressed overall'!

Clinging to the remembrance of his past achievements as a male, the 'chevaliere' was also doggedly insistent upon King Louis XVI giving her written citations—for the sake of posterity—commending the military service 'she' had given to his grandfather (which had admittedly been outstanding, in the guise of either sex). Éon particularly wished, since this was the greatest of all the honours he had earned, to be allowed to wear the Royal Cross of St Louis on certain military anniversaries, on clothes of either gender. 'But you earned them as a captain of dragoons,' Beaumarchais reminded him; to be reminded, in turn, that the *chevaliere* had in her time been a very successful captain of dragoons, which Beaumarchais knew to be irrefutable; for the 'lady' had proved herself to be the boldest of men.

Beaumarchais pointed out as tactfully as he could, that the decoration had never before been given to a woman, but the '*chevaliere*' insisted that the same body had received it from the late king, and 'she' had earned it under fire. With regard to the medals, there was another condition attached to a return to France that Beaumarchais knew would be particularly contentious; for it had been decided that Éon would not be allowed to bring in any weapons or uniforms, in the event that 'she' might be tempted to revert to wearing them to the embarrassment of the government—and so the *chevaliere* could not retain these regimental mementos as a reminder of 'his' glorious past. This was an especially hard demand for Beaumarchais to make, since he knew by now that for Éon to give up his arms was to ask him to give up the most singular part of his character; he had lived by his prowess with weapons.

Beaumarchais, always sympathetic to the tyrannized, compromised on this, and he agreed to the *chevaliere* retaining one modest uniform and its accoutrements. But he stressed that this indulgence would only be acceptable if Éon were to regard them as a widow might remember the treasured effects of a departed husband, which was, he must have reasoned, true enough, for the *chevaliere* would be mourning the only real 'man' in her life, her departed alter ego. As 'The Enigma of the Age,' d'Éon had never been known to be romantically involved with anybody of either sex, expressing a wary distaste for any sort of physical intimacy.

But Beaumarchais was always persuasive, and the papers had been given up, with Éon agreeing to seek no further quarrel with his government, and also accepting that he must go back into a woman's 'narrow world.' Beaumarchais attempted to persuade 'her' that she could still render King Louis XVI valuable service in this new role, since a female could take certain advantages that were denied to men, being now acceptable in different quarters. But the *chevaliere* recognized that she would never again be trusted 'as a woman.' She had been anonymous in Russia, and nobody had known her curious history, whereas 'the whole world' was now in possession of it.

When Éon finally agreed to be 'muzzled' by accepting his former gender, it was a considerable triumph for Beaumarchais; and when it was made public, the scandal convulsed bourgeois society on both sides of the channel.

That had been in the summer, and Monsieur was now officially 'Mademoiselle' d'Éon. Although no impartial authority had ever been called in to examine the lady-man's disputed parts.[9]

With that mission successfully accomplished, Beaumarchais was growing daily more occupied with what, to him, was something far more meaning-ful—nothing less than the 'nobler study, the more satisfying research' that he had already mentioned in his notes to King Louis XVI. The idea had, perhaps, been growing in his thoughts since before arriving in London, but his exposure to the *chevaliere's* many prominent English friends, including some blue-blooded freemasons and members of the 'Lodge of Immortality'[10] in the Strand, had helped to develop it further. Upon being welcomed into the house of the notorious radical and political agitator, John Wilkes,[11] whose home was a hub of secret activities in the capital, and a meeting place for the British revolutionary group known as the 'Friends of America,'[12] the plan had taken its final shape.

An English 'admiral,' Lord Ferrars,[13] played an important role in the activi-ties of the 'Friends of America', and he would become one of Beaumarchais's most important counsellors after they had been introduced to each other by Éon (to whom the peer had made loans secured on the possibility of one day receiving the *chevaliere's* secret papers). It was his lordship's willingness to blackmail his own government in the just cause of the American rebel colonists that had first made a strong impression upon Beaumarchais. For an aristocrat, and a member of the establishment at the highest level, to side with men who were seeking to free themselves from the very system that he served excited Beaumarchais greatly, and so he gave the 'admiral' his earnest concentration.

Yet he was still not entirely committed to throwing his own brand of fuel on to the conflagration about to incinerate British power in America. Drawn to the democratic ideal, the sparks had certainly been lit from the time he had conceived *The Barber of Seville*, but the full blaze of his feelings would burst into flame only after he had met up with a man he came to call his 'second self,' a radical writer of considerable talent, and whose egalitarian ideas would closely match his own. He met this agitator at John Wilkes's house also, and it was this man who would prove to be his earliest source of inspiration.

Arthur Lee,[14] the man Beaumarchais called his 'Virtuous American'—that is, until he grew to know him better—was one of four sons of a prominent Virginian family. Educated at Eton and the University of Edinburgh, study-ing science, literature and medicine, he had obtained his M.D. degree in 1764, afterwards travelling in Europe before returning to Virginia. He had resided in London since 1768, ostensibly to study law, but his real interests had always been in the field of politics and in writing about the art of policy making. In the pursuit of which he had plunged enthusiastically into the par-liamentary life of the capital, bringing it vividly to life in a series of articles of increasing acidity, as he became less and less enamoured of the level of debate in political circles (particularly when the increasing concerns of his fellow Americans were under discussion). As a result of these venomously sarcastic 'Junius Americanus Letters,'[15] in which he laid open the British political system for the sake of his readers back home, Arthur Lee had won a considerable reputation with some emerging political leaders in America.

He was an 'ambitious man; impetuous, witty, talkative, fond of scheming and intriguing,' and so possessed of all the qualities and defects to please a man like Beaumarchais, who shared many of his idiosyncrasies.[16] The two radicals had immediately hit it off, and they were soon conspiring together in intense conversations behind locked doors. The main theme of these discussions being the increasing need for the political and civil liberty of Lee's countrymen, and it was out of these conversations that 'the seed' of secret French aid to the American rebels 'was sown.'[17]

He soon learned that himself and Lee were not alone in pursuing this particular scheme. As he reported back to Versailles, a private subscription to aid the American colonists had already opened 'at the house of two of the wealthiest merchants' in the capital, where all the 'malcontents of London' were donating gold to send to them. A fund was also being raised to pay for military supplies, which—he had been assured—the 'liberty loving' Dutch were willing to send them. Beaumarchais had at once seen the wider possibilities of this scheme should his own countrymen decide to follow the same line, but on a more extensive scale. The harm that could be done to English authority in their American possessions would be greater than engaging them in open warfare!

The dissenting London merchants, he learned, also had their covert supporters in Portugal, '… in the very council of the King of that country.'[18] They were all of them scheming to prevent the Portuguese from settling their political differences with their enemies, the Spaniards, who were then in an uneasy truce with each other. For if the conspirators could succeed in breaking this it might encourage a new war between them, and such a war, as Beaumarchais also reasoned, would soon draw Great Britain into it.

For the British would have to take the side of their oldest ally, Portugal, to honour an ancient treaty between the two countries, and by sending their troops to the Iberian Peninsular they would lose vital manpower. All the fighting men in Portugal would be drained away from the developing showdown with the colonial Americans, leaving the colonists in a stronger position. Such repercussions would be catastrophic for King George III's cause, and would 'even more surely destroy the present ministry,' leading to the fall of the King's party; which was, perhaps, the 'constant object' of the London-based merchant plotters.

Lee even boasted that Spain had already received two American 'ambassa-dors' (from the Second Continental Congress).[19] Beaumarchais realized that, in his eagerness to involve the French in the Anglo-American controversy, Lee would exaggerate any situation that could help his cause, but he approved of this, since it was no more than he himself would have done in the circum-stances. In the early stages of their association he undoubtedly shared much of Lee's viewpoint, in that it was the *political* value of any projected financial aid that would be of lasting importance.

Yet Beaumarchais also quickly realized that any complications surround-ing aid to the Americans might be turned to the policy-making profit of the French. For while his government could never risk direct dealings with the rebellious Americans, or to side openly with them, any covert effort by the French would lead to a strengthening of the revolutionaries' resolve to free themselves from British influence, and this should be encouraged. There might be no territorial gains for the French, but as a result of their interfer-ence at this level a day would dawn when neither the French *nor* the British would hold sway between the American east coast and the Mississippi river. France had already lost her place on the northern continent, due to her mili-tary weakness, but the arrogant British could now also be dislodged from their possessions, and this could be achieved by surreptitiously arming the rebels, whilst giving them secret subsidies to aid them in their struggle. By these means, the French could win a unique war against their most ancient enemy without actually setting foot upon a battlefield!

III

'This Little Sowing ... '

In pursuit of this new undertaking, Beaumarchais decided upon a change of master, and he now sought to make the all-important Comte de Vergennes his sole channel of information to King Louis XVI. Through the exclusive agency of the foreign minister he was convinced that he would have a better chance to 'act upon the mind' of the young monarch—although he must, of course, still protect his back, and a written statement had to be drawn up and given to Sartine, assuring him of his servant's continuing fidelity. '… He should always believe that he is my unique confidant,' 'Figaro' assured his new master.[1]

His humble approach to Vergennes had been immediately successful, with the fleshy, imposing foreign minister (more majestic in his bearing than the King he served) responding warmly to his overtures. Vergennes had, in fact, been on the look-out for exactly such a man as Beaumarchais, and very soon it was as if the two 'had made a pact together.' They were bonded by their mutual hatred of Britain, whom they both saw as a bully,[2] and by an equal enthusiasm for agitating her—without the dangers inherent in direct confrontation.

Beaumarchais, however, was only blowing upon a guttering flame, for the Comte de Vergennes, more than most people in power, had never given up hope of drubbing the British in a new contest. From the start of his ministry, then only a few months old, he had followed much the same foreign policies as the Duc de Choiseul,[3] with regard to the fulfilment of this ambition. Having come to power too late to save France from humiliation in the Seven Years War, Choiseul had begun to build up what survived of the army and the navy, even as his government started to negotiate terms with the victorious British at the so-called 'Peace of Paris' in 1763[4]—a treaty that had left a lingering resentment in the French national consciousness, after a war in which the British had robbed their country of its most precious possessions in India, Africa and North America. Until his forced retirement in 1770, the Duc de Choiseul had placed great hope in the feasibility of a renewed war against Britain, possibly with the support of Spain. It was his failure to sell this policy to King Louis XV that had helped bring about his political downfall.

Vergennes, upon inheriting the foreign ministry, had taken up and pursued these same aims, his main ambition being to launch one more war of revenge against the country that had so humiliated his own. But, advised to do so with extreme caution by the Comptroller-General of Finances, Turgot,[5] who opposed spending money on any project that did not guarantee a one hundred per cent certainty of success, Vergennes moved more slowly than had the fiery Choiseul. Yet he was a man well-qualified for the task: 'Devoted to his duty, gifted with a subtle intellect, unscrupulous when the needs of France seemed to require duplicity, Vergennes hovered on the fringe of greatness.'[6] All that the minister needed to make his name resound throughout the chronicles of the age was a proper opportunity, and this opportunity may well have arisen with the events then taking place in America. Taking all this into consideration, Beaumarchais had decided that he was the very man to help the minister achieve his place in history.

Indeed, he was so enthusiastic in this cause that, for the first time in his political career, the normally wary schemer kept few secrets from his master. Even the letters he wrote to other ministers were first to be seen by Vergennes—an act of goodwill that was not reciprocated—and, from June to December 1775, there was a period of concentrated communication between the two men.[7] The convolutions of their relationship grew more intricate by the month, but the core of their association was always the question of the policy of secret aid to the Americans. There has been a long-standing controversy as to who actually instigated this policy, yet it is all there in 'Figaro's' letters to his new master—and, through him—to King Louis XVI.

The fact that Beaumarchais, with no proper position in the political hierarchy, should have aroused the minister to the extent that he did is a testament to his powers of persuasion. Vergennes—however keen a patriot—was considered to be nothing more than a career diplomat by his fellow ministers. Regarded as a man who would never overstep the mark, his growing interest in the developing resistance in America was seen as being completely out of character, for on all other reckoning he was regarded as a 'blinding reactionary,' a 'hypocritical and intolerant man.'

But Beaumarchais had always the measure of his patron, and he played upon his pride and patriotism superbly. His side of the correspondence reveals him at his most manipulative, with the servant constantly outsmarting the master. For example:

September 22 1775

For you alone, M. le Comte,

M. Sartine gave me back the paper yesterday, but said nothing to me of the affair. [He complains of being ignored, despite the importance of his message.] Now, in relation to the secret I let him think I was guarding for you, relative to my memorial to the King, I thought it better that I wrote you an ostensible letter, which you could carry, or send, to his Majesty. ['Figaro' is working behind Sartine's back, and the 'ostensible' letter is merely for show.] Then, if you are not commanded by the King to make a reply [to give him orders] I should at least receive one from your bounty, to console me for having taken useless pains. [That is, he will be in possession of a letter that links him to the matter in question.]

Please send me, I beg you, a blank passport, if you think I should await the orders of the King while I am in London, in case he has not had the time to decide the matter before I leave. [So he could make an unexpected return should the King finally decide to make use of him.]

Please be kind enough to inform me. Everything being understood between us, it will be to your advantage to write to me so obscurely that no one but myself can understand the point of your letter, especially if you should send it by way of the ambassador.[8]

Vergennes was to write to him using the vaguest expressions because their correspondence was—at that stage—without a proper code. Yet Beaumarchais felt it essential that only he and Vergennes should fully comprehend their business together. Moreover, when letters were exchanged through diplomatic channels, the messages needed to be better protected from interpretation.

The 'ostensible' letter, written purely for the purpose of making an impression upon King Louis XVI, was sent to him the next day, with a covering note from the Comte de Vergennes:

I see, Sire, by a letter of the *Sieur* de Beaumarchais … that he himself has already had the honour of reporting to your Majesty the impressions that he collected in London, and what profits he thinks can be drawn from them … [9]

The minister then goes on to ask for the King's orders, with regard to the question of exactly how their spy in London should proceed further, since Vergennes was not prepared to commit himself until the King had made that decision. So Beaumarchais was asked to delay his journey to London until 'tomorrow at noon;' that is, until the King had authorized the next move; even though King Louis—at his best, a kindly, flabby man—was, in fact, the least able person to advise Beaumarchais, at that stage, of the best way he could serve the government.

Beaumarchais, always impatient for results, was somewhat confused by the slow reaction to his important disclosures. The 'ostensible' letter is really a third appeal to the most important figure in the trio, and by pressing the King so directly—or as directly as he could—he had expected a swifter response, since he considered the matter to be of the utmost urgency. In a letter to Vergennes, he dared to talk openly of the distress the King's silence had plunged him into, although he was still playing by the elaborate rules of the game:

> I sent yesterday to the King, through M. Sartine, a short memorial ... It is an exact account of 'men and things' in England. There must have been a question of all this in the Council yesterday, and yet this morning you have sent me no word of it. So I must remind you that the worst setback to affairs of this kind comes from uncertainty, or loss of time.
>
> Should I await your reply, or must I leave without having received any? Have I done well or ill to penetrate those minds whose dispositions are becoming so important for us ... ?[10]

The ministers were maddeningly slow to move. They were, as always, willing to make use of their spy's zeal in collecting information, but they were in no haste to commit the government to the cause he now so boldly espoused. Apart from a few men that shared his vision, the inner circle of the French government had no real interest in the constitutional liberties of the Americans, even though they had a vital interest in their 'independence,' should it suit their purpose.

But nobody realized this better than Beaumarchais, and so he continued to urge that France should consent to give the Americans the secret, yet absolutely indispensable aid, which he was even then—in his eagerness—preparing (or, having studied the feasibility of such a policy, he had immediately started to follow his plans through, despite the fact that he could not yet rely upon the backing of the ministers). The fear tormenting him was, that because they lacked the means for an effective resistance, the colonists might reconcile themselves with the mother country before they could inflict any real damage upon her.

Apparently still preoccupied with the matter of *Mlles* d'Éon's new wardrobe, Beaumarchais reappeared at Versailles. On 24 November, in a letter to Vergennes supposedly relating to the subject of the *chevalière's* change of costume, he wrote: 'Instead of waiting for the reply, which should bear a definite decision, do you approve that I write to the King, advising him that I am here? Also that you have seen me "trembling," lest in a thing as easy as it is necessary, and perhaps the most important of all that he will ever have to decide, his Majesty should choose to say "No."'[11]

He implored Vergennes to secure for him an audience with King Louis, if only 'of a quarter of an hour,' before the King came to an irrevocable decision on the question of aid to the Americans. He was convinced that he needed only this short span of time in order to demonstrate 'the necessity of undertaking, the facility of doing, the certainty of succeeding, and the immense harvest of glory which this little sowing will yield to his reign …'[12]

He had now decided, after calculating the cost, that the 'seed' for this crop was a sum of perhaps $200,000, or a million *francs*. He proposed they send half of this amount to the struggling Americans as specie to bolster their sagging currency, and the other half was to be used to buy munitions of war, which would be sent to them through routes that he would set up in other countries.

In this first period of his involvement in the American cause, it is fairly certain that Beaumarchais simply saw himself as no more than a 'transmitter of funds,' and no other intention seems to have entered his mind. Although the wily and venal 'Figaro' was always lurking in the wings, and additional alternatives—which would accrue to his financial benefit—were always simmering in the thoughts of Beaumarchais, the financier.

Even the apathy with which his suggestions were received did not discourage him; for what, when Beaumarchais's enthusiasm was aroused, could ever chill his ardour? He simply looked about for some other approach to the problem, with an irrepressible belief in his own persuasiveness. What did it signify if his plans had been initially disapproved of, and might still be rejected? He could always rely upon the sharp point of his pen to change men's opinions—that compelling, spellbinding weapon.

Some time in September 1775, he took to writing directly to the King on the question now nearest to his present interests. This subject was the precarious British military position in the American colonies, as gleaned from his contacts in London; and he gave the King both a breakdown and a *lecture* on the subject (while condescendingly making his abstracts easy on the eye, knowing how ponderously the King tended to peruse his papers).

Beaumarchais was obliged for his intelligence regarding the situation in America to the Comte de Laureguais,[13] a common acquaintance of Lee and himself in London. In his letters to the king, he described the count as 'one of the best informed men on the inside of British politics,' who was proving useful to his Majesty despite being, like the *Chevaliere* d'Éon, an exile and in disgrace, (and brooding resentfully on the humiliation). A man of the highest nobility, a talented writer, would-be alchemist and a dedicated freemason, Laureguais had several years earlier been forced to flee abroad, seeking refuge from his many enemies at Versailles. Enmities largely created by his poisoned penmanship.

But he was still a patriotic Frenchman, Beaumarchais assured the King, and he had made good use of his exile, having become privy to many of King George III's ministers' best-kept secrets during his enforced stay in London.

And Laureguais had now revealed to him (although at this juncture, it was only his opinion, based upon privileged hearsay), that plans were being formulated by the British War Department to conquer the French and Spanish islands scattered throughout the Gulf of Mexico. Laureguais firmly believed that if the British were to let the thirteen colonies finally go their own way, they would make up their losses by seizing the French Sugar Islands in their place. '… The only thing that is not fixed is the time when such a move will be made,' Beaumarchais reported. 'But it cannot be doubted that it will be very soon.'

He advanced a number of reasons for such a dramatic shift in British policy, the most important (and most obvious) being that Britain could no longer subdue her American offspring 'without completely devastating them,' yet 'neither can she make peace with them without giving them their complete independence.' Either solution would result in some form of alienation between the two countries, and any kind of peace in such a situation would be destructive for British trade. Therefore, the only answer would be for them to snap up the Sugar Islands; 'it would be a hundred times easier than to conquer her own subjects.' Since the 1762 concession to Britain by Spain of the Florida peninsula, 'nothing prevents them from grabbing all the straits, from the 11th to the 28th parallels. They could block the Gulf of Mexico so that no ship could get in or out without their consent. They will be in exclusive control of the richest trade in the world.'[14]

Beaumarchais, being a student of such matters and also a realist, had absolutely no faith in the efforts of the French and Spanish fleets against a formidable adversary such as the British navy, even combined. France's naval forces had long shown themselves to be unequal to the task of protecting the Spanish Main against a numerically inferior sea power. The British may have been on the point of losing their influence and potency in North America, but Central and Southern America could still be at their mercy.

Laureguais, however, had come up with a 'sublime and secret plan' (which the canny 'Figaro' had already 'made known' to Sartine and Vergennes before he had approached the King, but which to this day remains unrevealed). 'If this project could be implemented, it will be through this one man alone,' Beaumarchais insisted, since Laureguais had a perfect knowledge of the strength of the British forces, resources, and banking systems. In view of the incalculable good the man could do for his country, Beaumarchais now begged the King to overlook his previous history, and to 'give ear' to this 'man of genius, courage and vigour'—a man who had 'bought experience and wisdom at the price of errors and long misfortune.'

The fact that this newly enlightened man, regardless of his straitened circumstances, still managed to travel freely back and forth between the English and French coasts—with a perfect disregard for expense or the possibility of arrest—was perhaps not known to Beaumarchais; but that he managed to keep up an extravagant style of living in London, despite appearing to have exhausted the wealth with which to support it, must always have been apparent. Exactly how the free-spending Laureguais managed to keep up appearances was a detail that the morally flexible 'Figaro' perhaps chose to ignore; he supposed he used much the same means as the former Chevalier d'Éon.

Faced with a stony silence from Versailles, Beaumarchais again approached King Louis XVI on 21 September 1775. This letter was submitted through Sartine, even though Beaumarchais was at that time back in Paris. Filling in his blank passport, he had slipped away from London, saying that he was 'going to the country'—without specifying which one. He had then 'run freely' from London to Calais and onwards to Versailles, in order to confer with Sartine and Vergennes 'on matters too important and too delicate to be entrusted with any common messenger.'

Britain was in crisis, he told the two ministers triumphantly: 'She could be near to ruin if her neighbours were capable of taking advantage of it!' He had learned this, he reported, because he had spoken to a man recently returned from Philadelphia[15] with vital information for the British government, and who had been in conference with certain members of parliament, 'shaken and frightened by what he had to say.'

The long-suffering colonists, the man had revealed, were now resolved to 'suffer anything rather than to bend,' having been pushed to the limit by British decrees. The northern states were already in a state of arousal and had 38,000 men, 'capable and determined,' under the walls of Boston, where they had reduced the besieged British army to a state of near starvation. Approximately another 40,000 Americans, well armed, and as determined as those who besieged Boston, were prepared to defend the rest of the country—and all this had been accomplished 'without taking one farmer away from the land, and not one worker away from the manufactories.' The main body of the American insurgents was, it appeared, largely drawn from the fishing industry, 'which the British have deliberately ruined. All those who worked in the ports have increased that army of furious men, whose actions are motivated by vengeance and outrage.'[16]

Beaumarchais reported that, although the British navy still controlled the coast, the American patriots were now virtually invincible, 'because they have so much "back country" available for retreats' (in 1775, who could have begun to estimate the huge size of the hinterland of Northern America?). Beaumarchais maintained that 'All sensible people [in London] are now convinced the English colonies are lost to the British'—which was also, happily, *his* opinion.

He even predicted a public flare-up in London, since the bitterness between the two political parties had 'reached excessive heights' now that King George III had declared the Americans to be in a state of rebellion against the monarchy. The Whig opposition had inevitably taken a con-trary—and obstreperous—position to the King's party, the Tories; and the rowdy Londoners were almost always on the side of the opposition. It was generally believed, Beaumarchais assured King Louis, that before the end of the parliamentary session—in this so-called 'democratic' monarchy—at least six members of the House of Commons would end up in the Tower of London. His good friend in London, Lord Rochford,[17] had told him 'with a sigh,' 'I am afraid, sir, that winter will not pass without a few heads rolling in the King's party, or in the Opposition's.'

On the other hand, the Lord Mayor of London, John Wilkes, had told Beaumarchais joyfully at the end of a sumptuous dinner, 'For a long time now the King of England has done me the honour of hating me. As I did him the justice of despising him. The time has come to decide which one of us has judged the best, and on which side the wind will blow heads down.'

Time, Beaumarchais believed, was definitely on the side of those who championed America. Lord North,[18] the Prime Minister—seen to be unhealthily dominated by the King—would have resigned on the spot 'if he could have done so with honour,' or so many people believed. In his letter to King Louis XVI, Beaumarchais did more than hint at the insecurity of the British king's position, and at the growing possibility of a rebellion against him in his own kingdom. In fact, he asserted boldly, he did not believe King George III's crown to be 'more firmly established on his head than his ministers' heads upon their shoulders.'

This outrageous statement was followed by some flagrant flattery of Louis XVI, with Beaumarchais, the courtier, hastening to assure his royal master that he himself possessed *no* republican sentiments!

IV

The Persuader

While Beaumarchais the courtier sought to convince his masters that he remained their 'ever humble servant,' the radical was setting out on a course that would soon involve them all. At the end of September the King, Vergennes and Sartine were still reluctant to 'follow him into the adventure into which he was drawing them, so to speak, with a towline,' but it was about this time that Beaumarchais had the inspiration for his fictitious export company 'Hortalez & Co.'[1] He had, in fact, already made contact in Holland and Spain with some influential men of business who would help him establish it; men well prepared to 'embrace the cause of the Americans against the English.'

From this time onwards all his efforts would become focused on a plan to dispatch funds and munitions to the insurgents, and he had already decided that the operation should predominantly be carried out from the neutral security of the Netherlands. It was essential that the most profound secrecy should surround the enterprise, not only to ensure its success, but also to prevent the French government from being compromised. As he wrote to the King in October 1775:

> While reason of State engages you to lend a helping hand to the Americans, politics requires that your Majesty takes elementary precautions against being seen to favour them—so that secret aid will not become a firebrand between England and France.

To prevent this possibility, Beaumarchais—'as a duty'—offers up his solution: the creation of an entirely fictitious armaments firm, which he proposed to call 'Rodrigue Hortalez & Co' ('Hortalez' was a minor character in his comedy *The Barber of Seville*) and of which he would be managing director:

> The primary purpose, [he informed the King], is to avert, by its being an entirely commercial arrangement, the suspicion that your Majesty or his Council may have anything personally to do with this business.

A second advantage, as he was keen to point out, would be that the King and his council would easily be able to follow the progress of the funding they supplied through the 'various changes and metamorphoses that commerce will make them undergo. Without fear that they may be diverted, or lost on the way'—that is, that the money supply would not end up in the wrong hands and proper commercial records would be kept.

King Louis had a regal distaste for trade, and as he did not respond to Beaumarchais's letter it seemed that the scheme had been summarily rejected. Yet its deviser was more than ever determined to involve the government, and—impetuous as always—he addressed another memoir to the King on 7 December; but this time couched in such respectful language, so warm and glowing, that its daring boldness might almost be overlooked:

> Sire, your Majesty's mere disapproval of a plan is, in general, a law for its rejection by all who are interested in it. But there are plans, however, of such supreme importance to the welfare of your Kingdom, that a zealous servant might deem it right to present them more than once, for fear that they may not earlier have been understood from a more favourable point of view …
>
> Monsieur de Vergennes informs me that your Majesty does not deem it just to adopt my proposed expedient. The objection, I gather, has no bearing on the immense utility of the plan, nor on the danger of carrying it out, but solely on the delicate conscientiousness of your Majesty.
>
> A refusal due to such honourable motives would condemn one to silence, did not the extreme importance of the proposition cause one to question whether the justice of the King of France is best being served by not adopting such an expedient. In general, I agree, every honest man should reject an unjustifiable enterprise. But, Sire, the foreign policy of a government can never be the same as that which serves the civil law of the citizens … I see no common ground between the two that can ensure the safety of the realm. Under the name of international law, the main axiom for any nation, (even according to Montesquieu),[2] is to do the best for oneself. This is the first law; the second is to do the least possible harm to the government of the day.
>
> The King owes to his subjects his justice and protection, as a strict and rigorous duty to them, but the obligations that he offers foreign states is never more than as convention warrants. The policies that preserve the relationships between alien states differ in almost every respect from the civil morality that governs the individuals in your Majesty's Kingdom …
>
> It is the English, Sire, which it concerns you to humiliate and weaken, if you wish to avoid being humiliated and weakened yourself, as has happened on every occasion in recent years. Have they not always waged war upon us without openly declaring it? Did they not begin the last war in a time of peace? Did they not humble us by destroying our finest seaport? (King Louis XIV[3] would rather have devoured both of his arms than not have redressed

such a humiliation!) The heart of every true Frenchman must bleed at such ignominy.

Pursuing the dynastic note of betrayed honour, he reminds the young king that his grandfather, Louis XV, forced by events beyond French control to accept the shameful peace treaty of 1763, 'swore to avenge these indignities.' He dwells on the pitiful state of the present kingdom in the world-view. Having robbed King Louis XV of the lands bordering the Mississippi, along with French Canada, had not the victorious enemy then contemptuously offered France two paltry islands in the Caribbean as a 'recompense'—insult added to injury. '... And yet your Majesty is so delicate and conscientious as to hesitate.'

He inevitably blows his own trumpet:

An indefatigable, zealous servant succeeds in putting the most formidable weapon in your hand, one that you can use without committing yourself, but which will still abase your natural enemies, and render them incapable of injuring you for a long time to come ...

I entreat you, Sire, in the name of your subjects ... in the name of glory and prosperity ... not to be deceived by the brilliant sophism of a false sensibility. This deplorable excess of fairness towards your enemies would be the most signal injustice towards your subjects, who will soon suffer the penalty of your misplaced scruples.

Finally, he admits to being:

so confounded by your Majesty's refusal that, unable to find a better reason for it, I am drawn to the conclusion that it is I, myself, who is the obstacle to the success of this important affair—at least in the mind of your Majesty.

Sire, may I assure you that my own interest goes for nothing in this business, that of serving you—and France—is everything! Select any other man of probity, intelligence and discretion, whom you believe can be relied upon to conduct the matter, and I will take him to England, to try and gain for him the same confidence that has been awarded to myself by our friends in London. He shall bring the affair to a successful conclusion, while I will return to France, to fall back into the quiet obscurity from which I emerged, rejoicing in having at least begun an affair of the greatest advantage to his country that any negotiator was ever honoured with.

Caron de Beaumarchais.

P.S. May the guardian angel of this government incline your Majesty's mind to the Project, for should he award us this first success, the rest will follow. I answer for it.

The King may have been amused at the idea of Beaumarchais 'retreating into the shadows,' but he may also have been outraged by the undertones of the letter. Once again the 'loyal subject,' despite the courtly language, was daring to lecture him. A lecturer, moreover, who because of several previous 'indiscretions' had been civilly degraded, and who was, even now, in the eyes of the Law debarred from fulfilling any public function! Once again, audacity did not immediately pay off, for no sign was given that the King had read the letter, or even received it.

Beaumarchais, after waiting several days, in a state of increasing frustration, resorted to another tack. He wrote to the King again, this time ostensibly seeking advice about a seemingly more *important* matter—namely what should be done about the *Chevaliere* d'Éon's male attire. But in it, he again left a wide margin for the king's reply; hoping, perhaps, that he would use this space to answer the previous questions. But the King confined his answers solely to the question in hand; and, as was his habit, they were brusque to the point of boorishness:

'Does the King allow *Mlle* d'Éon to wear the "Cross of St Louis" on her woman's
        clothing?'
Louis: 'Only outside Paris.'
'Does the King approve of my giving 2,000 *ecus* to the lady for her trousseau?'
Louis: 'Yes.'
'Does the King leave her to the entire disposal of her male wardrobe?'
Louis: 'She must sell them.'
'As these favours must be subordinated to certain dispositions of mind, which I
        wish to impose permanently on *Mlle* d'Éon, will his Majesty leave it up to
        me to grant or refuse, as the case may be, when it is useful to his service?'
Louis: 'Yes.'

To protect himself, Beaumarchais asked the king to acknowledge 'in good form' by way of a receipt, his valuable work in acquiring all the papers he had brought to him from England:

I have begged M. de Vergennes to ask his Majesty to be kind enough to add at the bottom of that instrument, in his own hand, a few words expressing satisfaction with the manner in which I accomplished my mission. This reward, the dearest to my heart, may one day be of great use to me.

The King, who possessed a Bourbon lack of gratitude, could not bring himself to write more than one ambiguous word in his spy's favour: 'Good.'

But Beaumarchais went on to broaden the scope of the letter, having reminded the King of his grandfather's debt to him in the past. He now prompted him to recognize that his services would be equally useful in the future:

> 'As the first person I shall see in London will be Lord Rochford, and as I do not doubt that he will ask me secretly what the King of France replied to the King of England's prayer—which I transmitted to you—what shall I answer on your behalf?'
>
> Louis: '… That you received no answer.'
>
> 'If this Lord, who is in close relationship with the King of England, insists upon taking me secretly to His Britannic Majesty, shall I accept or not? This question is not idle and deserves to be pondered upon.'
>
> Louis, again ambiguously: '… That may be.'

Beaumarchais, always aware of his enemies at the French court—and who almost certainly extended their influence into England—quite naturally attempted to guard his back:

> '… I must warn your Majesty that the Comte de Guines has attempted to make me suspect with the English ministers. Am I allowed to say a few words to him regarding it? Or does his Majesty wish me to appear unaware of all the covert plots which have been devised to harm me, and my operations, and consequently the good services of your Majesty?'
>
> Louis: 'He must not know about it.'

Inevitably, Beaumarchais ended with a demand dictated by his real need, for which the rest of the letter was only a cloak:

> And, now, I must ask before departing [to London] for a positive response to my last memorial. For if ever a question is important, it must be admitted that it is this one. I answer on my head, after having well reflected upon the question, for the most glorious success of this operation; the greatest, perhaps, of your entire reign. Which, I can assure you, will never compromise your person, your ministers, or any of your interests. Can any one of those who influence his Majesty against this measure answer 'on his head' to the King, for the evil which will infallibly come to France if it is rejected?
>
> In that case we shall be so unhappy in that the King should constantly refuse to adopt a plan that is so simple and so wise. I implore his Majesty to take note

of the date when I first arranged this superb design, in order that one day he may render me the justice due to my views. When it may be left to us to bitterly regret not having followed my proposal.

On 15 December, Beaumarchais wrote to Sartine, complaining about his deep loathing of the continued bargaining with *Mlle* d'Éon. He insists that he is not lacking in zeal, and feels that he has certainly proved himself in this regard; but, after the latest news from England, he is afraid that he will return there too late to take any active role in the American development: '… I have perceived that in that sort of affair the danger is extreme in the case of failure.' He is well aware, 'from experience,' he notes, that even in the case of success, the triumphant negotiator can very often be rewarded only with 'all kinds of unpleasantness.'

On the same day, he wrote to the King, expressing his frustration with the continuing business of *Mlle* d'Éon's conversion, 'a task that has brought me neither thanks, honour, or profit,' and he begs King Louis to allow somebody else to do the job. 'I have several times barely escaped with my life,' he reminds the King proudly, adding bitterly that this 'is of little importance once the danger is passed. So much so that no one barely deigns to listen to my reports.'

The audacity of the secret agent would in the end prevail over the prudence of the King, but for the moment Beaumarchais was obliged to start for London, knowing only that the *Chevaliere* d'Éon must sell her male attire; his hopes for the new project for the moment shattered. However enthusiastic Vergennes may have been, intrigues at court controlled his actions, making him feel the danger inherent in the scheme. The count was visibly the butt of serious attacks from his fellow ministers with regard to the question of aid to America, and Beaumarchais was in consequence held at a distance. 'Everything seemed compromised.'[4]

Vergennes was also under attack from another, and more dangerous, source—Great Britain. On 8 December 1775, he wrote to Viscount Stormont,[5] British ambassador to France:

I received the letter your Excellency has honoured me with, on the 5th of this month, and I have taken cognizance of your warning about the few American ships that have recently appeared in several European reports; the captains of which have confessed to trying to procure arms and munitions. I also take notice of your request for King Louis to circulate his ports with orders necessary to prevent the export of war munitions on any kind of British ship, and even the ships from other nations, if they are bound for America.

I have, Sir, transmitted your request to his Majesty and his Council. The
King has ordered me to reply that he will never desire more than to give the
King of England the most convincing proofs of his sincere and constant friendship ... He has given orders to restrain any ship departing from his ports with
martial goods for America.

As a result, perhaps, of this development (the French were appalled to
discover just how close a watch the British were keeping on their ports),
Vergennes tried to check the increasing fervour of his most active enthusiast.
Beaumarchais wrote to him on 1 January 1776, complaining of the minister's
coldness towards him. Adding, with a touch of the purest 'Figaro,'—

Great experience of men, and the habit of misfortune, has given me that
watchful prudence, which makes me consider everything, and direct matters
according to the timid or courageous character of those for whom I do them.

The New Year began, then, with little encouragement for the cause of
American independence. But although Beaumarchais almost lost heart in the
first days of January, his faith was partly restored when he realized that the argument was slowly inclining towards him as the weeks progressed. The timid policy
of King Louis XVI towards the Americans, bolstered by the objections of his
more cautious ministers, began to give way, apparently encouraged by the 'quiet
and uniform influence of M. de Vergennes.' Beaumarchais was led to believe the
minister was 'imperceptibly' overcoming the scruples of the inexperienced king,
'who never fully comprehended the far-reaching importance of the question.'[6]

Yet, even as his pet project began to attract the backing of a few influential
courtiers, Beaumarchais also began to see that he was, for whatever reason,
being quietly sidelined. He wrote to Vergennes, again complaining of his
'chilliness' towards him. He had examined himself, he wrote; and concluded
(naturally) that he 'did not deserve it.'

There was, as so often in his correspondence with his masters, a discreet
hint of the blackmail that would have been familiar to Figaro in his dealings
with his betters:

In the country where you live, Sir, [he wrote to Vergennes], they neglect no
opportunity to create new preconceptions against whoever makes himself useful. Never forget, M. le Comte, the wind that appears to blow me away in a
swirl of slander will also enfold you in it more and more. In this country of
intrigues, a good servant, with some wits about him, is more useful to you than
twenty court 'friends' whom you have to keep satisfied.

The fact is that our great affair is going astray. While we argue over accessories, I assure you that the enemies of your administration (and the State) do their best to take advantage of our indolence. They are striving to extinguish in our friends [the American rebels] the hope that we can be useful to them. In a few weeks it will, perhaps, be too late to remedy it.

Think of it, M. le Comte. I will go tomorrow night to warn M. de Maurepas[7] about it, and, if around 8pm, your door is not closed to me, I will hand you the statement of the funds used to balance the d'Éon affair.

Even his New Year's greeting sounds ambiguous: 'The renewing of the year adds nothing to my respectful sentiments.'

V

Undiplomatic Relations

Events in America throughout 1775 had slowly led Vergennes himself to conclude that the colonists were seriously considering an open battle for independence, in a 'shooting war.' More importantly, he believed that they were, at last, now capable of successfully challenging the British—with some help from a friendly nation. All they lacked was the sophisticated military hardware they would need to face a better-equipped adversary, along with experts to advise them on how to make the best use of it. Even without Beaumarchais's constant reminders of the advantages to be gained, the foreign minister now believed that something might be done by his own government to sound out this new revolutionary awareness in America, which could be used for his country's benefit in a subversive war against Britain.

Vergennes's initial response to the gratifying reports that reached him from across the Atlantic was to revive the use of secret agents in the thirteen states, a practice that had been developed by his predecessor, the Duc de Choiseul. For Choiseul had maintained a spy service in the American seaboard states, to record the mood of the colonists as they grew increasingly dissatisfied with British rule.

The 'detailed reports' of Choiseul's chief spy, the so-called Baron de Kalb[1] (born a Bavarian peasant, yet mysteriously ennobled by nobody knew whom), had been the 'observations of a shrewd and impartial investigator'— although Kalb made the mistake of passing on the *truth* of what he found in America, which was not what Choiseul really wanted to hear. The duke wished to be told that the colonists could be easily roused to action, whereas Kalb—whilst registering their increasing anger against the British government—also insisted upon their sense of loyalty towards the 'Old Country.' The project had been suddenly dropped in 1770, when Choiseul reached the conclusion that the Americans were not yet ready to separate themselves from their oppressors, and the matter was further stifled after the duke's downfall. (Choiseul had been 'retired' by Louis XV's last mistress, Madame du Barry, of whom he made an enemy in 1770, not realizing the extent of her influence over the infatuated king.)

Now, five years later, Vergennes, realizing that the hoped-for rupture between Britain and the American people was at last imminent, decided upon an exploratory mission to some of the colonies; to be led by a man in whom he could trust, Julien Achard de Bonvouloir.[2] From London, the Comte de Guines had enthusiastically recommended him to the minister, describing him as 'a gentleman of impeccable breeding … who is familiar with the American people on their home-ground.' Unlike, of course, the would-be aristocrat Beaumarchais, who had no any experience of the American situation *at source*, whereas Bonvouloir had already visited all the English colonies; and, in fact, had just returned from there.

Moreover, while travelling in America in 1774, the presentable young Frenchman had so much impressed the Americans that they had tried to enlist him into their untrained rebel army, but without success. The insurgents knew they were desperately in need of men with military expertise, and Bonvouloir had presented himself to them as an ex-officer. As a result of the exchanges with his impressionable, if naïve hosts—while gracefully disentangling himself from any commitment—Bonvouloir had established sources of information throughout the thirteen states.

'He has given me excellent reports of all he has seen and heard,' Guines wrote to Vergennes, 'and he would like nothing better than to return to America.'

Despite representing himself as a French officer of some experience, Bonvouloir had, in fact, been nothing more than a volunteer in the Cape Regiment;[3] and he had served in it with no real distinction before being given a medical discharge, leaving San Domingo 'for a change of air.' Yet Vergennes agreed to Guine's request that his protégé should now be given an authentic commission as a lieutenant of infantry—a commission that he could flaunt in America, 'for any advantage he might find useful during his [secret] mission among the colonists' (although official records show that Bonvouloir did not become a gazetted officer, and a *lieutenant de fregate* at that, until he was inducted into the navy on 10 July, 1779).

But Bonvouloir had all the requisite qualifications in the judgement of King Louis's advisers and so, as their representative, he sailed to America from London on 8 September 1775, having been briefed by the French ambassador to send back reports in code on the situation in the colonies, and to evaluate the possibility of covertly supporting the rebels. Vergennes had advised Guines that Bonvouloir's instructions should be verbal, and must be confined to two essential aims. 'Firstly, to make a faithful report to you of the prevailing disposition of the colonial public mind;' secondly, to re-assure the Americans that they need not be mistrustful of the Canadians, whom many Americans remained convinced were still faithful to their late French rulers.[4] 'They must be made to understand that we have abandoned all our ambitions in that area,' the foreign minister wrote.

Despite his promotion to a lieutenancy, Bonvouloir was ordered to masquerade as a 'merchant of Antwerp' when he reached the eastern seaboard; and he was also commanded by his French directors to strictly limit his language to English, in which he was proficient. Above all, it was vital that he worked in absolute secrecy. His contacts were first-class, in view of his earlier tour, for he was introduced to people at the highest level upon arrival. Reaching Philadelphia, the 'capital' of the emergent America, Bonvouloir was immediately granted a meeting with Benjamin Franklin[5] and three other members of the recently created 'Secret Committee,' which had been appointed to put the procurement of war supplies on a methodical basis. This panel had been established even as the Frenchman was crossing the Atlantic, given wide powers and large sums of money, and ordered to keep its proceedings strictly secret (which it did with such effect that it destroyed many records to protect its integrity).

The 'Flanders merchant' took pains to disclaim an official connection with *any* European government, saying that he was there only to explore the possibilities of making 'some private deals' to supply the Americans with military equipment. But the cannier members on the committee sensed the presence of French authorities behind his sales pitch, which is apparent from some of the questions they submitted to him in writing:

'Could the gentleman inform them of the official French attitude towards the position of the colonists; and, if it is favourable, how can this be authenticated?'

'How can the Committee go about acquiring two qualified French engineers?'

'Would it be possible to get arms and other war supplies directly from the French authorities, paid for in American products, and would French ports be open for such an exchange?'

Bonvouloir adroitly fielded these question and others like them. He reported to his superiors that he had resolutely maintained his position as a 'private citizen,' and had promised only that he would present the committee's requests 'where they might best be satisfied'—all of which the Americans recognized as a diplomatic fabrication. But, as a result of these talks, the possibility of secret aid had been implanted in the minds of the Americans, and it began to flourish more openly at Versailles. Bonvouloir's report of 18 December 1775 came at a time when American military fortunes were high enough for the French to feel that the rebels were strong enough to be worth backing.

Americans, though, before their Revolution, had been largely antagonistic to the French who had settled as their neighbours in America, and they now had no desire to incur a debt of any kind with their late rivals, financial or political. They had hitherto regarded France as a natural enemy—as she had indeed proved often enough to be throughout the recent colonial wars. The expulsion of the French from North America had been as much one of the main aims of the British settlers as it had been for the British government; now, it was feared that if their old enemies were once again to meddle in their affairs they might seek to regain the territories they had lost. To ask for any sort of aid from France was an intolerable suggestion to many in the Revolutionary Party, and it was necessity alone that would finally drive them to take such a step. Not until the late summer of 1775 was a motion raised in the Second Continental Congress, strongly supported by John Adams,[6] to send some sort of spokesman to France.

Acting independently, the Secret Committee—having seen through Bonvouloir's pretence of being a freelance salesman—decided that two could play the same game. It was secretly agreed that an undercover agent should be sent to France, to explore the possibilities of military assistance, of whatever kind; and, as it happened, the right man for the job seemed to be at hand. On 26 February 1776, the Congress enacted an embargo on exports to Britain, and on 2 March, Silas Deane[7] was appointed secret envoy to Versailles— to also go 'in the character of a merchant'—where he was to do what he could to procure French aid. Deane, an energetic if not particularly brilliant young lawyer, had in some way made a political error in his home state of Connecticut, and had failed to be re-elected to the Congress he had twice served, which left him free for this new role. Although Deane's talents may have been lost upon his constituents, they were fully apparent to his political colleagues in Philadelphia, and he was the first American selected to represent the United Colonies abroad.

Silas Deane was, in fact, an extraordinary man in many ways. He was celebrated for his enterprise, and his intensely ambitious nature had long been recognized. Born in Groton, Connecticut, in 1737, the son of a blacksmith, he had put himself through Yale University in what would become a 'time-honoured' American custom—by taking up any employment that would furnish his college fees. Graduating in 1758, he had been admitted to the Bar in 1761, and from the following year he had started a rapid rise to political prominence, while gathering a fortune and prestige along the way.

He was a handsome and affable young man who had, admittedly, been greatly aided in his progress by two advantageous marriages. His second, to Elizabeth Saltonstall—the granddaughter of a former Governor of Connecticut—had eased his entry into politics. But, as a successful lawyer and a prosperous merchant, he had made his mark on the pre-Revolutionary scene without further aid, and in the first session of the Second Continental Congress he had served with distinction on the committees that were appointed to reorganize the American navy. Setting his political acumen aside, he was well qualified for the role of a commercial agent, having 'a capacity for penetrating analysis in matters of business,' although, as would later be revealed, he was also unfortunately 'endowed with an ardent cupidity.'[8]

It was this greed that would prove his eventual undoing, and irregularities in his early business dealings may have had something to do with his failure to be re-elected to the Second Congress. But if his new employers, the Secret Committee, were aware of his failings, it would seem that they were prepared to overlook them. It may well be that he was chosen for this European assignment as he was the only capable person then at liberty for the task, and in March 1776, Deane set off for France.

His instructions, which were explicit, were to be carried out with the utmost tact. His main objective was to discover the *exact* level of military assistance that would be made available from France, either openly or secretly, and what form this assistance would take. Having determined that, he was then to establish what sort of diplomatic connection the Americans could *safely* form with the French government.

In this last regard, he was ordered to make it absolutely clear that there would be no political agreement between the two countries, other than that which could be established between two sovereign states. Regardless of whatever kind of help was offered to them, the rebel colonists would not submit themselves to any form of French authority; they were not about to exchange one form of control for another. Following on from that, there would be no military link-up. Congress would welcome individual soldiers, or even military groups, but they would allow no sizeable contingent of French troops to set foot on American soil, and the agreement was to be strictly commercial in its initial phase.

VI

'More Convincing Arguments'

It did not take much delving for the ex-spy to uncover the details of the Comte de Vergennes's secret survey into the American political scene. Within days of doing so, Beaumarchais had started to make his own inquiries in the thirteen states, and when he received a report from the agent that he had sent there, the conclusions reached only endorsed his own judgement. As he swiftly informed the King:

> For the sake of diplomacy, the rebel Congress must continue to believe that your Majesty does not want to have any connection with it. The fiction must be maintained that a clandestine organization will entrust certain monies to the prudence of a faithful agent, who will then furnish military assistance to the Americans, by the safest and speediest ways, in exchange for tobacco and other goods.
>
> Secrecy is of the essence.
>
> There are two vital points, which must always be remembered. One: the ease with which your Majesty may obtain as much gunpowder as you have occasion for, to be sold on to my company at a moderate price. Two: the impossibility at the moment for the Farmers-General[1] to procure tobacco, at any price.

If these two points were granted, Beaumarchais suggested that the business would proceed as follows:

(a) The King is to place one million *livres* ($200,000) at the disposal of his agent, who will style himself 'Rodrigue Hortalez & Co,' this being the trade name under which I have decided to conduct the whole business. Five hundred thousand *livres* will be changed into gold *moidores*,[2] or other Portuguese pieces, the only foreign money that is now acceptable in America, and which will be immediately transported there. For it is necessary for the Colonists to have a little gold at once, in order to put their own paper money into circulation, otherwise it will stagnate and be valueless. (It is the leaven that must be added to the heavy dough to make it rise and properly ferment!) The profit to be made from this half a million *livres*[3] would be in the return of Virginia tobacco, which the Congress must supply directly to Hortalez & Co when its ships drop anchor at any port that can be guaranteed to be open to them. The Farmers-General having previously agreed with the agent to purchase the tobacco from him at a fair price. [Although Beaumarchais, not wishing to appear as being commercially exploitative, insisted that this was of little consequence in the grander scheme of things.]

(b) The agent will then use the remaining half a million *livres* in procuring arms and gunpowder, and in conveying it without delay to the rebels. But instead of buying gunpowder in Holland at the current price of twenty or thirty *sols turnois*[4] a pound, (even higher when sold directly to the Americans), it would be more advantageous to procure it from his Majesty's registrars, on the basis of four to five *sols* a pound. Which should be a saving all round, if it pleases his Majesty. The real artifice of this operation consists in secretly procuring all the necessary military stores from your Majesty's arsenals.

(c) However, if Hortalez & Co is forced to buy the gunpowder at the dearer rate of twenty *sols* a pound, the company would be unable to send more than 500,000 pounds-worth of powder in the initial shipments, since even this would absorb the remaining half a million *livres*. The second transaction would work in the same way as the first one regarding the gold coins, the same return would be expected from both: payment in tobacco, with a price having been agreed in advance with the Farmers-General.

Again, the courtier Beaumarchais stressed that the price paid for the imports was of 'no great consequence,' but pointed out the obvious advantage of buying at the cheaper rate, which would mean that the company could buy some 20,000 *quintals*[5] of powder, instead of a quarter of that sum. And this—when sold on to the Americans at twenty *sols* a pound, the accepted European price—would leave the Congress in debt to Hortalez & Co (that is, the French government, or the King) to the amount of two million *sols turnois*.

... The profits, returning to France in the shape of tobacco, would enable the firm of Hortalez & Co to settle with the real owner, *videlicet* your Majesty, for the sum of 2,500,000 *livres*. And in addition, the profit on the sales of tobacco remains to be calculated. This may rise, in round numbers, to above 500,000 *livres*. The return on these two sums will be placed at the disposition of Hortalez & Co, an actual capital of three million *livres*, with which to renew the operation.

Firstly, American paper money can be restored to health by an injection of one million, five hundred thousand *livres* in gold. The rest can be used to supply the Americans with mortars and cannon, along with 60,000 quintals of gunpowder. But this 60,000 quintals, although costing Hortalez & Co only

15,000 *livres*, will nevertheless again make the Americans the King's debtors to the amount of nine million, in return for both the powder and the Portuguese gold received by them.

Beaumarchais then blinds the king with more 'economic science':

> This is enough to show your Majesty how the spin-offs of this affair, managed according to the customary principles of commerce, must increase in circulation not at the double progression of 1.2.4. etc., but the triple progression of 1.3.9. For the first million realized gives three, but these ploughed back into the business must give nine more, and these nine lead on to twenty-seven and so. As I think I have clearly proved.
>
> Your Majesty must not become alarmed if this operation looks complicated, my pen may have run away with me in my enthusiasm for the project. I can assure you that no commercial speculation is run or succeeds in any simpler or more natural way!

But the objective, as Beaumarchais insisted, was not to launch the King upon a lucrative speculation at the expense of a people seeking liberation from a tyrant—God forbid! No, the idea was always to realize ever greater amounts of money from each transaction that would then be returned to a central fund, and put to the further assistance of the Americans, so that each operation could be recommenced on an increasing scale.

He then went on to the practical matter of transportation, for which he intended to use Dutch, rather than French, vessels. By hiring Dutch ships, the source of the supplies might be more effectively concealed, even if these merchantmen were to be intercepted by British cruisers—whereas a French ship could only ensure a safe passage to the French Cape. Certainly, one could use the Cape as a depot for trade with America, but it was a more roundabout way and would add weeks to the delivery date.

Beaumarchais also reasoned that if it should become known that Hortalez & Co was using the French Cape in this way, it would give grounds for suspicion that Versailles favoured the enterprise, and was even *connected* to it. He later set this fear aside, and even saw an advantage to be gained from taking this route; 'Considering that any real proof of that fact can never be produced, we can disregard it.' This was his conclusion, after due consideration, and he saw at least one clear benefit:

> So let us suppose that a French ship be employed and freighted, in the service of Hortalez & Co, and is then sent to the Cape to do business in that area.

Congress—or rather Mr Adams, the General-Secretary of the Congress—will, then be informed by an American agent in London [Arthur Lee] that a ship carrying gold and munitions will arrive upon a certain date. An American vessel loaded with Virginia tobacco will also dock in the same harbour. The American captain has the authority to receive our gold and munitions, with instructions to transfer his entire returns in tobacco to the supercargo of Hortalez & Co. Or, at least, to leave a promissory note for the debt outstanding.

Beaumarchais argued that, if an American ship was captured during the short run between the North American mainland and San Domingo,[6] nothing could be established beyond the fact that some American merchant was engaged in a simple commercial transaction with Hortalez & Co; although questions would be asked if the ship was boarded and proved to be carrying arms.

He also passed on to Vergennes a malicious idea of Arthur Lee's; that 'it would be rather pleasant' to help America fight her battles with the use of *British* money, 'which would be very easy.' It would indeed be very easy, for all that was required would be for King Louis XVI to adopt an already existing usage of the British Customs House, whereby a tax of 75% *ad valorum* was exacted on all French vessels entering England through the Channel ports. Adopting a like measure, the King should decree that, in future, all English vehicles and horses landing at French ports should pay a tax equal to the one levied in England. There were many expensive carriages and horses brought over to the Continent, and a tax in proportion to their estimated value would raise a satisfying amount of revenue, which could then be used for the American venture.

Beaumarchais reassured the king that, if he could manage 'this little matter,' the government would no longer need to be concerned with the furnishing of secret funds to Hortalez & Co, since the company would soon have enough financial backing to flourish in style:

The cost [is] to be borne by England, and not by your Majesty's subjects. It accords with the principle, adopted by economists, that fancy products and merchandise ought not to be admitted into any country unless they create a revenue equivalent to their consumption.

He was enchanted by the piquancy of the idea: 'It would plant a few flowers amid the dry wastelands of explanations!':

… The decision, [he again reminded the King], depends upon your commands, the execution upon my prudence, and success upon luck. Which seems to me to be the most beneficial of all.

> In case your Majesty does not adopt it, my service in the matter will at least
> have the advantage of showing, if not any extensive knowledge, at least a zeal as
> active and pure as it is unalterable.

His active zeal, though, appears to have perturbed those of the King's closest
advisers—that 'hornet's nest'—who were not in favour of interference in the
Anglo-American quarrel. Once again, Beaumarchais had to throw himself on
the mercy of his masters, seeking protection. From London, on 14 January
1776, he wrote to Sartine:

> This reflection is for you alone. Please take precautions to keep the Ministry
> clear of suspicion. They [the King's anti-American friends] only want to throw
> matters into more confusion, and to take advantage of any divergence of opin-
> ion, in order to lay hold of the King. Should they succeed, then you would
> certainly be lost.

Lost, it would seem, because Sartine was by then starting to approve of
plans for secret American aid. Beaumarchais, used as he was to court
intrigues, now assured the minister that, although he regarded himself as
'nothing,' he would still protect himself: 'I will see to it that future developments will no longer be at my expense, on the part of the malcontents.'
But he knew that he could not stem the resentment that still prevailed
against him, and he depended upon the King to keep him safe from an
ever-increasing number of enemies: 'Truly, that's the least of what is due
to me.'

But fifteen days later, Beaumarchais felt it necessary to write directly to
King Louis, (although through a ministerial dispatch):

London, 29th February 1776

> Sire, the famous quarrel between England and America, which is soon going
> to divide the world and change the [internal] systems of the European powers,
> imposes on each of them the necessity of examining the possible outcome of
> this separation, to see whether it can best serve or harm them.
>
> The most concerned of all is certainly France, since the English have long
> coveted our Sugar Islands. Their defence must without fail bring war to us,
> unless—through weakness—we consent to sacrifice our possessions in the Gulf
> [of Mexico] to another shameful peace. Perhaps more destructive to us in the
> long run than the war we dread.
>
> The moment of violent crisis is rapidly approaching, and I am obliged to

warn you that the preservation of our American possessions depends solely upon our willingness to aid the Americans. As I hope to demonstrate.

The English state is being torn apart, yet all must agree that no one can flatter themselves with the hope of bringing the Americans back into the fold, and neither will any effort to subjugate them succeed. The violent debates here, without promoting any cause, only serve to show that everything is at deadlock.

Lord North, afraid to steer the ship of state through such a storm, has shifted the weight of the affair on to the ambitious Lord Germaine [sic].[7] Germaine [sic], stunned by the clamour, and struck by the indisputable arguments of His Majesty's Opposition, tells the party leaders they cannot dare to answer to the Nation, saying that the Americans will [still] come to acceptable terms. The Colonists will never accept the Navigation Act,[8] and return to the same condition they were in before the troubles of 1763. If they do dare to answer for such an unpopular measure, then they may at once assume the duties of the Ministry, and the Welfare of the State, at their own risk and fortunes.

The Opposition are, perhaps, inclined to take the Minister at his word. But if they are ready to say 'Yes,' they are held back only because they worry that the Americans, encouraged by successes, and perhaps emboldened by some secret Treaties with France and Spain, might refuse today the same conditions for peace that they were begging for only two years ago!

For only the second time in his memorials, he mentions Arthur Lee, if only by the initial 'L'. This accredited secret agent of the American colonists, Beaumarchais writes, had been greatly discouraged by the apparent uselessness of his attempts (through himself) to obtain supplies of powder and munitions. He had warned Beaumarchais—who now warned his masters—that he must ask 'for the last time if France is absolutely determined to deny us any help.' If so, he asserts, they will be the 'laughing stock of Europe, because of our incredible inertia.'

Arthur Lee, Beaumarchais writes, is obliged to give a definite answer on this matter to his compatriots. 'He awaits France's final reply, in order to give us his,' and it would seem that he had been instructed to give France very gratifying commercial terms: 'As the price of secret aid, a treaty of commerce that will let us enjoy, for a number of years, after the peace, all the profits with which they have [previously] enriched England.' Congress had also offered to act as the allies of France within the American sphere of influence, particularly with regard to the protection of the French Sugar Islands; '… a guarantee of France's possessions, according to our strength.'

Lee insisted, 'I need only ask Lord Shelbourne[9] [a party leader] for the time it would take a ship to go and inform the Congress of England's proposals and to bring back their answer, but I can tell you right now what the Congress will reply. They will immediately declare their resolve to offer the Nations of the World, in order to obtain their help, the conditions that I am offering you secretly today.'

Beaumarchais's influence can be seen in Lee's proposal, for Lee also attempts a form of political blackmail:

> To avenge ourselves of France, and to publicly force her to make a declaration regarding us, which will compromise her excessively, we will send to French ports the first prizes that we take of English shipping. Then, whatever you say or do, the war that you dread so much will be inevitable for you, whatever you may decide. If you admit the ships into your ports, you are bound to break off with England. If you send them away, Congress will at once accept the peace proposal from the Mother Country. The Americans, outraged, will join their forces with those of England and overtake your islands, proving to you that the fine precautions you were taking to keep your possessions were useless in any event, since your caution has robbed you of them forever.

Lee had, said Beaumarchais, requested him to return to France, to give the king's counsellors 'this picture of the situation.' Lee himself would retire to the English countryside in the meanwhile, so that he would not be forced to give his colleagues in America an answer before he had received the French reply. He was equally prepared to go to France, if necessary, to confirm these 'mad declarations.':

> There you have it, Sire, [wrote Beaumarchais, firmly seconding Lee's opinions]. The awful, striking picture of our position. Your Majesty sincerely wants peace?
> The way to keep it, Sire, is the object of this memorial.

And with wearying patience, he once more lays out the various hypotheses:

I.   Great Britain will either win or lose in North America.

II.   Britain will let the colonies go their own way, and separate in peace.

III. The Parliamentary Opposition, returned to power, will try to get the Americans back into the fold.

IV.   Even if Britain triumphs over the Americans, it will be at such tremendous cost they will be forced to take over the French Sugar Islands in order to counter the expense. They will, thus, become absolute owners of the Caribbean.

V.   King Louis XVI will then be left with the only choice of starting an
      unfruitful war, for which it may already be too late. Or else he must sue
      for peace, and lose two hundred and eighty million *livres* in revenue.

VI.   If the Americans win, Britain—desperate at seeing their standard of living
      reduced by three fourths—will then compensate by taking over French
      possessions in the Caribbean.

Beaumarchais quite clearly, and unpatriotically, suggests that even if exhausted
by their American losses, the British could still take on the French navy and
win!

Beaumarchais also proposed that King Louis XVI should obtain the recall
to London of Lord Stormont, the British ambassador, who, 'because of his
relations with various courtiers at Versailles, is in a position to inform, and
does inform London, on a daily basis, of all that is being said in your Majesty's
Council'—which, since the British knew much of what was being decided at
Versailles (even as it was being decided) would seem to have been the case.

He suggested that King Louis find some pretext to withdraw the French
ambassador, the Comte de Guines, from London, so that Britain would be
forced to send for Lord Stormont in reciprocation. King Louis should then
delay the appointment of Guines's successor, which would create a diplomatic hiatus, since it would take some time for Stormont to be replaced at
Versailles,

> ... a long time before he [Stormont's successor] would be in a position to do
> us as much harm as Lord Stormont does now. Once the crisis is over, the most
> ineffectual of our lords could be sent in all safety as our ambassador.

The King's Council took the advice of their London spy on this issue, and
Guines was brought back to France on a diplomatic technicality. But, to their
extreme vexation, it did not bring about the recall of the able and over-active
British ambassador.

VII

Figaro in London

Beaumarchais wrote to Vergennes from London on 16 April 1776:

> While all England is gathered in Westminster Hall to witness the trial of the old, adulterous and bigamous Duchess of Kingston,[1] I am going to report to you on a rather serious conversation I had with my Lord Rochford.

The peer had sent him a couple of passes for the duchess's trial, which was the most sensational social scandal of the day. Since tickets for this event were in high demand, the fact that Rochford offered two of them to Beaumarchais reveals how highly he regarded the Frenchman, although they may have been in the nature of a bribe, as the letter goes on to demonstrate:

> 'Sir,' he [Rochford] said, 'Because I wish to extract the proof of confidence and friendship from you, I am going to show my trust in you by revealing something I have not yet shown anyone.'
>
> And that something, M. Le Comte, was a letter to Lord Rochford from the King of England. It was full of kind regards and tender sentiments, and even great familiarity. In it, his Majesty asks Rochford to accept the Vice-Royalty of Ireland.[2] The King requires, he says, a very sure man in that island, for in the present state of affairs 'we must fear that Ireland will follow in the footsteps of America.' (That is, to demand independence of the Crown).
>
> My Lord agreed to go, but only if he had to spend just six months out of the year in Dublin. He is to report directly to the King, and only to the King.

Rochford had confided in him, Beaumarchais went on, because he had felt that the matter (the possibility of Ireland following the example of the American colonies) in some way concerned France, '... which worries us today.' It worried Beaumarchais that Rochford possibly believed him, also, to be involved in the business, and that he may even have believed him to be an undercover agent acting in the interests of both America and Ireland.[3] But he was wrong in this, at least partially.

Disturbing news had been received from Bristol, Rochford explained. The captain of a ship that had been detained in the port was found to be carrying letters from the American Continental Congress to a merchant in Nantes, named Montaudoin, and among the letters was an order to exchange the captain's merchandise for war munitions of all kinds. It was King George's good fortune, Rochford said, that the ship had been taken straight to Bristol by a seaman 'faithful to his King.'

The order proved that a correspondence had been going on for some time, and the tone of the communication also indicated some form of protection by the French government. This, plus the fact that two French gentlemen—Pliarne and Penet[4]—were known to have been secretly negotiating with Congress on behalf of French ministers, had seriously alarmed King George's Council—the revelation of which also disturbed Beaumarchais! Pliarne and Penet were said to have 'hidden relationships' with pro-American people in London.

Rochford assured his friend that although 'a few misinformed people' had also tried to connect Beaumarchais with this clandestine trade, King George did not believe him to be involved with it (which was why the King had permitted Rochford to discuss the matter with him). 'Everybody' in London was convinced that Beaumarchais was there only to settle the matter of the 'Lady Knight of Éon,' who was at that time taking refuge in Lord Ferrer's mansion—Staunton-Harold in Leicestershire—after having kept to her fortified house in Soho for almost two months in order to avoid the many wagers that were being taken as to her true sex. Interest in the question had risen to new heights, the level of betting was stupendous, and the 'Enigma' was in greater danger than ever of being seized and brutally examined. *Mlle* d'Éon now accused her former 'protector'—Beaumarchais—of 'despotism' in his judgements, and she openly blamed him for being ordered to give up the masculine role; 'All of which is unbearable to me,' she complained.

Beaumarchais, flattered to be taken into Lord Rochford's confidence, informed him that he already knew about the ship, (without an explanation of how he had come by the information). But when Rochford complained of the French authorities allowing the free use of her ports to Americans, and asked if the merchant of Nantes would be punished for his arms dealing, Beaumarchais presumed to answer for his superiors.

Flying in the face of earlier assurances given to Britain by his government, he was emboldened to argue that, since France was not at war with anyone, her ports were open to all the merchants of the world. The quarrel was only between 'Englishmen,' and so Britain had no right to restrict free trade between other nations, and no treaty existed that obliged the French to open and close her ports at their behest. At the same time, he insisted that 'the noble principle of my King is solidly proved by the neutrality he has assumed;' even though 'everything seems to invite France to take advantage of your internal disputes, and to recover from England all that they took away from us during the last war.'

But he was equally at pains to show that, while 'some' Frenchmen *may* have dealt with the Americans 'for private assistance,' they were not, '*absolutely not*,' accredited agents of his government. If any merchants suggested such a thing, 'they would be disowned and even punished.' That is, of course, if they could be legally arrested. 'As you can see, M. le Comte, I am playing it straight,' Beaumarchais wrote with some amusement to Vergennes, while acknowledging more seriously, '… It will be too bad for those [spies] who are caught in London or elsewhere.' It would be too bad for *him*, certainly, since he was already more actively involved with the movement of arms to America than any other 'honest' merchant.

Astonishingly, he then informed Lord Rochford that he was supplying Portuguese gold coins to the American colonies, and Rochford, puzzled by this, sensibly pointed out that, as they had not been legal tender in Britain for the past two years, it could not be a good transaction—and why did it bring Beaumarchais to London in particular? 'Because it is more convenient for me to deal in London, where I know everyone, than in Lisbon, where I know nobody,' Beaumarchais replied, admitting that he was hoping to make a profit on the deal (for which purpose he had conferred with several London bankers since his arrival—which was later checked with the Royal Exchange where it was found that he had entered into a genuine arrangement regarding this enterprise). Precisely *why* Beaumarchais believed that by openly confessing to doing deals with the Americans—who seemed to be seeking an alternative to the British-backed currency—he was in some way 'covering his tracks,' is hard to explain. It would have been much better, surely, just to maintain the fiction that he was in London on the Lady Knight's account.

The two men parted on amicable enough terms and Beaumarchais suggested that Rochford took a certain Duflos[5] with him to Ireland, to act as the head of his household, as he had already done successfully in France (successful, certainly, for the French, since the man had proved a rewarding informer). '… Our Duflos, M. le Comte,' crowed Beaumarchais, 'is absolutely devoted to me, and through him you will always have dependable information about the most intimate details of the household of the Vice-Royalty of Ireland. I am rather like Figaro, and I do not lose my head for a little noise.'

He also took the opportunity to inform Vergennes about three Dutch vessels that had been intercepted by the British on their way to America.[6] Captured, they had been taken to Deal and Dover, and their crew had been interrogated when the cargo proved to contain military equipment. The British government was afraid that if the matter was brought up in open court, the jury might decide for the Hollanders against British interests, since the ships had actually been seized against international maritime law—a jury that would be 'encouraged by our friend John Wilkes' who led the opposition to the government on the American matter. The ministry, in the end, secretly agreed to reimburse the Dutch merchants for the entire shipment of munitions, once it had been confiscated, and the question of a trial was quietly set aside. For, as Beaumarchais wrote, 'No one wants to go to the Law with our friend Wilkes.' … 'Advice to the reader, M. le Comte.'

Other advice to the reader was inspirational; for a scheme of the Dutch captains, it had transpired, was their use of two separate bills of lading: 'One of them ostensible' [with a false cargo], 'the other secret' [with the true freight, or part of it, noted]. The shipping companies then made use of one or the other according to their need, and Beaumarchais thought such a scheme could very well do for Hortalez & Co.

He also reported that a large contingent of Hessian[7] troops—conscripted at the command of King George III—were leaving for America, to join forces with British soldiers. The Germans had pledged allegiance to the British king on 22 March 1776. The Americans, he reported, had by now succeeded in acquiring twelve vessels, ranging from twenty-two to forty-two guns, besides twelve of fifteen pieces and more than thirty of twelve pieces. 'This constitutes a navy almost as respectable as that of England,' he exaggerated optimistically, and it was also his opinion that since, in the last two and a half months, the British had only managed to capture one ship—the one that had been taken to Bristol—the level of evasion was quite remarkable, and very encouraging for his own scheme.

He also reported that the 'King's Guard,'[8] who had been held back because of a rumour that spies were at work in the Irish port from which they were to embark, had now received orders to leave for America. '… They started to go on board yesterday, and they are sailing tomorrow.' '…That is all for today, M. le Comte, I have quite emptied my bag!'

Except to ask for a favour, that was. Beaumarchais's law suit against the Comte de la Blache was coming up for trial in Aix en Provence,[9] and he was asking for an extension of time before it went to court. 'For,' as he pointed out, 'it would not be fair for me to be judged in the south when I am three hundred leagues north,' (and on the King's business). 'A word from M. de Miromésnil[10] will suffice to relieve me of my worries.'

On 19 April 1776, Beaumarchais wrote secretly to Vergennes, conveying exciting news from America:

The South Carolinians, who have only mumbled up to now, have finally spoken out as clearly as the other colonies; she has her little fleet of six vessels, well equipped. She has 6,000 troops in good order, and more than 200 guns forming batteries around the town of Charleston, which the inhabitants don't wish to see burn down, as did her sister town in Massachusetts.[11]

A certain colonial, Menil de St Pierre, a Norman by birth, a good gentleman but a bad winegrower, heading a little colony he calls New Bordeaux (where he grows grapes that refuse to ripen), has raised a regiment of French, Danish and German refugees. This he has offered to the city of Charleston, his neighbour. But they have refused his generous proposal, since they hold his concessions to be from the English government, and since he has already forsworn his first country, France.[12] I imagine that it is this Norman's proposition, perhaps repeated before the Congress, which has given rise to the rumours of Frenchmen being sent as soldiers to America by our government. If I can prove this to be true, I will use it well with the peer I am 'indoctrinating'!

Vergennes replied on 26 April. The King, he said, had roundly approved of the way Beaumarchais had countered Rochford's accusations concerning the ship that had been taken to Bristol. The British were jumping to conclusions, and Vergennes knew of no treaty that bound King Louis to make British interests his own; 'And there is no example of it in the behaviour of England, when she had the chance to harm us.'—

The King, faithful to his principles, will not take advantage of England's situation to increase her difficulties, but he cannot cut off the protection he owes to the commerce of his subjects.

The orders forbidding the shipping of munitions from French ports could not be made more general, said Vergennes, but what was 'smuggling' to the British were 'matters of trade' with France:

It would be against all reason and propriety to claim that we must not sell these articles to whoever is prepared to buy them, simply because they might pass at second-hand into America.[13]

Moreover, the British had enough forces at sea to intercept the ships they suspected of carrying 'contraband.' The French navy would not impede the British in their sea-patrols—in fact they could not have done so, even if they had wanted to—but neither would they make a claim upon any American ship the British seized.—'Provided they don't make bold to arrest them in view of our fortresses, and under our guns!'

The merchant Montaudoin was not to be punished for his 'enterprise'. His majesty's council was actually more concerned about the unknown 'noble ambassador' who had presented himself before Congress claiming to act on the King's behalf,[14] which had deeply offended his Majesty. If his government wished to enter into a correspondence with the American insurgents, they would send a representative more capable of making himself less conspicuous! Vergennes knew nothing of this man, but he thought it might be some ruined merchant who, seeing an opportunity to make some money, had gone to offer his services to the Congress, perhaps to establish a mercantile correspondence.—

The English Ministers are better informed than we are about what goes on in our ports, and I would be obliged if they would let me know who this pilgrim is. If it is true that he represented himself as an official French emissary, he will certainly be chastised; the King is not inclined to permit such a criminal abuse of his name. If, every time you hear such valid complaints, Sir, you will not be compromised in making sure that justice is done.[15]

Vergennes seems to be giving Beaumarchais permission to take whatever action he deems fit against such men, but how far was he expected to go in dealing out such justice? It is also clear from the tone of the letter that Beaumarchais is expected to reveal its contents to Lord Rochford, as a reassurance of the French king's neutrality.

In another letter, of the same date, Vergennes informed his spy he already knew that the first Hessian mercenaries had left Germany for America. He also now believed that if North Carolina did join the rebels, it could well change the campaign plans. 'England is powerful,' he writes, 'but perhaps not enough for what she has started!'

On the same day, Beaumarchais was writing to Vergennes. He had, he said, been 'reasoning' with 'the man you thought it advisable to keep from coming to France' [Arthur Lee] who had been 'astounded rather than surprised' at the minister's rejection of the news he had brought from Spain concerning the rebel commissioners being received at the Spanish court: 'He believes he is well informed, as I do myself, because it is not in their interests to deceive him.' But Beaumarchais thought it more plausible that Congress had only sent their 'ambassadors' to some Spanish colony in the Americas, or to their fleet commander in the Caribbean, instead of all the way to Madrid.[16]

Lee expected to hear further on this through his contacts in Holland, from where it would be forwarded to him by the safest channels; 'Meanwhile, he keeps asking me if we don't want to do anything for them.' Lee fervently believed that an American success was important to France, and therefore France should aid them. Mostly, he urged, the rebels were in need of French military engineers, but Beaumarchais had assured him that this would be exceedingly difficult to manage, because such men could not be sent into a theatre of war without having first been commissioned. 'Men talk, and we would be compromised ... merchandise does not talk,' he cautioned. Lee had then suggested that the French should give them the money to find engineers elsewhere—from Germany, perhaps; or Sweden, or Italy. The French, he pledged, would not be embarrassed by such a loan; it would all be settled in the deepest secrecy.

Londoners, Beaumarchais reported, were growing increasingly jittery, alarmed by the slightest scrap of news to come out of France, however absurd. An alleged new treaty between France and Spain instantly plunged the Stock Market into panic, and the 'silly rumour' that the French had captured British-held Jamaica had also caused financial hysteria. 'The least scare concerning us has this effect on the Exchange.'

In the Commons, though, most members had the sense to laugh at Lord North when he said that intelligence between the British and the French was near perfect, because such information was more necessary to the French. They laughed again when he asserted that the British nation had never been more prosperous, although the laughter was replaced with indignation when the Opposition spoke out. '... Feebleness and fright,' Beaumarchais reported, 'that was what was to be seen there. The ministers always hassle about the intentions of the French, and he [Lord North] cannot answer one word.' For example:

> Why do the French have 7,500 men on Bourbon Island? [La Reunion, in the Indian Ocean].

> Why are the Spaniards at Hispaniola, aboard nine men-o'-war, by which they are probably protecting trade from the Continent?

> Why do the Spanish have two more fleets ready to sail, when they have an American fleet at Cartagena? [And another one at Cadiz].

There were no replies to any of these questions, although it was taken for granted by most members of parliament that there was a growing certainty of a coming war between France and Great Britain. Charles James Fox,[17] a leading member of the Opposition, asked:

What forces do you intend to use against a fleet of forty-five American privateers, who are protected by 'tornadoes' and ten ports, as well as twenty foreign
men-o'-war, always ready to help them with munitions? Protected, moreover,
by two powerful European nations, who will soon be ready to assist them
openly, and even to recognize them as allies?

'It is clear, M. le Comte,' Beaumarchais wrote, 'that the one who keeps
silent here, does so because he has nothing to say in reply. Fear and danger on
the one side, weakness and confusion on the other. That's the true picture.'

He pointed out the extraordinary value to the investor of a new government
loan, which was purely a panic measure. For each 100*l* lent to the government
there was to be a substantial return, plus three sweepstake tickets worth 10*l*
each!—adding three per cent interest, which the government would pay on
the return, Beaumarchais calculated that it would make a profit of fourteen
per cent!—

These proofs of the difficulties the government is encountering are without question, M. le Comte. And when it can be easily demonstrated that the British cannot
carry through more than one campaign at this horrendous price, can it be true
that you will do nothing to bring the Americans up to par with their enemies?

Once more he begged Vergennes to stress to his colleagues that the French
could win a war against their traditional enemy, possibly by the outcome of
just one campaign. An American success against the British, he believed,
would reduce their bitterest rivals to the status of a second-rate power and, as
a result, return France to their natural state of supremacy, in Europe at least—
it would give them hegemony, as before, on the whole of the Continent.

He could not repeat too often (although he did so indefatigably) that
this should be the most important policy to occupy the King's council. Had
they not yet worked out what an American defeat would mean to France?
Beaumarchais had: 'Three hundred millions in revenues, men and ships, our
islands, and much else besides.' The English would reign supreme, and be a
new danger:

... For really, with their forces reunited against us, their troops in fine fettle, and
made more audacious by such a huge success, it is too obvious that they will
impose war upon us. Those same Frenchmen who could, for the outlay of just
two million *livres*, plunge them into a defeat that would be as shameful as it
would be ruinous.

In spite of the risks he knew he was running by writing 'such daring things,' Beaumarchais stated that he always felt twice as French in London than he did in Paris; 'These people's patriotism reawakens mine!' Knowing that he was suspected (despite Lord Rochford's assurances to the contrary) and aware that he was constantly watched, his precarious situation fired his imagination.

As always, he was as much under suspicion at Versailles, and he begged Vergennes to speak to Sartine 'on the matter of my security;' for it would seem that a number of people in the French financial world—bankers, brokers and gold dealers—'secretly contracted by the ministers,' were prepared to testify that he was negotiating a currency with them. This was, he swore, the purest deception on their part, since they had never seen him 'pass from the order to the purchase'—and which, now, they never would see, 'whatever truth there was originally in the tale.' So there *had* been some truth in the story ...

Two Irishmen had already been arrested with regard to the accusation, and Beaumarchais might be in the all-too-familiar position of having to defend himself against charges very soon; 'Unless his Majesty is willing to own me. ...Until then, I am just a merchant dealing in *piastres* and *moidores*.' He had no fear of losing his case, should it ever be brought to trial. 'But another suit! I am tired of them, I swear to you.'

He finished his letter by informing Vergennes that parliament had debated the question of a British 'observation' frigate sent to take note of any fleet that should come out of the northern French harbour of Brest,[18] and to follow its course. Lord North, as with other questions raised by the Opposition, had remained silent about the matter. 'It would be best if you consulted with M. de Sartine about it,' Beaumarchais urged. It did not need a spy, of any calibre, to understand that British suspicions were by now thoroughly aroused against his country.

Beaumarchais wrote to Vergennes on 26 April:

> After I had closed my last package, I then received news which I am going to dictate, because I am too tired to hold the pen. It has been confirmed that General [Charles] Lee[19] has taken all the weapons away from the 'shaky' people [the politically undecided] in New York City, where he leads an army of 20,000 men.

General Lee had been detached from the Boston army in the previous January to raise volunteers in Connecticut for the defence of New York. Upon reaching the city in February, he had seen immediately that the strategic problem practically defied solution, as New York was 'so encircled with navigable waters' that whoever had command of the sea must also command the town. The broad deep estuary of the Hudson River offered the British navy almost unlimited tactical licence; while, on the other hand, the river would prevent any significant American troop movement to or from New Jersey. The crooked waterway of the East River also presented the British with numerous possibilities for amphibious operations. Lee reasoned that the city could not be made into a tenable fortress, but if defended by 'people of spirit' it could be made into a field of battle, which might 'cost the enemy many thousands of men to get possession of it.'

By the time Beaumarchais received this information in London, the situation had changed in New York. Congress had sent Lee to Charleston, and his duties had been taken over by General George Washington,[20] who speeded up the construction of fortifications that Lee had planned but not worked upon. The Americans had thrown up numerous strongholds, and—as Beaumarchais noted—there were over 19,000 troops present to man them, and all fit for duty. But Washington had little artillery, no cavalry, and no naval support, while the Continental Army was composed of mostly untried militia, poorly armed and badly equipped. Beaumarchais might have stressed the last two details in his report, for his own purpose, but he also passed on the message that these recruits were, for the most part, being led by amateurs.

News of events in New York had arrived by means of a ship which had berthed at Merroy[21] in Ireland, bringing many letters, all of which were intercepted by British government agents. The ship, the *Poly* had been seized by customs officers, for the offence of carrying hemp and hemp seed, which had been procured in America. But after a representation was made to the Lord Lieutenant, to the effect that such a cargo fell under the exceptions provided in the 'Confiscations Act,'[22] the ship was released—although the nature of the intercepted letters was not made public. Beaumarchais had come by this information through his highly-placed Anglo-Irish friends, sympathetic to the American cause.

He had also learned that a great many of the convoy vessels dispatched to America had actually been 'thrown' upon the American coast, which meant that they had not made safe harbour, although they were not necessarily shipwrecked. Among the survivors of these partially-destroyed vessels were two detachments of the 45th and 56th regiments.[23] These mishaps had created a shortage of 'wholesome victuals' in Boston, and necessary items were increasingly hard to find. The same situation prevailed in the camp of General Washington who, because of his failure to make an expected assault upon Boston during the past winter, had come very close to being recalled. 'That's how things stand there,' Beaumarchais informed Vergennes.

That was not exactly how things stood in America, however, for Beaumarchais was often misinformed, sometimes intentionally. For instance, some of the intercepted letters at Merroy were from Benedict Arnold[24] who, in the previous year, had been attached to the raiding party of Richard Montgomery,[25] a general in the Continental Army. The general had been killed instantly during an unsuccessful American assault upon British-held Quebec on 1 January 1776, but Beaumarchais has him captured in Montreal in September and killed on 13 November. Arnold, co-leading a vanguard of twenty-five men, was taken out of action by receiving a leg wound when the British opened fire, which Beaumarchais notes correctly, but he also records that Montgomery was killed along with sixty of his men, with 300 more being taken prisoner.

This again was a gross exaggeration, for only five officers and thirteen men were cut down, and only 300 men took part in that particular raid. 'Arnold has led a troop he has gathered close to Quebec into retrenchments, where they cannot be found out,' Beaumarchais reported. Of the 1,800 British troops under General Guy Carleton's[26] command in Quebec, only five were killed and thirteen wounded in action. All told, the Americans had mustered about 800, of which 426 were captured and another 60 killed or wounded. The loss of General Montgomery was a particularly hard blow to the cause, since he was recognized as being an officer of exceptional promise.

The reason that Lord Howe[27] initially refused to go to America, Beaumarchais also reported, was that he did not want to leave England without first being given the power to negotiate a political reconciliation with the colonists. This duty he wished to share with his brother William,[28] who was acting Commander in Chief of all British forces in America, since both men did not wish to be limited to the use of armed force, and William was already on record as saying that he would never accept a position of command against the colonists. Such an authority appeared to have been granted him by the government, but King George III did not agree to it, insisting upon absolute submission to his will by rebellious subjects. '… As if such a thing were possible!' Beaumarchais commented ironically.

Howe's final instructions of 6 May 1776 authorized him as a special commissioner, in partnership with his brother William, to do little more than offer pardons. They could grant the 'King's peace' and remove the restrictions upon trade, but before doing so, they were to exact reasonable assurances that there would be no revival of the revolution. These 'reasonable assurances' included the disbanding of all the rebel political and military parties, the surrender of all forts and military outposts, and the restoration of the King's officials. 'As if such a thing were possible,' indeed! In case of failure, which would mean further humiliation for the damaged British government, Beaumarchais noted that 'Lord Bute is waiting behind the curtains, whether or not somebody backs him up.'

In a speech to parliament, Lord North compared the present situation in America with the first British campaign against the French in Germany, in the previous war, 'which was followed by most glorious conquests.' He blamed the present lack of success on the 'sluggishness' of the nation, 'which allowed all energy to rest with friends and defenders of [America].' Lord North predicted that he would soon be in a position to prove what he had just stated, and he pledged the British nation would get together—to 'stand up, ignoring the animosity of a few individuals who, through lies and iniquitous actions worthy of the worst punishment, had dared trouble the peace of their countrymen.'

Both Lord Littleton and Lord Carlisle[29] had asked to be sent as ambassadors to Spain, a country that was increasingly seen to be vital to British interests in the Americas. Lord Grantham,[30] the present ambassador in Madrid, was said to be on the verge of being recalled, (he would stay on until 1779). The Duke of Manchester[31] was supposed to be replacing Lord Stormont at Versailles, and Stormont was being considered for Ireland. 'What I told you about Ireland is still secret,' Beaumarchais reminded Vergennes.

Four frigates, of 32 cannons each, were being outfitted at Chatham,[32] and were said to be ready to sail for America; two of their captains had joined their ships already:

Lord Germain has been working for a month on a plan for America, which he will set before the House. It is predicated on continuing the war, more vigorously than ever.

Troop movements are supposed to have taken place in Sweden,[33] which gives some concern to the Ministers … for the existing treaty between England and Russia binds them so tightly in the North, that war cannot be waged without the consent of Great Britain, who is neither willing nor able to split her forces.

Should Britain be asked to go to the aid of Portugal and Russia *at the same time*, he gloated, she would lose more men who were vital to the American campaign.

VIII

Setting up Shop

After more than a year of vacillation, the course of action that Beaumarchais had long been recommending at last seemed acceptable to his superiors, and was even going to be acted upon by them. On 2 May 1776, Vergennes wrote to King Louis XVI:

Sire,

I have the honour of placing at your Majesty's feet the paper that authorizes me to supply a million *livres* for the use of the English colonies in America, if you deign to ratify it with your signature.

I also enclose, Sire, the draft of the reply which I intend to make to the *Sieur* de Beaumarchais, and, should your Majesty approve it, may I beg that it may be returned to me without delay? It shall not go forth in my handwriting, or in that of any of my clerks and secretaries, but in that of my son's, which cannot be recognized. Although he is only fifteen years old, I can vouch for his discretion.

The next letters to Beaumarchais that immediately follow this message to the king are all in the handwriting of this son. The minister was learning a trick or two about the art of concealment from his 'Figaro.' He went on to say:

As it is of consequence that this operation should not be detected, or, at least, imparted to the government, I propose, with your Majesty's consent, to call hither the *Sieur* Montaudoin.[1] (The French merchant from Nantes, who was already in correspondence with Congress, and whom Vergennes was encouraging to extend credit privately to the Americans). The ostensible motive will be to ask him to account for his correspondence with the Americans, the real one will be to charge him with the transmission to them of the funds which your Majesty is pleased to grant them. Directing at the same time that he adopts all the precautions that he would take if he had advanced the funds on his own account. On this head also, I take the liberty of requesting the orders of your Majesty. That being done, I will write to the Marquis de Grimaldi,[2] [in Spain] and inform him in detail of our operation, and propose to him that his country should double it. [Which was the sum that Beaumarchais had hoped would be advanced to *him*.]

The prime mover of the plan was again to be set aside, at least temporarily, and another 'merchant' entrusted with the implementation of it. On the same day that Vergennes was revealing such bad faith, he was writing to Beaumarchais, possibly defending his action: 'It is as easy to talk as it is difficult to act well, even the British ministers will confirm this axiom.' A man such as he must look at matters from every point of view, he added. By doing so, he had since come to realize that the 'advantages' Beaumarchais so blithely spoke of could in fact turn out to be a 'source of harmful consequences, each one deadlier than the other'—therefore, extreme caution was required. It is possible that Vergennes and his ministers felt that Beaumarchais was too well known, and too close to the court, to be employed in the business that he had initiated, whereas the merchant of Nantes was more anonymous.

He was not, Vergennes assured Beaumarchais, refuting his foresight, and he was certainly not to believe that his ideas were being rejected because they had been imperfectly grasped; but 'there are gradations it is prudent to follow.' In a post-script, he confirmed that Beaumarchais would definitely be authorized to start the gold shipments, but that the dates might be rather delayed. Vergennes was also concerned by these consignments because their cost would be 'very high.'[3]

Beaumarchais was then in London, and he wrote to Vergennes on 3 May, although he had little to report of any consequence except for the 'news of the evacuation of Boston,'[4] which had arrived three days before—the evacuation itself having taken place on 17 March, when the English troops had left on board ships bound for Halifax, Nova Scotia. '… Having destroyed Boston without removing their great guns, and without being bothered, while embarking, by the local people, who no doubt were glad to see them go,' Beaumarchais reported.

The British government, he also stated, was trying to make it appear that this retreat was in fact a scheme previously ordered by their ministers:

… But it does not work; it is too obvious that it is the want of victuals that prevented the English from staying in Boston any longer. It reminds me of last winter, when my informants told me that English troops were suffering all kinds of shortages,[5] and yet Milord Stormont countered, with a sublime imposture, that King George's men were only 'taking it easy.' As indeed they were, were they not? With their boots warmed by the blazing log fires, drinking spiced punch, while the rebels were starving in the cold snow! Alas for us; every probability turns up eventually; and then the consequences are always so embarrassing.

The Boston evacuation and General Lee's[6] arrival in New York with a force of 23,000 men confirmed what Beaumarchais had prophesied in his last mail. The Americans were doing astonishingly well on all counts, held back only by the lack of powder and engineers. 'Ah, Monsieur le Comte,' Beaumarchais pleaded, 'powder and engineers, please! I don't believe I have ever wanted anything so much!'

Rochford had told him that he had decided to turn down the viceroyalty of Ireland, because he did not want to live there continually—a condition that Lord North had insisted upon, having spent some 200,000 guineas in order to establish Ireland's present form of government. 'It's too bad that he will not go,' Beaumarchais wrote, 'for we could have learnt directly from Ireland all the interesting news about that island!'

He could also report that Laureguais was 'back in place, having been forced to use the newspapers against a man named Texier'—that is, by conducting a verbal duel in the press since he was too proud to actually cross swords with a social inferior. While on the subject of social embarrassments, Beaumarchais took the opportunity to thank Vergennes for the help he had given in the Aix affair, during which the count had managed to have the La Blache suit against Beaumarchais postponed, and for which he was deeply grateful.

He could report nothing on the subject of the *Chevaliere* d'Éon, who was still taking refuge in the country. 'She is raving on, and I would get angry if I actually listened. But her brother-in-law has arrived in London; he is a peaceable man, and if my heroine is not a detestable and ungrateful creature, he might bring her back to reason.'

'England,' he concluded mordantly, 'offers a microcosmic picture of the universe, where general harmony is founded on the continual warring of all beings against each other. No other country in Europe can compare.'

He also enclosed a letter from the Comte de Laureguais.

An official statement confirmed what Beaumarchais had earlier estimated to be the military situation in America eight days before:

> By their dissimulating, [he wrote to Vergennes], the [British] government has saved itself for only a short space of time from the first embarrassing moment when it must tell the truth. It is obvious today that General Howe received no order from the Court, and that he was driven from Boston by force and by want.
>
> … But there is something else, [he added]. Far from having received orders or assistance, Howe has been without news from England since October last. How else explain that he writes on March 14th to Milord Dartmouth,[7] who,

since October has no longer been the Secretary of the Colonies? It also seems that all the useful wares [new armaments?] the English have been sending to Boston have been forced to stop over in Antigua,[8] without being able to go through.

Figaro was wrong in his supposition about the evacuation of Boston, however, for the British had considered moving their forces out of the city since the summer of 1775. Moreover, they most certainly did not destroy Boston upon leaving, even if the 64th Regiment had blown up Castle William; although, while they may not have burned the city, there had been a great deal of looting by departing soldiers and Loyalists.

But Beaumarchais was accurate in the picture he drew of the disorder in London that had been created by the news from America:

… These reports, which are far from insignificant, kept the King's Inner Council[9] in session last Thursday until after 3.00am … The opposition triumphs, and what a triumph! Englishmen against Englishmen, are they not?

He saw catastrophe approaching, and he was not alone. The Chevalier Ellis,[10] 'one of the King's party,' had bitterly criticized Lord North in parliament. 'I do not know what it is that makes the noble lord try spreading a confidence that only he—not anyone in this Council—possesses,' he had said. 'I believe that everything is at its worst.' Ellis's speech was, Beaumarchais reported, 'prodigiously impressive,' and the ministry was at bay. The papers claimed that the first division of Hessians had already left from Portsmouth, but Beaumarchais was still unsure. It was rumoured that Lord Germain, Secretary of State for the American Colonies, was going to the port to urge the general of the Hessian forces to set sail; which he did not want to do, it was reported, until *all* of his troops were under his control.

Beaumarchais could not resist gloating: 'I say the time is near when the Americans will be masters in their own country;' and he could also not resist returning to his pressing theme:

And if the Americans now have the upper hand, as everything leads one to believe, are we not going to be sorry, my dear M. le Comte, that we did not yield earlier to their entreaties? They will have won without us, and they will make a good peace with their present enemies, which will be against us. Surely, they will avenge themselves for our cruelty towards them?

But hey! What are two or three million *livres* advanced to them without our being compromised? For I can swear to you on my sacred word to see to it that they receive, through Holland, all the assistance they want, without risk and without any other authorization but the one now existing between us.

With the spirit of Figaro looking over his shoulder, he suggested that it might even be enough for the French just to *look* as if they were prepared to assist the Americans:

> … I know that even the Virginians have an abundant manufacture of saltpeter, and that the Congress, since South Carolina has joined, has decided that the powder which was manufactured only in Philadelphia will now be made on location. Moreover, the Virginians have 7,000 trained troops and seventy militia soldiers, plenty of iron, and they manufacture as many weapons as the rest of America put together. But they need engineers! Engineers and powder, or the money with which to get them! That's what I've learned from all my conferences.

He stayed in London, awaiting news from either Vergennes or Sartine, and was deeply conscious of the inadequacy of his pretence of being a dealer in foreign coins:

> I beg you both to realize that only the Bank of England trades in gold in this country, and they know to the very penny what competition I give on these matters. They grumble about my standing, which is the very basis of my security here. If you truly hear me, you will understand that it is important for me to be accredited as a genuine gold merchant.

So anxious was he about his vulnerability, and the danger he was in, that he sent off the letter in greater secrecy than ever. He had it taken to Calais, 'by someone who is reliable and devoted to me.'

Vergennes was understandably pleased with the news of the British evacuation of Boston. But—always overly cautious—he was not convinced that it was a matter for rejoicing yet; and like the Americans themselves, he was puzzled by the withdrawal to Canada when the British had made it known they intended to attack New York. But Beaumarchais had his own view on this:

> They will have a new campaign plan to make for the moment these operations should start. The result may very well be that, even if the campaign is not totally lost it will slacken, and they will do well to save themselves a few advantages, which they can use against the insurgents another year. I don't know if

the latter lack anything for their defence, but I do know that they were clever enough to get from a neighbour of ours [the Dutch] a huge quantity of munitions. Whatever precautions may be taken to intercept that aid, they won't lack as long as they are able to pay as well as I hear they have done so far. If you were to ask me where their mines are, I'll tell you ingenuously, Sir, I do not know. But they must not lack any resources when [Dutch] merchants are so eager to serve them.

Beaumarchais had completely washed his hands of the *Chevaliere* d'Éon: '… I have exhausted whatever gallantry seemed to be required from me due to the misfortunes of her sex. It is surely up to her to enjoy the happy lot that is now assured her.' But the Lady-Knight of Éon was then the least of his problems in London, as he tried to substantiate his cover, seeking out private individuals who wished to speculate in Portuguese coins. He was correct in believing that few people supposed this to be his real reason for returning to London.

Beaumarchais, then, had been correct about the news from General Howe, and he also correctly reported that, on receipt of it, the General Council had met without delay. Two ships, both confusingly called *Elizabeth*, had docked with news from America, the second one containing 700 letters. 'Tomorrow,' Beaumarchais wrote with great satisfaction, 'all the news from America will be in the English papers. The truth is beginning to come out.'

He also reported that General Howe's brother, Lord Richard, had left Plymouth on his vessel the *Eagle*, and he added with relish that Lord North had provoked a furious debate in parliament by asking the House of Commons for one million pounds on behalf of the king. A Colonel Barré[11] had then demanded that General Howe's dispatches be put on the Common's table, to be scrutinized by the members, before anything could be decided, and a further debate of several hours ended in North's refusal to display them. There were 174 votes for the King against showing them, 56 only for the opposition.

But Edmund Burke[12] had given the lie to Lord Germain, who had firmly stated that General Howe had neither parleyed nor capitulated. 'Show your letters,' Burke demanded, 'and I will get mine out, and the nation will know which one of us is deceiving the people!' Lord North then made a further fool of himself by suggesting that it were of no more consequence for the success of British arms to move 6,000 men from Boston to Halifax than to get them out of Halifax to reinforce Boston. For this vacuous sample of politician's claptrap, he was loudly booed.

Burke afterwards poured more scorn upon the government. '… Then my lords, look upon General Washington's attack as a godsend, because if Heaven had not within fifteen days dropped quails and manna to our troops in Boston, they would all have starved to death. But we must hope that Halifax, better equipped by our noble care, will furnish them with torrents of milk and honey, since Halifax is the Promised Land of that campaign. And when the expenditure we made to take Boston and give it back has been shown to be over 1,700,000 pounds sterling, and last year each soldier has been costing the State more than 220 pounds sterling, you ask for our money but only *promise* us success.'

'Et cetera, et cetera,' Beaumarchais crowed. 'Such is the tone of the daily meetings, M. le Comte, in that tumultuous parliament!' As Beaumarchais did not always attend these sessions, he must have had a remarkably attentive spy in the House, and one with an extremely retentive memory.

The House of Lords was equally tumultuous. When the Duke of Manchester made a motion to ask for the communication of General Howe's dispatches, in order to make the chief ministers concerned accountable 'on their heads' for the unsuccessful prosecution of the war, it led to a debate that lasted far into the night. The Lord Mayor of London accused Lord Sandwich[13] and the admiralty, before parliament, of having loaded some of the King's vessels with contraband for America. With only thirty-six voices in favour of his motion, he still managed to prove a case for the fraudulent exportation of colours, fine fabric, gauze, etc., and again, the House did not adjourn until 3am.

Beaumarchais learned that the southern state of Georgia, having declared for Congress, had burnt ten British vessels in Savannah, nine merchant vessels and one frigate; the loss of this cargo, destined for London, was estimated at 120,000 guineas.[14] He had also been informed that the Americans had at least twenty armed vessels, 'privateers,' moored at the mouth of the St Lawrence River, placed there for the single purpose of intercepting any assistance to Quebec. General Lee was said to be marching northwards towards it 'all day long,' and the privateers had been ordered to destroy anything that was of no value to them.

> … There is a rumour current among the opposition that an Admiral Hopkins[15] has taken over the Isle of Providence, and that he is looking askance at the English Islands, [Beaumarchais reported]. It was his fifteen sail fleet that had been seen near Jamaica.

But he had only half his facts right in this instance, for Ezekial Hopkins, the first commander-in-chief of the newly assembled Continental Navy, had at that time only eight ships, mounting 110 guns, against 78 British vessels carrying over 2,000 guns, in American waters. Although he managed to capture Nassau, the chief port of the Bahamas, along with an armed enemy schooner, his efforts were undone when the British frigate *Alfred-Glasgow* sailed boldly into the midst of the five ships under Hopkin's command at midnight. In a remarkable three-hour fight, this single British ship inflicted great casualties on the Americans.

But Beaumarchais was nearer the mark when he wrote of King George's ministers 'not knowing where to turn.' They were very upset, he reported, about not having been able to prevent an American ship from putting in at Dover, '… thus releasing bad news and flooding the country with it, which had dismayed them extremely.' Indeed, the situation was growing so acute that he could barely keep up with the disasters, or the rumours of them, that were reported daily in London.

> He wrote later in May to warn Vergennes that 'Mr Frenchman' [the codename for Laureguais] who appeared to me to be an essential ally in England, is now absolutely devoted to the cause of Monsieur Turgot[16] [Controller General of Finances 1774–76]. It is up to you to decide whether it would be appropriate to place in London someone who shares M. Turgot's views rather than yours. On this important matter you must take no one's advice but your own!

Beaumarchais also pointed out that certain 'people' (ministers at Versailles) were said to be anxious about 'a certain long conversation' the Spanish ambassador was supposed to have had with King Louis XVI. He did not know the subject under discussion, and so he could not speculate upon it, but he was aware that matters were being openly discussed in London and that they were happening unnoticed under Vergennes's nose at Versailles, and felt it his duty to report to the count. Clearly the British spies in France were more efficient than French secret agents in England, (other than himself, of course). Tying the two things together, he also reported that British spies in France were worried about 'alleged ministerial changes in the air.'

Beaumarchais certainly knew, and Vergennes himself must have suspected, that the Duc de Choiseul's friends, meeting in supposed secret at the Salon Guemenee,[17] were plotting to replace the count with the Baron de Breteuil[18] as leader. Even the Lady-Knight of Éon, supposedly long retired from spying, was aware of this. For she had told Beaumarchais that she was in no hurry to return to France, as she firmly believed that when 'her friend'—the Baron de Breteuil—was made foreign minister, she would get fairer treatment from him than from 'the present one.' Her friends, she said, had 'arranged all in

France for her greater comfort and security, and so they had advised her about the imminent change.' Beaumarchais hoped that it would be 'unfounded advice.'

He also assured Vergennes that he was being 'prudent' in the dealings with his London hosts; but he was guilty of startling indiscretions. A poor quip that he made at some private gathering, at which the bad news from Boston had been announced, was now being repeated all over Mayfair. 'The English,' he had joked, 'had caught the "Boston disease!" The Americans had procured an "evacuation" for them, which, far from being an easement, had proved to be a deadly flux.' The jest was a fairly poor one, but even the London papers were printing it—fortunately without any reference to its author. 'This will teach me to turn my tongue seven times before I speak,' he promised his superiors.

More seriously, the news had reached London that the Duc de Choiseul was soon to recover his position as foreign minister, which could only mean that a war between Britain and France was imminent. 'I don't know why people can't disassociate war from the name of Choiseul,' Beaumarchais recorded dryly, for the fact was that the duke had always been recognized as the most militant of Louis XVI's probable office-holders, and certainly, the rumour of Choiseul's imminent re-appointment created great consternation among the rank and file of the British parliament, with Beaumarchais recording that the reaction of the public was sad, even gloomy. '… I would almost bet that the Stock Exchange will fall tomorrow, as a result,' he asserted.

The British government perhaps believed in this rumour, as it was now known that the French ambassador to Britain—the Comte de Guines—was to be sent to Vienna, and that a Monsieur de Cligny[19] was set to replace Turgot as the Comptroller of France. Cligny was known to be a 'creature' of Choiseul, now even more heavily rumoured to be headed for the top post in the French administration, with Breteuil to sit behind the Comte de Vergennes's desk.

But Beaumarchais was sorry to see that the British were acting as if they knew all the secrets of the French cabinet ahead of time, for he thought that it gave an air of 'flightiness' to whatever was done in France. Vergennes was, he wrote, the only person he had confided in with 'all this nonsense;' but, should these rumours prove true, he was alarmed to think of the consequences and repercussions in London, where ministers firmly believed the Duc de Choiseul always made war when in power; or, at least, was always prepared for it, 'in order to keep himself in place.'

Beaumarchais reported that a packet boat from Virginia had brought news so distressing to the British government that they announced the trunk containing these messages had fallen into the sea during a storm, rather than make the tidings public. 'Admirable cunning!' mocked Beaumarchais, adding that the day before, when a ship arrived from Canada, the authorities had ordered a gun to be fired across its bows to prevent it coming into harbour. A small craft had then sailed out to meet the boat and a seaman had jumped into it, after which the ship sailed away, (he knew not where). The sailor was sent post-haste to London, but the purpose of the dispatch he carried was unknown. 'Hence the current refrain: "Why the mystery? Why the mystery?" Indeed, and the news must be very bad for them to be so secretive about it.'

He planned to leave London, he wrote, on the Tuesday following the dispatch of this report to Vergennes, but just after he had sent the letter off, he received a message from Arthur Lee. They had known each other for almost a year, but this was the first time that Lee had written to him, and on this occasion he addressed him as 'Monsieur Hortalez,' the name that Beaumarchais used as his cover as an arms-dealer. The use of it in the context of the letter, though, makes sense:

 Be persuaded [Lee assured 'Hortalez'], that the Comte de Laureguais cannot in any manner embarrass you. I pray you to consider, in your arrangements to the Cape, that the want of tobacco [in return] ought not to hinder your sending out your supplies to America. For tobacco is so weighty an article that it will greatly impede the sailing of the ships, and the essential object is to maintain the war.

Lee, to protect his identity, dictated his letter to a woman friend, and it was signed 'Mary Johnston.'

IX

'Mary Johnston'

Beaumarchais was back in Paris on 24 May, arriving at three in the morning in a state of near collapse; but his first thought was to obtain an appointment with Vergennes. 'My black servant¹ will be in Versailles when you arise, and back in Paris by the time I get up. I hope he brings the news that I have been awaiting most impatiently, the permission to assure you in person of my continuing loyalty, etc.' He was so physically tired that he feared the minister would not recognize his handwriting.

But he was not given an interview until the fifth of June, at which time he was already planning his return to London, and the interview was to be strictly confined to the continuing funding of his activities 'in the enemy camp.' He had already persuaded Sartine that the delay in providing him with Portuguese gold coins, 'my *piastres*,' had given him a competitor in London, which caused the price to rise 'to my detriment;' the matter had not been concluded to Beaumarchais's satisfaction by the time he met Vergennes. He also wanted the minister to arrange a short interview with Maurepas. … 'I will whisper to you the purpose of it, and you will be free to ignore it or not, as you choose.'

But he wrote to Lee from Paris on the sixth of June with good news:

I will perform my promises to you in the way I pointed out. I am about to send to the island of San Domingo, a ship loaded with merchandise to the value of 25,000 pounds sterling; besides cannon, powder and stores; but these last articles will only arrive in small parcels on account of the risk involved. On your part, do not fail to send a ship loaded with good Virginian tobacco. Then let your friend send an intelligent, discreet and faithful person to the ship, with powers to receive the money or the merchandise and powder, and also to make remittances in tobacco, which I can no more do without than your friend can do without what I send him ['Your friend' being their code for Congress]. If there is no tobacco available, let him give his notes [bills of exchange] to my house for what he is not able to pay in tobacco, but to make certain and solid arrangements with my agent at the Cape for the future.

The captain, on arrival at the Cape, must inquire of the main magistrate there, who is the merchant entrusted with the affairs of Roderigue Hortalez and Co, and he will introduce him to the correspondent of your humble servant.

Finally! He was able to make this commitment because he was at last in possession of the all-important authorization. He delivered a receipt for it:

> I have received from Monsieur Duvergier,[2] pursuant to Monsieur de Vergennes's orders, dated 5th of this month [June], the sum of *one million*, for which I will be accountable to Monsieur de Vergennes.
>
> Caron de Beaumarchais

And he was able to write to Lee (alias Mary Johnston) on 26 June 1776:

> I refer to my previous letter of June 6, whose precautions I earnestly ask you to follow. The difficulties encountered here with various ministers have caused me to form a company which will handle the assistance in munitions and powder to our friend without delay, in exchange for returns in tobacco at the French Cape, and always under the name of your servant.
>
> Rodrigue Hortalez & Co

Why Beaumarchais only now admitted to having formed this company, when Lee had already addressed him as Monsieur Hortalez, is not made clear. Perhaps Beaumarchais was already using this particular alias when dealing with his secret associates in London.

At Versailles, on 13 June 1776, Beaumarchais was still trying to obtain a private interview with Maurepas[3] before he again left for England on the following Sunday (provided that he had been granted an audience). The main subject, he told Vergennes, would involve the secret affair about which he had talked for such a long time at their own meeting earlier. 'But as it is "top secret",' Beaumarchais wrote, 'even for you, who has agreed to ignore it, I beg you to obtain this interview [with Maurepas] for an important affair whose purpose must remain unspecified.' He planned to travel to the coast via Versailles, and—if it were granted—he would make a report of his meeting with Maurepas 'as agreed.' So much for Vergennes's indifference to the matter.

Beaumarchais had not yet given the minister his letter in ciphers, which 'follows immediately *infra*,' because, having arrived in Versailles, he found he had forgotten to put the letter into his 'secret portfolio.' But he promised that Vergennes would receive it (with a French translation) in his morning post the following day. Beaumarchais hoped that he would receive orders from Maurepas at their proposed meeting on the Saturday morning, and he would drop in to Vergennes's department to 'offer you my thanks'—ostensibly for the count having set up the interview, but really to brief him on his conversation with Maurepas.

Before he left, Beaumarchais received a letter from Lee in London, replying to his own letter of 6 June. Still masquerading as 'Mary Johnston' (and the letter written in a female hand), Lee wrote:

> I will do my utmost to answer your wishes; but I advise you, as I advise my friends, to consider always that the communication of sentiments [code for tobacco] is difficult. For that reason we ought to do all in our power, without insisting on a certain and immediate return.

The stressing of this last point would come back to haunt Beaumarchais at a later date, by which time he had committed himself—and his fortunes—to the American cause to the point of no return.

'Mary Johnston' continued in ciphers:

> Consider above all things that we are not merely translating a mercantile business, but that politics is greatly concerned in this offer. I have written on your account to our friend Vrayman' [which may have been their cipher for Laureguais].

Beaumarchais was still in Versailles on the sixth of June, and advising Vergennes that Laureguais could possibly be returning to France. Astonishingly, for a man who was still unwelcome at Versailles, he was willing to undertake this dangerous mission to show the chief ministers 'how displeased he is about your inaction.' Beaumarchais himself, he assured Vergennes, had kept a strictly 'negative attitude' towards Laureguais with regard to the subject of any kind of action in favour of the Americans when in conversation with him: '… Based on the King's principles and the danger of the insurgents boasting about our aid, and bringing about a general quarrel [with the British].'

He was, he ended, leaving within the next two hours for Bordeaux and other ports, where the Hortalez business was about to be started. He expected to be back within fifteen days, 'if nothing stops me.'

'Mary Johnston' wrote a third letter on 21 June, again in code. In it, the American situation—as it was known at that time—was laid out, and a further argument for French aid was offered:

> The army of the British in America consists of 40,000 men, and their fleet of 100 ships, of which but two are of 74 guns. Their officers, both sea and land, and their engineers are very good, and they are well supplied with artillery and

stores. Only consider then, sir, how difficult it will be for the Americans to resist such forces if the French do not assist them by sending French officers, engineers, and large ships of war. You may send them out without the least risk to yourselves.

If ten French ships of war, dispatched secretly to the Cape or Martinique,[4] are joined with the American fleet, they might scour the American coast and destroy the whole of British sea power in that area, dispersed as it is at present. Thereupon, their army on land, thus deprived of succour, would be easily defeated. And by this one stroke, the English navy would be mortally wounded.

Do you feel that this will kindle a war between your two nations? But how will the English be able to support a war without fleets, without colonies, without seamen and without resources? On the contrary, if you suffer America to fall again under the dominion of England, the latter will be forever invincible. Adieu.

Nothing was said in this letter, of course, that Beaumarchais did not already agree with, and it is not known if he passed on Lee's message, although the letter was clearly meant to be read by his superiors. Beaumarchais had, in any case, other matters on his mind by this time, fast proving to be his first concern, and where he had experienced something of a triumph. After only one day in Bordeaux, he reported to Vergennes, he had 'already arranged everything' [with regard to the shipments to America], and was now also writing to Sartine, sending various requests for his orders—'Which I beg you to help expedite, suggesting to him to let me have them as soon as he has signed them.' Because of the urgency of the situation, he entreated Vergennes to answer by return post (as always, a forlorn request when dealing with government ministers).

The earlier interview he had been given with Maurepas appears to have been unsatisfactory; or at least, as always, inconclusive—despite the fact that Beaumarchais believed he had convinced the King's chief minister that he had 'found a way to accomplish a great thing, which he might consider impossible, but which he seems to infinitely desire,' as he told Vergennes. In fact he had totally miscalculated the chief minister's character, for Maurepas, cynical by nature, had only one policy: to maintain peace at home. The Duc de Levis[5] described him as 'having no feeling at all for the public good.'

Nevertheless, Beaumarchais advised Maurepas that 'this great thing, which would honour your humanity and bring glory to your person and your administration,' should not be decided upon until he had a chance to speak to the head of the King's household, Lamoignon de Malesherbes.[6]

He was staying, as he invariably did, in some style at the fittingly named Hotel des Princes at Bordeaux, which he would not leave, he said, until he had received orders from Sartine, '…and accomplished them.' For the first time in writing to the foreign minister, he placed a little seal under the edge of the envelope of the letter that he sent to him, asking that his letter should be sealed in the same fashion 'before you pass it on.' He would, he said, from henceforward 'always proceed in this manner.'

To his immense satisfaction he had just heard that he could levy, 'without harming the [King's] service,' some 500 quintals of powder at the Chateau Trompette (a local arsenal). He was therefore including a petition to the Comte de Saint-Germaine[7] on this subject, insisting that they answer quickly and positively.

He was back in Paris at the beginning of July, having left the south without waiting to hear from the dilatory Sartine (or, presumably, the equally laggard Saint-Germaine). His carriage had broken down some eight miles outside the city, and he had abandoned it along with all his clothes, so anxious was he to meet up with the minister of marine, and receive the orders he had requested. If they had not already been sent to Bordeaux, he would receive them from the ministers' hands personally, though what he would do if they had already been mailed, he did not say. He was immensely pleased with the way he had carried out 'the business of the King,' and he was anxious to make his report to Vergennes.

On the other hand, with regard to his own ongoing legal matters, he was far from pleased with the action of the *parlement*. They had rejected his application to appeal against the sentence of 'civil death' that had been passed on him on 27 February 1774; so to add to his problems he was still socially 'beyond the pale.'

He had been further incensed to learn that Miron,[8] the husband of one of his sisters, had approached Vergennes about this matter, 'in an excess of indignation,' importuning the minister to act on behalf of his maligned brother-in-law, who wrote to the count apologetically:

> What does this have to do with you, whose actions have always been so benefi-
> cial to me? You can believe that I know everything, the *quare* [the why] and the
> *quo modo* [the how]. They [the *parlement*] felt it was better to get rid of me than
> to employ me. But the truth will out, and then let anyone blush who needs to!

He assured Vergennes that he was not to be concerned about the possibility of the Sartine packages having already left for Bordeaux, so having passed

him in transit. 'It will only be over-abundance,' he stated, 'and at any rate there will not be a moment lost'—since he planned to see the minister when at Versailles. Should Vergennes himself not be free to see him on the following day, the carrier of his letter had been instructed to wait for further orders. Beaumarchais had not gone on to Aix, as planned, from Bordeaux, 'For one must run to what's most urgent, and I never employ anyone else when I can perform better myself.'

Yet on 13 July he employed Vergennes as a go-between in a matter too delicate for him to handle personally. '… I beg you to hand this draft of a letter to M. de Maurepas the first time you see him. As I have become a "time merchant," and as it is a precious commodity, I waste as little of it as I can.' The 'power of intercession' enjoyed by Vergennes was, Beaumarchais wrote, always 'infinitely dear to me,' and so he begged him to accelerate matters by handing the letter personally to the chief minister. He had four concerns he wished to be facilitated:

I. To see Saint-Germaine.
II. To decide on the artillery to be sent to America.
III. To 'tap' the Spanish ambassador for his country's views.
IV. To protect himself from his opponents (as always).

One of whom was about to make his presence felt in the 'affaire Hortalez' which, despite every effort that Beaumarchais had made to keep it under wraps, was still known to a few interested individuals. Among them was a man who would quickly prove his sternest critic, the noted botanist Doctor Barbeu-Dubourg.[9] An acquaintance of Benjamin Franklin, it was perhaps due to this American connection that he had been selected by the French government to serve as intermediary on the matter of secret aid. As such, he met Beaumarchais on 13 July in the morning, and because he had been authorized to do so by Vergennes, he 'conferred with him freely,' (by his own account). Unknown to Beaumarchais, though not for long, this report of the meeting—and Barbeu-Dubourg's impressions of his host—was swiftly submitted to the count.

'Everyone knows his wit and his ability, and no one recognizes more than I do his honesty and discretion, his zeal for whatever is noble and good,' Barbeu-Dubourg began; but his praise ended there. After casting a number of aspersions with regard to Beaumarchais's private life, he ended by saying that, while he definitely considered him 'a gentleman most qualified for political negotiations,' he was at the same time 'the least qualified for the negotiations of business' (despite Beaumarchais's past trading successes and his constant brushes with government authority).

The botanist, something of a puritan, was perhaps most agitated by what he saw of his host's manner of living. He had been scandalized, he wrote, by the writer's blatant love of luxury, but even more so by the fact that 'he keeps young ladies,' (a veritable harem!). It was also said of him—and the doctor was happy to pass on this information—that Beaumarchais was a 'money-killer,' and few merchants or manufacturers in France considered him to be anything other and, in consequence, would hesitate to do business with him.

The truth was, that as well as learning of the intimacy between the creator of the disreputable 'Figaro' and the all-powerful Vergennes, Barbeu-Dubourg had also been astounded to discover that such an unlikely man had now been given the sole charge of *all* the commercial operations in the American affair. 'Export and import, munitions as well as ordinary merchandise, from France to the "United Colonies" and from them to France, with the management of all business, the regulation of prices, the contracting powers, etc.'—a truly astonishing situation, he thought, and one he found personally outrageous.

Barbeau-Dubourg 'perfectly agreed' that the result of these arrangements, as already laid down, would be the advantage of carrying out all these operations 'a little more secretly,' but he also argued that with one man taking over this immense trade, it would give rise to cries of 'monopoly.' An arrangement like this could only exclude other people from it, 'people who had gone to much expenditure, endured so much fatigue, and run so many risks for the service and on request of the Congress.' Such a 'monopoly' would inflict a great wrong on many people who 'deserved better.'

Beaumarchais, stung, immediately counter-argued that none of his arrangements would inflict any loss on the people that Barbeu-Dubourg sought to defend, despite his opponent 'putting forth all his eloquence to prove it to me from A–Z.'

Barbeau-Dubourg had hoped that other ways might be found to preserve the secrecy of this operation, pointing out that Beaumarchais would not be able to dispense with the hiring of any number of employees who might prove considerably less discreet than those recruited by more conventional merchants, 'whose main objective is always to hide their speculations from everyone.' He therefore begged Vergennes to reconsider the situation, 'to ponder it carefully.' There might be a thousand persons in France much less talented than Beaumarchais, but who would be better equipped to carry on the count's objectives, if only by inspiring more confidence in those they would have to deal with in France or America.

As the newly accredited mediator for the 'American cause in Paris,' Barbeu-Dubourg had taken the recent arrival—Silas Deane—under his protection, although so far without proving useful to him; or to Deane's old friend

Dr Edward Bancroft,[10] when the Americans met up in Paris (as instructed by the Secret Committee in Philadelphia). Of the two, the thirty-one year old Bancroft seemed more fitted to act as European agent in France, if only because he spoke French with more fluency than Deane, who had been his tutor in America.

In fact Bancroft was Deane's intellectual superior in almost every respect, and over the next few months he would become the dominating influence on his former mentor's actions, while remaining always in the background. A natural maverick, he had been apprenticed to a physician in his native Massachusetts as a youth, but had run away at the age of eighteen, first to Barbados and then to Suriname, where he had made a study of the tropical flora—his particular interest being in the extraction of colours and poisons from the plants of the jungle; preoccupations that would come to play some part in his later activities. At the age of twenty-two he had published the results of his researches in his 'Essay on the Natural History of Guiana,' and people had begun to take notice of the brilliant young man (who had gone on to be awarded a degree in medicine from the University of Aberdeen). In London, he had been taken up by Benjamin Franklin, then acting as agent for Congress in England, and in very distinguished company he had become a founder member of the Royal Medical Society of London.

More ominously, Bancroft had also acted as a spy for Franklin while in the English capital, and he had now been sent to Paris to perform the same role for his old friend, Silas Deane.

'I have advised Deane and Bancroft,' Barbeau-Dubourg informed his superiors, 'that they should talk little to others they may meet in society, and even to change their names.' In fact he seems to have advised them to drop out of sight, for he intended to 'tell everyone, including Laureguais and Le Ray,[11] that I have not seen them again, and that they were sent back suddenly [to America], and without fanfare.'

Such a thing could not have been kept from him, and Beaumarchais had learned of Barbeu-Dubourg's letter within three days of Vergennes receiving it. He responded with his usual vigour when attacked, tackling his critic head-on, at his most mocking:

Pray, what do our affairs have to do with my being 'well known,' a big spender, keeping girls, etc? The girls I have been keeping for twenty years were five—my four sisters and a niece! In the last three years, two of the 'kept women' have died, most regrettably, so I no longer keep but three—still rather lavish for a person like myself, I suppose.

But what would you have thought had you known that I am keeping men as well: two nephews, very young and rather pretty. I even shelter the unfortunate man who fathered such a scandalous philanderer.

As to luxury, it is even worse. For three years, finding lace and embroidery to be too plain for my vanity, have I not been conceited enough to insist upon the most beautiful muslin for my wrists? Superfine black cloth is not too grand for me, and I have sometimes even gone to silk, when the weather was warm. But I beg you, please don't write to Monsieur Vergennes of these things—as you could ruin me with him!

I am sure you felt that you had good reason to write to him about me, even though you do not know me. And I have it in mind not to be offended by your action, although I have the honour of knowing you! You are I think, Sir, a gentleman so eager to do a good deed that you felt you could permit yourself a bad one in order to succeed. This is not exactly the morality of the Gospels, but I have seen a good many righteous people making do with it. It is in this spirit that the Fathers of the Church, in order to convert the pagans, would sometimes take liberties with quotations from the Holy Book, a sort of sanctified slander, which they would call 'pious frauds.'

He assured Barbeu-Dubourg that he was not angry with him, and nor was he afraid of any consequences arising from the doctor's report, 'Because M. de Vergennes is not a small man, and I can rely upon his reply.' Beaumarchais seems not to have questioned why his exemplary employer was now saddling him with such an obvious sneak as Dr Barbeu-Dubourg:

I grant that those I will ask for business advances may distrust me, but for those who really care for the common friends we are involved with here, let them think twice before they turn their back on such an honourable man as myself. A man who offers to do all the favours, and advance all monies useful to these needy friends.

Do you hear me plainly, Sir?

Beaumarchais signed his letter as the doctor's 'most humble and obedient servant,' brazenly adding, 'doing business under the name of "Rodrigue Hortalez and Co."'

They had, despite their obvious reservations about each other, arranged a meeting for that very afternoon, where they were to be joined by Silas Deane and Edward Bancroft—neither of whom the good doctor had, with some inconsistency, judged it best to keep out of such 'dangerous company.'

Beaumarchais may have airily signed his letter to Barbeau-Dubourg as the chief representative of a fictional organization, almost flaunting his covert operation, but he was canny enough to recognize the doctor and his associates as a threat to his security. With his suspicions of his fellow French conspirators now aroused, he lost no time in advising Arthur Lee not to confide in the Comte de Laureguais in London, 'in spite of what Doctor Dubourg might have told you.' He could not even commit his fears to paper, when he replied to Lee's two letters of 14 and 21 June, but said that he would answer for them in person when he travelled to London, which he was to do in the very near future.

Yet on the same day he *did* write a letter to 'Mary Johnston,' and he sent it first to Vergennes in the hope that it would be transferred to London in the diplomatic pouch. He had not, so far, discussed the details of his initial conversation with Barbeu-Dubourg with Vergennes, but he now wrote that 'the good doctor' had started out in a hostile mood, but had ended by confiding in him. He also gave the count a copy of the reply he had sent to a dinner invitation from Barbeu-Dubourg. 'The good doctor, seeing I was not angry with him, has decided to talk to me freely. In much the same way that Turkish women, unable to deceive their husbands, find pleasure after all in loving them!'

But to increase his sense of annoyance, he found that he was *still* not free of 'my heroine,' for d'Éon's brother-in-law had called on him with new complaints from the Lady-Knight, who was still in England. Beaumarchais begged Vergennes to deal with this new pest; 'I feel he could do with a little lesson from you with regard to his sister-in-law,' he told Vergennes. The *chevaliere's* advisers in London were still asking for 100 *ecus*, about 300 *livres*, and the lady's entire annuity was to be insured in England.

X

'The Connecticut Patriot'

Beaumarchais wrote to Silas Deane, who was staying at the Hotel Grand Villars, on 18 July 1776:

> I do not know, Sir, whether you have someone available to translate from French, dealing with confidential matters. I myself will not be able to do it freely with English until someone arrives from England, to serve as an interpreter between us. I can inform you, however, that I have attempted in several ways to open a secret and secure commerce between the Congress and a company I am organizing for that purpose.

He went on to tell him of his approach to 'a person in London who claims to be devoted to the interests of America,'[1] but that their connection since Beaumarchais had returned to Paris had proved very difficult to maintain. Forced to communicate in the form of ciphers, he was still waiting for an answer to his last letter, 'in which I have tried to set down the basis of this Great Affair.'

He had been reliably informed that Deane was entirely trustworthy, and so he was anxious to 'resume' the negotiations they had started, 'but in a more secure and serious manner.' His transactions with his 'London correspondent'[2] had proved to be 'tentative' so far; and he was anxious to point out that his own means were not 'extensive as yet, but they can increase infinitely if we succeed in establishing together an agreement based on suitable conditions and exact execution.'

Beaumarchais also confided that he felt unable to grant Dr Barbeu-Dubourg the same confidence as he could Deane, when it came to talking freely about any future plans. But he felt certain that, once Deane had compared the other offers he was certain to receive with his own, he would be reassured by the 'disinterested zeal that binds me to the American cause.' He was also confident that Deane would appreciate the profound difference between 'dealing with ordinary merchants, working on the strictest conditions, and the good fortune of meeting a generous friend.' One moreover 'whose pleasure it will be to prove to your nation and to you, their secret representative, how devotedly I am, Sir, yours ... etc.'

Had Beaumarchais known that Deane would confide most of their arrangements to his old friend Edward Bancroft, he might have felt less inclined to trust him. But at this time, neither Beaumarchais nor Deane had any reason to distrust Bancroft; for what neither knew—and what Deane could never have suspected—was that, by the end of the year, Bancroft would become a spy for the British, assuming the name of Edwards. He would betray his countrymen purely for the satisfying salary he received from the British government and for the promise of the post of Regius Professor of Divinity at King's College, New York, once that city was back under British control. Given the special mission of spying on Americans in Paris, once he had established himself there, his reports would be sent to Paul Wentworth,[3] another double spy, in London.

Even though they had met only the day before—on 20 July—and he had already established his credentials, Deane sent Beaumarchais a copy of his commission from Congress, along with a lengthy extract from his 'instructions.' Although clearly censored by his employers (in order to ensure his safety), the extract fully satisfied Beaumarchais that Deane was solely authorized to make the purchases needed, though Deane carefully pointed out that he had been expressly instructed to make his first applications to the various ministries. He was to procure the supplies required through them, by an outright purchase or by way of a loan, and it was only if these attempts failed that he was to 'apply elsewhere'—yet he had not exhausted these official approaches before turning to Beaumarchais.

'With respect to the credit which will be required for the goods and stores, I hope that a long one will not be necessary,' Deane advised Beaumarchais optimistically; 'Twelve months has been the longest period of credit my countrymen have ever been accustomed to.' He added, with some confidence, that, as Congress had 'engaged' for large quantities of tobacco from Maryland and Virginia—as well as 'other articles in other places,' to be placed at the disposal of the French—he had every hope that very considerable remittances would be made within six months. These were to be shipped over as vessels became available, and Deane was positive these repayments in goods would be requited well within a year.

He would urge Congress to do all they could to meet these terms; but, as he also pointed out, 'events of war are uncertain and our commerce is exposed to be affected thereby.' If the remittances were for some reason delayed, was Beaumarchais in a position to wait for whatever sums might remain due to him after the credit 'we shall agree upon' had expired? The usual interest allowed to the supplier would, of course, be paid as arranged.

He sent Beaumarchais an invoice, listing the type of clothing and the many articles of 'furniture and stores' necessary to be supplied for an army. He could, he apologized, not particularize them 'at present,' but since the number of uniforms required was known, he had made out the detail for them. For the moment he requested 200 brass cannon, and small arms and clothing for about 25,000 servicemen—obviously, larger quantities would be required later.

But as he was still uncertain that Beaumarchais could actually undertake such a large commission, and 'on what terms'—even after meeting the enthusiastic and already proven entrepreneur—he would not, at this stage, presume to go further. Both the letter and the invoice had to be translated, in order for both parties to be sure of an *exact* rendition of it, but he would do himself the honour of waiting upon Monsieur Beaumarchais later—where, presumably, both men would also need the presence of a translator to make sure they both fully understood each other in speech as well as in writing. Deane's spoken French was only ever adequate and, on his forays into London, Beaumarchais had always depended upon those he met being able to speak enough French to supplement his feeble grasp of English. His informants in London were, after all, largely from ministerial circles, and French was accepted throughout Europe as the language of diplomacy.

In return, Beaumarchais was keen to point out to Deane that his means were 'not extensive,' and he was, in fact, as dependent upon the colonists as they might be upon him. It would certainly take 'an uninterrupted circulation of returns'—that is, by cargoes of sugar or tobacco—for his shipments to put him in a position to renew his efforts on their behalf; and as he expected that, to 'spread their effect,' even larger amounts of money would be required to continue the operation, it was essential that the Americans exchanged the weapons he sent them with goods that would raise money in France.

He candidly admitted that it would be impossible for him to 'follow exactly' the order and description of the supplies that Deane had stipulated as being essential, since not all of them could easily be procured. But he would do his best to 'approximate' Deane's requests when he made out the orders, 'although the objects will arrive at our ports unevenly, and the totality may not be completed until several shipments have left our shores.' He did, however, concede that the American vessels bound for France could be loaded with whatever the warehouses in their ports could contain, '… since any choice can only be made after all these goods have arrived in America.' He also pointed out that the 'risks of the sea or such other perils' might prevent him from directing his ships straight to the North American continent, otherwise the ships would be sent to the Gulf of Mexico. The same would apply to the return voyages:

> As to the value of the merchandise, I plan to base it on the exact worth of their
> sale in Europe, all expenses deducted. I can promise you that if your principles

are faithful to these conventions, as I hope they will be, I will always use these returns for new advances [of arms].

He thought a year rather too long for the balance to be paid, but agreed that the current situation did not permit them to contemplate a shorter term, and he would accept this state of affairs without making it a condition of their agreement. Of course, by agreeing to this arrangement, the Americans must realize that nothing could be 'subtracted' (by which he presumably means taxed at source) on all cargoes arriving in France—'Which we destined in advance for the satisfaction, in whole or part, of the debt that you are contracting on behalf of your country with my company.'

The price of the goods he provided would depend on the amount of effort and expense involved in getting them to their destination. 'As I believe that I am dealing with a virtuous people, it will suffice for me to keep an exact accounting of all my advances. The Congress will choose either to pay for these goods at their exact pecuniary value, at the time of their arrival, or to receive them according to the purchase price, the delays and the insurance, with a commission in proportion to the efforts made for their dispatch. These, obviously, cannot be fixed at the present, as it is impossible to foresee the sort of obstacles and hindrances that we might have to overcome; or the costs involved.'

With a typical flourish, he ended his letter stating, 'I mean to serve your country as if it were my own,' and he hoped to find 'in their friendship' the true reward of his endeavours.

When he asked Deane to come to his house to arrange further details, he requested that he did so 'with discretion,' in order to avoid the attention of the many British spies then in Paris. Beaumarchais was aware that his house in Paris was under some sort of surveillance by them, and he was always anxious not to alarm his superiors 'through allowing the [British] ambassador to complain about us'. It could, as he explained, 'create some bizarre difficulties. Our first priority is always to slip between everyone's fingers, and not cause anyone to "squeal" while we go to our work.'

Deane himself wrote to Conrad A. Gerard,[4] the Comte de Vergennes's clerk, on 22 July 1776: 'Enclosed, I send you a copy of the Article of my Instructions, which was the subject of our last conference.'

In the first of the untruths by which he would seek to mislead his official French contacts, he stated that he had not yet met Beaumarchais. But he was confident 'from the character I have received of him from you,' that he would be able to do business with him, 'in preference to any other person.' With the first hint of disloyalty to Beaumarchais, he slyly pointed out that the goods to be bought from him amounted to a considerable sum, upon which the colonists were willing to give a commission for negotiating the business—with the result that 'This concern may turn very well to his account, *without his having much trouble in the affair*' [my italics].

Two days later he was reassuring Beaumarchais in much the same terms that he had used with Gerard. At the same time he felt it imperative to emphasize that the invoice provided was for clothing only, and already amounted to between two or three million *livres*. Cannon, arms and other equipment would raise this sum much higher, and Deane could not answer for remittances being made for the whole of such a cargo within the timescale proposed; though the interest on the balance would make for a satisfactory compensation! With respect to the cargoes to be sent from America, he thought his superiors would make no objection to their being sent to Beaumarchais's agents in France, when they arrived.

Deane had discovered that French *military* stores were regarded as prohibited articles and could not be exported 'in a private manner.' Apprehensive about this, since he could neither purchase nor ship such items openly without giving the alarm, it was Deane himself who then suggested that various deceptions should be practiced. Such stratagems were particularly important, he urged, because he knew that the British ambassador was aware of his presence in Paris: 'He is attentive to everything done by me. His spies watch every action of mine, and will probably watch the movements of those with whom I am connected in this situation.' Beaumarchais was in perfect agreement with him; and he further agreed with Deane when he argued that, 'Being a stranger in great measure to your language, I can foresee many embarrassments, which I know not how to obviate.'

He must, however, have been amused by Deane's naïve assertion that he thought Beaumarchais, despite his 'superior knowledge and address,' would also be perplexed by the intrigues that might arise from their covert activities. 'Figaro' was, of course, perfectly aware of the interest that was already being evinced in his operation by all manner of secret agents; even if he was not, as would later be shown, completely in command of the situation.

Deane was concerned that the military goods should be 'good and well laid in,' and that they should be shipped to America without being unnecessarily detained in French ports: '… The fate of my country depends in great measure on the expeditious arrival of these supplies. I cannot therefore be too anxious on this subject; there is no danger or exposure so great but what must be hazarded if necessary to effect so capital and important an object'—a sentiment that Beaumarchais would have been in complete agreement with, had he been at hand to agree with it; for when Deane went to ask for his thoughts on the subject in person, calling upon him that morning in the company of Bancroft, he was told that Beaumarchais had left for Versailles.

Here, Beaumarchais was having trouble in procuring the goods that he so vitally needed. He complained to Vergennes that the artillery commander at the Chateau Trompette fortress in Bordeaux was refusing to deliver powder to his commercial associate in that city; the commander of the artillery guard at Blaye[5] was similarly refusing his orders. In both cases it was demanded that 'M. de Hortalez' should appear in person to sign the affidavit to replace the stock in store. Beaumarchais had explained to them that Hortalez—that figment of his imagination—had already signed an affidavit with the minister of war, 'But they persist in saying they have their orders on this matter.'

Beaumarchais sent Vergennes a copy of the letter he had sent to Saint-Germaine, pleading with him to send the orders he must give in Bordeaux and at Blaye for the release of the powders; barring which, he protested, 'it will be impossible for me to proceed.' But this particular problem, as he pointed out, was being aggravated further in that the navy minister was also ignoring his requests, and he informed Vergennes that he planned to send Sartine a copy of the order for the different ports. '… And so we will start over on new expenditures,' he added, already anticipating that the two ministries would fail him.

He had again met Deane (presumably in secret), and they had 'parted quite happy with each other,' arranging to meet once more, when Deane would bring a further 'statement of his needs.' Interestingly, since Deane now appears to have decided that his best chances of success lay with Beaumarchais, he requested him not to inform Dr Barbeu-Dubourg about their meetings—because, as he put it, that good man was keen to supply him 'from among his friends' (people Deane clearly did not trust), a detail that was already apparent to the ever watchful 'Figaro'.

Beaumarchais also asked Vergennes if he had managed to get him the cannon, from the discarded ordnance of the Royal Armoury,[6] for which he had been asking. '… What do 100 pieces of four really matter among the 1,700 pieces at least of this calibre that fill the King's warehouses?' he questioned fretfully. The problem, too, of the royal coat of arms on the French cannon[7] could be easily settled—since *they could be safely removed*! 'Do I have to go [openly] to the foundries to procure the weapons?' he asked; '… That would be even more dangerous.' As indeed it would, since he was now aware that agents hired by the British embassy were by now tracking his movements daily.

But while the problem of procuring the armaments still continued to inconvenience him, it was not his most pressing preoccupation, since he was more engaged with the political game than with commercial matters at this stage. Even as he left for Versailles, where he hoped to meet the ministers involved with clearing his shipments, he was planning to meet the Spanish ambassador, whom he hoped to involve in the Hortalez business—and that would be an entirely different state of affairs.

Beaumarchais went on complaining about the delays to the delivery of the goods he had requisitioned, of course, but with little effect. He was now being stalled by the Keeper of the Seals,[8] who was 'cavilling about forms,' putting every sort of difficulty in his way; acrimonious disputes that soon reached into the very highest levels of the administration—the members of which were supposed to be without knowledge of the covert dealings of Beaumarchais's fallacious company, even unaware of its existence! '… All these obstacles tire Monsieur de Maurepas, and will exhaust his goodwill,' Beaumarchais pointed out, 'and I suffer accordingly.'

It was only Maurepas's weariness threatened his endeavours, for he was also obstructed at an even higher level. The problem this time was a formal declaration by King Louis XVI, no less, concerning an item of weaponry that Beaumarchais had requisitioned, but which was already said to be obsolete, and which his Majesty wished to be withdrawn, even from the Americans. There was also a disagreement about the wording of a new form of letters patent. 'Although,' Beaumarchais raged, 'those that I have given them were done under the chief magistrate's eyes. There is no end to it!'

There was indeed no foreseeable end to it for him with the press of business more than devouring the time of day, as he put it; and for nearly two months he was unable to procure valid orders for the harbour commissioners of the ocean ports. An even worse disaster overwhelmed him on a private level, though, for during the ten days he spent in Bordeaux, seeking to have his ships cleared, he lost two private civil lawsuits in Paris, and in all he squandered one hundred days in working to set up 'this essential undertaking.' 'Patience!' he advised himself stoically, but he was totally dejected by this lack of success.

The opponents of his scheme who were privy to it, (far more than he could have expected to be 'in the know,' although the cynic in him might have envisaged such a possibility) were also trying to impede his progress—largely by suppressing the newly created discount bank[9] even before it was opened; a move that would have affected his transactions, since he had invested in it heavily. Beaumarchais was more concerned that this 'new nonsense' might

damage him in Maurepas's report to the King, and he wrote to the minister
to say as much. In the meantime, for reasons of security, these matters must
be kept as classified as possible, and so he instructed the minister's advisers
to act as he had earlier advised Vergennes. 'Lift one side of the envelope, and
after reading my letter, put a little wax under that side before passing it on to
Monsieur de Maurepas'—he was growing increasingly fearful of his messages
being intercepted by officials.

He also begged Vergennes to let 'his thunder be heard against the infamous things' that his opponents were preparing against him, for he knew that
the minister's voice would carry much farther than his own. It was essential
that he and Vergennes should 'join together' in this matter, if only to stop
the minister from yielding to their opponents on a matter of interest 'to the
State and to yourself,' (although by this time Beaumarchais may have been
convinced that the count's concern with developments in America were now
interchangeable with his own convictions).

In the meantime, he was dealing with Silas Deane, having to warn him off
from carrying out his own personal search for cannon and other armaments:
'You are too new in this country' (and too painfully conspicuous, he might
have added) 'to succeed in procuring any of these objects.' Besides which,
artillery of good quality was only to be found in the King's arsenals and warehouses, and even Beaumarchais himself was proceeding with caution in his
dealings with these royal sources. He disguised the various buyers' names,
misrepresented the use intended for the weapons, and lied freely about their
eventual destination.

Moreover, he knew the vital importance of using go-betweens as his nego-
tiators; nothing that was arranged on behalf of Hortalez & Co should be
directly traceable to himself, or to Deane. 'Several persons are going to handle
this required secrecy on my behalf,' he advised his American collaborator,
while he himself would do whatever was necessary, 'including giving bribes,'
provided it could be done discretely—bribery being a form of persuasion
that Beaumarchais was perfectly able to handle, having long experience of
this particular form of corruption; which would have shocked the 'virtuous
American,' Beaumarchais believed, had he been honest with him.

In fact, Deane, he stressed, was not to worry about either the collection
or dispatch of the cargo, for his subordinates would take care of the details.
Although Deane here raised an important point, for he thought it impracticable that sophisticated artillery should leave for America without servicemen
trained in its use to accompany it. His compatriots, he counselled, were not
warlike men, being largely drawn from the land, and they had a particular
need for professional soldiers to instruct them in the arts of war; 'For,' as he

said, 'all pertaining to military tactics must be largely unknown to such an essentially peaceable people as American citizens.'

Beaumarchais thought Deane's argument was worth acting upon, and because he was then still on good terms with Arthur Lee, he informed Deane of Lee's project of sending French officers and engineers to advise the American colonists. Enthusiastic about this proposition, if Deane agreed to it, he proposed to 'secretly entice' the best men, 'especially among the officers of fortune,' who would be the most promising material (since in France at that period the higher ranks in the army were reserved for the nobility, the 'officers of fortune' were very often foreigners who hired out their services, and who were often better trained than their commanders).

But from wherever they were recruited, it was, Beaumarchais thought, an important condition for their success that they should be sent to America in all secrecy:

> Once arrived in our ports, these men, along with arms and munitions, will find ships ready to embark them without the knowledge of others. For the dockside is where, too often, the alarms connected with secret embarkation is sounded, for that is where the enemy keeps their spies. Our main concern must be that each ship must be far from our coasts whenever the notice arrives and gets to our ministers' ears. ... What can't be [safely] done during the day must be done at night!

In the same way that Beaumarchais had vouched for supplies not to be sent to America until they had first been thoroughly tested and found to be of the highest quality, he now included the military men who accompanied the goods.

The gratified Deane replied immediately, fully agreeing with Beaumarchais, writing ingratiatingly:

> Your knowledge of men and their connections is so very extensive and sound that I must depend upon you for the choice of the proper persons, and such whose talents may be of service to my country.

He was confident that the American ships would arrive in time to meet the stores and goods, but he feared that there might be an insufficient number. He was going to write to his correspondent in America to try to procure more ships, and he thought it possible that he could also engage some of them from 'my friends here.'

As it happened, he wrote, his friend Doctor Bancroft was setting out for London that same day, so he could possibly meet up with Lee. 'If you have any commands, he will gladly receive them,' Deane told Beaumarchais the spy, (who was about to meet his match with this sharp and shifty manipulator).

But, for the moment, Beaumarchais was more concerned with 'that cruel babbler' Dr Barbeu-Dubourg. He had met him again at Gerard's house in the company of Silas Deane, 'whom he drags around with him everywhere,' when Deane had said on this occasion that he was there to separate his personal 'rights' from those of his adviser. He had proposed to Gerard that the 'political part' of the American business should be left to Beaumarchais, as well as anything to do with prohibited goods, but he reserved for himself and his 'camp' all *commercial* operations. Beaumarchais had naturally been dumb-founded by the sheer audacity of this suggestion, which he attributed to the influence of Barbeu-Dubourg.

'You may judge what impression all that rambling must have had on Gerard, who certainly knew nothing about these new arrangements,' he reported to Vergennes, little knowing that the two men had been communicating with Gerard from the beginning. Beaumarchais had, he said, felt like 'beating up the good doctor'—who had also been particularly antagonistic to any proposals put forward by him throughout the meeting—when they left Gerard's house together (he had restrained himself with difficulty). '… It is up to you, M. le Comte, to deliver us from that deadly scatterbrain. I'd give up everything, were I obliged everyday to put up with his contradictions.'

But it must also have occurred to him that Vergennes, by making such use of the 'deadly scatterbrain,' was displaying an insulting lack of confidence in his own ability, and he must have questioned the situation, if only to himself. If so, he was mollified a few days later when, on 11 August, he received an acknowledgement for the one million *livres tournois* that Duvergier gave to the Spanish ambassador, with which Beaumarchais could now obtain the sum of 'one million plus' from the Treasury.

Deane told Beaumarchais on the following day that he now had absolute proof of the British ambassador knowing about his presence in Paris, and that Lord Stormont had received orders from London to remonstrate forcefully with the French government about it. Even the English papers were reporting on his alleged relations with certain French ministers, and Deane was convinced that he was being 'tailed' by a spy from the embassy, even though he had done nothing 'imprudent.'

'He assumes that he never opens his mouth when he encounters an Englishman,' Beaumarchais commented wryly. 'He must therefore be the most silent man in France, since he can't say ten words in front of a Frenchman.'

More interestingly, Deane had also been informed that Lord Rochford had left London for Paris, 'and has probably been here since yesterday,' a fact unknown to Beaumarchais; who immediately planned to seek him out, and possibly uncover whatever secret commission he had been charged with. He could rely on his familiarity with the peer to extract *some* sort of information from him.

Meanwhile, Beaumarchais was relieved to have two important ministers taking care of complications for him without him being personally involved, since he had pressing legal affairs in Paris and they were going poorly. When Maurepas seemed to have finally been brought to believe in 'the cause,' Beaumarchais had adopted a new motto with regard to his own difficulties: 'If all is not going well, all is not going badly either.' He would, he said, be on his way to Bordeaux (to secure new armaments) as soon as he had renewed his 'letters patent'—the papers that would give him back his civil rights.

In the meantime, he was so busily engaged in Paris that he could find no time to reply to two letters that were sent to him by Vergennes; although he sent the minister letters and copies for the Spanish ambassador, stating that their file was closed. But he did find time to write to Saint-Germaine, in which he satisfyingly reported that he had seen the Comptroller General, the Farmers-General and Silas Deane, and 'everything was set.' It was, however, disconcerting to learn that Deane was convinced that certain vessels had come to France only to give him much needed funds through the sales of their *salted fish*!

A new commissioner from Maryland, one Carmichael,[10] a friend of Deane's, had just arrived from Holland, and Deane brought him to meet Beaumarchais. They were going to write to Congress, saying that they had both agreed to pay for general officers—engineers or artillery—along with lieutenants and other ranks necessary to the American service. There were also several conferences, usually in Beaumarchais's office, between Deane and the 38-year old military man Philippe Tronson de Coudray[11] who, by September 1776, would attain the rank of *chef de brigade*, and appear to be headed for the top of his profession. A man of tireless energy, with a lively mind and strong connections at court, he had tutored the King's youngest brother in the arts of war. He naturally dazzled the impressionable Deane, but even Beaumarchais found himself stirred by his 'spirit of cooperation' ... at least, in the beginning.

It was as a result of these meetings that the two commissioners, several artillery officers and a courier dined with Beaumarchais on 17 August, at which occasion each man was asked to bring with him the work he had prepared for Congress. Some brought dispatches they had written, while others brought the assurances they would leave in the care of the officers chosen to cross the ocean.

Beaumarchais himself drafted a letter in their presence containing their whole plan of 'active, reciprocal and perpetual trade' between the firm of Hortalez & Co and Congress—but which was to be sent to them 'in a handwriting other than my own.' As an added precaution, the courier present was instructed to commit to memory all the written information that he would be taking with him, 'so that in case there was a need to throw the papers into the sea, he would at least be able to give his message verbally when he arrives.' When he returned, he was to bring a letter from the Congress to Vergennes (presumably also committed to memory).

It was resolved that all the ships coming from American into French harbours would have their cargoes addressed directly to Hortalez & Co, in order for that house to have priority over all others. Beaumarchais had been surprised that neither Deane nor himself had received any direct news from the five American ships then moored in Bordeaux, two of which were 'warships'— that is, transports for military goods—while the others were undecided as to what type of stock to take. They were said to be waiting for the arrival of ships which had departed after them from the port of New London, Connecticut, and of which there had been no news—at least for Beaumarchais and Deane; the Comte de Maurepas had received *his* some days ago.

Beaumarchais was then about to apply to Saint-Germaine for artillery, but he could not put in his application until he had decided exactly what he wanted, and from where he wished to take the weapons. The arsenals at Strasbourg and Metz were too far away from the Atlantic ports, and moreover, if he drew his wares from there, only Holland could receive such an order, since it would have to be carried along the Rhine—an unsatisfactory adaptation; for could he now trust the Dutch, who had become his rivals somewhat? He also had to arrange with a general supplier of artillery carriages to pick up the armaments.

There were, in fact, so many things to go forward—not counting his dealings with the uniform manufacturers—that he was forced to hire new personnel to cope with the increased pressure of work.[12] 'I will drown in detail,' he wrote, 'if I don't get help soon.' Some of his new employees would travel between Paris and the coasts, while others would reside in ports and others in the manufactories. He had already promised his tobacco to the Farmers-General, and American hemp would also sell very well. Oddly, despite his increasing problems, he was at last beginning to see his affairs in a clearer light.

The only outstanding business still bothering him, in fact, had nothing to do with his new company; it was the matter of the letters patent with regard to the restoration of his civil rights. 'Judges, lawyers, friends, relatives, even newspapermen, hurry to ask me if that's only a false rumour,' he bewailed. 'They've restricted the suit that was killing me, following three days of debate in the Council, and after six weeks I still cannot have the first document necessary for the hearing that is to resurrect me!'

The Comte de Maurepas reassured him continually that it was an accomplished fact, 'It's all over!' He was to receive the necessary letters of re-establishment by Tuesday, yet he was still waiting the following Friday, and another delay of three days could force him to lose three more months, since the Council would then be adjourned. He told Vergennes that he was not angry, only very sad to see that his civil status was still equivocal and its return uncertain.

Yet despite all his endeavours, it would not be until the end of the year that the first of his ships would be ready to sail, and British intelligence watched every port, waiting to report any suspicious movement to their embassy in Paris. Even so, the first of 'Figaro's Fleet,' the *Amphitrice* was ready to put to sea on 4 December 1776.

XI

Secret Correspondence

Beaumarchais had already sent a letter to the Committee of Secret Correspondence in Philadelphia on 18 August 1776 with regard to the new commissioners they were dispatching to France. In it he assured them that their representatives would find a reliable friend in him, a sanctuary in his house, money in his till, and every means of facilitating their public or secret operations throughout the country and beyond: '… I will remove wherever possible any obstacle that European politics might oppose to your wishes.'

He was happy to report that he had already procured for them 200 pieces of brass cannon, all four-pounders, which he would send at the earliest opportunity. He had also secured 200,000 pounds of cannon powder, 20,000 'excellent' guns, some brass mortars, bombs, cannon balls, bayonets, plates, cloth, linens 'for the clothing of your troops,' and lead from which to make musket balls.

He promised that an artillery officer 'possessed of the greatest merit,' who would be accompanied by other officers—artillery men, engineers and gunners, 'all that I deem necessary for your service'—would leave for Philadelphia, 'even before you have received my first shipments.' These were the best gift that his attachment to their cause could offer:

> Your present commissioner and I have agreed upon the terms we felt suitable for this officer, and I have found the commissioner's powers sufficient to warrant this officer's leaving under the conditions laid down by Mr Deane. The terms of which I have no doubt that Congress will comply with …

He wished to stress that, because of the secrecy with which these matters should be dealt, all orders should be addressed to 'Hortalez & Cie,' to avoid the possibility of dangerous gossip.

Beaumarchais, though, could not resist making a sly attempt to outflank Silas Deane by pointing out to his superiors that he had made an error of judgement with regard to the type of goods to be transported from America, (although Deane was not really responsible for their mistake). Beaumarchais respectfully assured the committee that the shipload of *salt fish* they had sent was in fact useless to him, since such a sale was actually prohibited in France. But he had still agreed to help Deane make his 'purchases' from the unlawful sale of this forbidden cargo, putting himself at risk of prosecution, and would they accept this act as a further token of his goodwill towards them? He would be grateful if they did not repeat this particular mistake; he had done everything possible to get the French authorities to allow the fish to be unloaded and sold on, but he had trodden a fine line in doing so.

He would, he also assured them, have an agent posted in every French port to wait upon the American captains and to offer them his unique services. These men would receive the letters and bills of lading from America, and his agents would then transmit the whole to Beaumarchais in Paris. He was prepared to accommodate them still further, by taking charge of any commissions 'you would like to be forwarded safely to any country of Europe,'—after he had conferred with Mr Deane, of course.

Having assured the Americans of his commitment, Beaumarchais now laid out his own demands, getting down to business with customary frankness. He wanted them to send him, before next spring, at least ten to twelve thousand hogsheads of Virginia tobacco of the finest quality. Moreover, they themselves must be responsible for the safe delivery of these cargoes. It should be clear to them, he pointed out, that he had already allocated 'many millions' to their trade alone, and he could not operate if the return voyages were not entirely at their own risk.

He had arranged for them to trade through the French islands in the southeast Caribbean, and his correspondent would be waiting for their orders there; and with regard to cost they would have nothing to pay other than freight and insurance. The risk of their ships being captured by their enemies must be borne, pursuant to the explicit contract he would make with Silas Deane, who should receive 'as soon as possible' full power and authority to accept deliveries. In turn, Deane would receive the accounts from Hortalez & Co, examine them, make payments thereon, or enter into arrangements which would bind the committee, 'as the leaders of your brave people, to who I am devoting my work. In short, he should have the power to deal with me continually about your affairs.' He also declared that he would do his utmost to clear up any difficulties that might arise with regard to any infringements of foreign treaties, embarrassing to the French government. What he had just outlined, however, was only a general agreement, subject to any augmentation or restriction which future events might require of each of the interested parties.

Beaumarchais ended by warning them that 'in the nature of their relationship' it was also advisable to use discretion on their own territory when discussing these matters, even when they reported their business to Congress; because 'everything that goes on there is very soon known to the King of

England, I don't know how!' It only took *one* indiscreet citizen to give an exact account of their deliberations over St James's Palace for that to come about. He seemed to be almost advocating a temporary dictatorship, for it was his firm belief that the more 'concentrated' executive power was in critical situations, the more effective it was, and the fewer leaks there were to fear.

With his usual optimism, Beaumarchais gave the Secret Committee in America to understand that matters in France were going more smoothly than they in fact were. Silas Deane was actually having great trouble finding enough vessels to take on the 'stores and goods' (unspecified), and it was, Deane complained, beyond his powers to procure ships 'without making their destination and object too public.' It was he who now proposed that Beaumarchais should acquire all the ships needed, (or at least to act as 'security' for payment of their charter).

On 29 August, Beaumarchais's commercial agent, Theveneau de Francy,[1] arrived back from London, and his employer hoped that his presence in Paris might ease conversations with the American, since Francy spoke very good English. Deane and Beaumarchais both admitted they did not 'chat together as quickly as our mutual curiosity warrants it,'[2] and their conversations presumably became easier once the agent could act as intermediary.

But Francy then discovered, through reading the ledgers and their correspondence, written both in English and French, that some error had been made with regard to the artillery—an error that had been brought about by the artillery officer 'of the greatest merit,' Tronson du Coudray, who readily admitted it. Coudray had, independently of his association with Beaumarchais, been selected by the government to 'cull' the royal arsenals for weaponry that might be sent to America without impairing French combat effectiveness. He was, in fact, then working with the great artillery general, J.B. de Gribeauval,[3] whose new and superior system of artillery had just been adopted in France, leaving the country with vast stocks of perfectly good but outdated materiel to liquidate. It was partly because of this that Beaumarchais had decided to allow him to supervise the artillery and engineering officers who would go to America as technical advisers. Deane, equally impressed, had signed a contract with him allowing Coudray to be commissioned a Major General in the Continental army, with the title of General of Artillery and Ordnance, and with complete control over the men who would be shipped to America. But Coudray was capable of even greater errors of judgement—as he was soon to reveal—not the least of which being a singular lack of discretion.

There was, however, some good news for Beaumarchais on the home front, although not in connection with the progress of his American plans.

A judgement was made on 6 September 1776 on the letters patent respecting the restoration of his civil rights, and to 'a general applause' he was found not guilty; or 'de-blamed' as the wording had it. Beaumarchais wrote at once to his patron in the matter, the Comte de Vergennes, begging him to present his heartfelt gratitude to the King—'I am surrounded by 400 people who clap their hands, kiss me, and make an infernal noise, which sounds to me like a superb symphony!'

On the same day he also introduced Vergennes to the owner of an Anglo-French journal called the *Courrier de l'Europe*,[4] (in which Beaumarchais had a secret interest, and which was published in England). The latest issue of the journal was, he reported to Vergennes, still awaiting authorization to circulate in France after having been censured by the authorities in Boulogne.[5] The editor wished to apologize to the minister in person over a 'bad paragraph' that had been inserted into the pages without his knowledge. He intended, he said, from now on to limit all the articles that were relevant to France, to the 'strictest decency.' Beaumarchais recommended that, 'with precautions,' the government should favour a future publication in Paris, 'since most of the articles in it are taken from English newspapers, and so will be up to date on English moves and London anecdotes.' Vergennes, recognizing that such a publication in Paris might be useful in any propaganda war, graciously agreed to allow the owner to produce a new edition—one which would, of course, be scrupulously censored.

By his second letter to Congress, Beaumarchais was advising its members on how best to proceed in Europe. Portugal had made a blunder in closing all their ports to the Americans, which in fact proved to French advantage since it gave them an edge with the Spanish, who were always resentful of their Iberian neighbours. Beaumarchais now came up with the outrageous suggestion that the Americans should declare war on the country that had so shamefully insulted them, although not in the European area! They should immediately send an armed fleet to Brazil, the largest of the Portuguese colonies, to harry the coastline, where this 'bold and sudden step' would put Spain on their side; 'henceforth you would become the allies of Spain, since our enemy's enemies are always more than halfway our friends.'

'Have no doubt,' he urged, 'that Spain would open her American ports to your warships and grant asylum to your privateers there, receiving the prizes they may make on the Portuguese.' In fact if their declaration of war against the Portuguese in Brazil did draw Spain in openly, 'such a diversion would soon force the English to deplete their armed forces when they went to the aid of the Portuguese':

Then, if you gathered your own forces, you would have an immense advantage upon them. And you would be even more successful if Spain went into it openly, for France has always come to the aid of Spain with ships, troops and money whenever Spain is engaged in a war. This is because of a family covenant between our royal house and theirs, and therefore England will have to lend to Portugal a more considerable assistance. The English will also no longer be able to prevent my country from opening her ports to you without reservation. Which, in turn, will permit you to obtain with us, by way of trade, plentiful supplies of every sort.

Our Foreign Minister will say to the British ambassador, 'What can we do? The King, our master, is going to the aid of Spain not because he wants to make war, but because he has to comply with the treaty between us. Do you want us to close our ports to the Portuguese in order to provoke the Americans, with whom we have no quarrel, thus making them pounce on our American possessions when they rise up against us also? In order to oblige the English, are we to fall into the absurd situation of making war upon the Americans on the one hand and helping Spain against Portugal on the other, in concert with the same Americans?' This, gentlemen is what our Minister would say, and I believe that the English would have no reply. Who knows how far things would go in England as a result of such a confusion of various and remote interests?

Immoderate as the suggestion was, Silas Deane—with whom Beaumarchais was now on intimate terms—was favourably disposed towards it; indeed the American was deeply impressed by its mad logic. 'He always knows a good proposition when he sees one,' said Beaumarchais smugly, and the arch-contriver had little doubt that Deane would shortly be writing to Congress to back up his proposition.

On 18 September, Deane dined at Beaumarchais's house, in the company of Coudray, to discuss the terms of boat charters. '… If they are such as I was led to believe are on offer, I think you must not hesitate,' Beaumarchais told the American.

Coudray would also bring with him a proposal that he had prepared. This proposal concerned financial reimbursement, and proved a tricky proposition; for while Coudray wanted more money in return for his undeniable expertise—'because he was a nobleman'—he considered such details below his dignity, and was therefore prepared to leave Beaumarchais to do his bargaining for him. '… You cannot engage good people to leave their country if you do not offer them more advantages than they would have by staying at home,' the latter told Deane; and Coudray—being young, gifted, and energetic—was absolutely their best choice. The matter had to be decided at dinner that night.

Beaumarchais requested Deane bring them whatever news from America he possessed; 'We need to know that people there are true to the cause of freedom, if only to keep up our own enthusiasm.' He also suggested, when they were assembled, that they 'pray together'—if only for a favourable wind to blow a few tobacco loads across the Atlantic!—otherwise, the organizer of this business would be facing financial ruin.

Meanwhile the question of secrecy was becoming paramount. Three days later, Beaumarchais sent a letter to Vergennes via one of his undercover agents, a 'Mr Swinton',[6] who had been ordered to deliver it to Monsieur d'Ogny,[7] the man in charge of the minister's communications. The letter, in fact, was concerned with the postal costs for Swinton's English packages, but Beaumarchais was also bothered about the official examination of each communication, a policy that seemed obligatory with the postal ministry, however secret the information contained.

He told the minister that his other agents were looking into the matter of whoever 'had blown up the munitions affair,' dealings he had entered into with the utmost secrecy, but which had since been widely disclosed. Barbeu-Dubourg was, of course, his prime suspect, since he was constantly annoying him by 'always going public on the subject.' The Baron de Pullecourt,[8] who had a well-disciplined corps of 600 men, 'would like to lead them to the traitors,' Beaumarchais reported; and so he sent the baron to interview one of the two people he considered responsible for the disclosure: Monsieur le Ray de Chaumont[9] or Doctor Barbeu-Dubourg; 'the choice was his.'

The Comte de Chaumont was the trickiest person to investigate, since he was a wealthy government contractor and an important figure in Paris, and not in any way perturbed by the Baron de Pullecourt's inquiries. He condescendingly assured the baron that the French ministry would be pleased to use him—and his 600 henchman—in some way in the future, and that the assurance would be given in writing. This news displeased Beaumarchais, who did not wish the baron to be suborned by a man he saw as opposition. 'It is as if,' he wrote, 'while we are closing the door on one side they are opening the window on the other; the secret is bound to escape. Those babblers must be silenced!' He was particularly disturbed by Chaumont's offer of 'official' employment to Pullecourt. 'Let them commit themselves if they choose, but not the ministry.'

But apart from distrusting Chaumont and Barbeu-Dubourg, Beaumarchais now became unsure of the baron, who may have found the count's offer tempting. As he wanted to keep him on *his* side, rather than on that of

Chaumont, he asked permission from Vergennes to put Pullecourt in touch with Deane, to draw him further into their camp. He had, so far, told the baron little about the exact nature and progression of Hortalez & Co's affairs; only promising to inform him more fully at a later date.

But when he arranged the meeting between Deane and Pullecourt, Barbeu-Dubourg wished also to be included—a request that Beaumarchais had no desire to grant, since he now knew that the doctor had his own commercial agent, Penet[10]—a partner of Pliarne of Nantes—who had also been contracted to supply Congress with secret arms in the winter of 1775. It was Beaumarchais's declared intention to put a stop to this rival action, and he had already requested Vergennes to stop Penet's 'prohibited' shipments, in order to 'make an example of it;' now, he wanted him to impose a ban on all their shipments, because Hortalez & Co was already losing trade. It was, he insisted, extremely important to silence Barbeu-Dubourg with regard to his parallel dealings. Just as it was also as important to muffle Le Ray de Chaumont; but this, he knew, would be more difficult.

While he was struggling with these new complications, momentous news arrived from Nantucket,[11] Rhode Island, on 25 September 1776:

I. The Congress was still in Philadelphia and was not contemplating leaving.

II. The Americans had irrevocably declared their independence on July 4th, 'and have not wavered since then.'

III. The Americans had taken over the two important forts of Ticonderoga and Crownpoint.[12] They were waiting there for General Burgoyne, who was master of Montreal, but who could not advance because he lacked the boats to cross the lakes, 'which are going to freeze over while they are being built.'

IV. On 12 or 13 August there had been 'a very bloody scrap' in New York. General Howe, who was encamped on Staten Island 'in view of his Excellency, General Washington, who was on Long Island' had resolved to attack the Americans. In order to facilitate this, Howe had made a pretence of landing his troops on one side of Long Island while actually landing upon the other. His men had taken over a hill and surrounded the American army. The two sides having opposed each other for some time, the American generals had then realized their troops were going to be butchered in that sort of blockade if they did not attempt to regain the advantage. They ordered their soldiers to 'pounce' upon the English, swords in hand, and rush through their ranks while they were still unprepared, which the Americans had done 'with awesome courage.' They then attacked the English from behind, forcing them to retreat to their ships. The losses had been about equal on both sides, and amounted to some 11,000 men, both American and British. But the former had taken three British generals prisoner, along with several artillery officers, and many enemy soldiers.[13]

V.   It was not true that the provinces of Maryland and the county of Sussex on the Delaware River had declared for England, as reported by the *English Gazette*.[14] On the contrary, the entire thirteen colonies, which comprised the *whole* people, had declared for independence. Florida counted for nothing, as did Nova Scotia, because they each contained so few inhabitants.

Beaumarchais was keen for Vergennes to pass on the news to his fellow ministers, for now that the situation in America was so utterly changed, Deane was expecting two other commissioners to join him in France with new instructions. 'Soon, it will be time for you to say either "Yes" or "No,"' Beaumarchais told Vergennes; '… I'll go and hang myself right away if it is the latter.' But he hoped that the King's council would be wise enough to save him from that fate!

He had also sent the news bulletin from America to the Spanish ambassador, and had forgotten, in his excitement, to add that 'no peace negotiation is expected as the result of the powers given to Lord Howe.' His lordship had made such an attempt when he first arrived off Massachusetts Bay in June 1776, but 'he had been laughed at for his pains and been sent a copy of the Declaration of Independence.'

'Bravo! Bravissimo!' 'Figaro' crowed.

His sense of triumph did not last, however, and he was outraged by an incident that happened much closer to home, when an American ship was seized by the authorities in Bilbao, off the coast of northwest Spain. Beaumarchais feared the crew would be mistreated, and that the Americans would be led to believe they could expect no help from Spain, (and hence their ally, France)—'A proposition' he declared, 'the English try desperately to give credit to!'

He was concerned that such a development, coming so quickly after their triumphs on the home front, could persuade the Americans that their victories were of no lasting value, and so might still make them agree to a truce or open negotiation with King George III. Might they not even come to a total reconciliation with the British, who would then not fail to inflate such a coup, and even 'build a golden bridge for the Americans to reunite with the Motherland?' Beaumarchais therefore recommended that a messenger be sent hot foot to Madrid to advise that, whatever the cause for the ship's arrest, the court had set it free, or at least had taken no action against the crew.

He argued that the Spanish should remain uninvolved, 'Until a complete success by the Americans in New York teaches the Spanish government that it can safely offer its assistance to a brave people who no longer need it.' 'They may beat about the bush, abandon the Americans to their own courage, fail to help them smash our only enemy,' he added cynically, 'as long as they are believed to be ready to help them.' But it would be fatal for France if the Spanish were 'to arrest a brave privateer, and so tear down the veil that makes Spain's attitude at least equivocal. In honour, there is enough at stake here to make one lose one's mind from grief and fury!' He begged Vergennes to write to the Spanish Court at once. 'For by God, if they don't want to help, at least not let them do any harm! Is it too much to ask?'

By this time Beaumarchais had convinced himself that the French held the destiny of the planet in their hands, since by aiding the Americans they could change the whole world system; he could see so much good, glory and benefit escaping them if they continued to hold back from their manifest role in this affair. He regretted wholeheartedly that he had no influence on the resolutions of the two most dominant European courts and their councils, and he knew that he had spoken out too dangerously in his keenness to neutralize the Spanish, but Beaumarchais also trusted in Vergennes's innate patriotism to keep his forthrightness from further harming him at Versailles. 'I trust in you too well to be afraid that I will offend you in giving vent to my anxieties,' he wrote in his defence. He had, he said, 'been carried away by strong feeling.'

Meanwhile, he went on with the business that was now beginning to consume his every moment. On 14 October, he sent Deane the freight contract for 1,600 barrels of gunpowder, 'or more if necessary,' on conditions that had been agreed between Deane and Monthieu.[15] He could not deny that he had tried to get out of paying his half of this freight's advance payment, 'because my circumstances are becoming very straightened;' but Beaumarchais had soon found that, despite his guarantees, 'half in advance are the conditions without which we cannot obtain any ships.'

As soon as the contract was signed, Beaumarchais assured Deane he would 'sweep away the bundles of goods and weapons' and deal with the artillery pieces, 'which are worrisome because nothing can disguise their shape on route.' He was going to try and arrange a detour, 'at some extra cost,' so that these articles could be floated by river, 'which will save us from inquisitive eyes, eyes that are beginning to follow us.'

Deane was to bring the contract with him when he came to lunch; 'If you have not made any changes, we will sign it.' There had still been no news from America about the awaited shipments from them, and Beaumarchais was impatient for his tobacco. 'I am sad about it,' he told Deane with resignation, 'but it is a long way from sadness to discouragement.' Discouragement indeed, for Beaumarchais was now experiencing difficulties with Count d'Aranda,[16] the Spanish ambassador to France, since there had still been no answer from Madrid with regard to the funds set aside for the American cause. Beaumarchais reminded the Spaniard, for the umpteenth time, of the advantages to be gained from a 'perpetual alliance of the two nations whose friendship they are seeking today.'

He went on with his customary punctiliousness, although he was speaking as a 'private individual,' to outline what might be a future treaty of alliance between Spain and France with the United Colonies of America, 'if the latter was agreeable to the former countries':

I.   The thirteen United Colonies to be recognized by France and Spain as independent states, and treated as such. Possession of the portion of North America ceded by France and Spain to Great Britain in 1763 to be guaranteed by them.

II.   The U.S. in return, to guarantee to France and Spain all their possessions and rights in America, north or south of the Equator.

III. If France or Spain, singly or together, invaded the Caribbean Islands now owned by Great Britain, the U.S. was to help these two powers and guarantee them possession of these acquisitions.

IV.   Fisheries in Newfoundland (known as the cod fisheries), to be free to the French and Spanish and the citizens of North America, but to no one else. Each of the aforementioned nations to have its own islands or possessions specified for handling and drying, and salting fish, with such absolute provisions made that there could be no misunderstanding on the subject.

V.   There to be absolutely free trade in those islands between France, Spain and the new United States, and each country will agree to protect one another against outsiders.

VI.   To strengthen this alliance, every English ship found on the coasts of North America, including the islands, to be regarded as a good prize, in peace or war. Access to the North American ports to be forbidden to English ships. This article not to be modified except with the consent of the three consenting parties.

VII. During the present war between the U.S. and G.B, France and Spain to send or maintain a fleet in North America, to defend the coasts and protect the trade of the U.S. Should French or Spanish possessions be attacked by the English, the U.S. to go to their assistance.

To Beaumarchais it must have seemed only logical to draw up such an agreement between all three countries, even though his own government and that of Spain were still acting with excruciating slowness.

XII

Departures and Arrivals

On arriving back in Paris on 9 November, Beaumarchais found a letter awaiting him from Dover. It reported that the British had taken possession of New York, with the loss of seventeen men, and the Americans had lost over four hundred (as they were retreating), but they had set the city on fire, destroying a large portion of it.[1] There is no proof of this, although the conflagration undeniably caused the British army great inconvenience, since they had counted on billeting troops in the city; even though they had managed to put the fire out with the aid of the citizens. The whereabouts of General Washington's troops were still unknown, so the British had been unable to involve him in a conventional battle; but it was conceded that things were going badly for the Americans at this point, and press-gangs were going about their work 'with the utmost violence' in all British ports in a bid to raise fresh troops to send across the Atlantic.[2]

Although appalled at this news, Beaumarchais renewed his attempts to send further armaments to the embattled Americans with twice his usual vigour, urging Vergennes to give him greater powers with regard to the contracting of new weapons. It seemed clear to him that it was the lack of artillery causing the Americans to lose ground. 'They have courage, but no science,' he wrote, and he begged Vergennes to send more engineers, 'which will soon give them other means of retrenching and defending themselves.'

Tronson de Coudray, who had not yet left for America, and was chafing at the delay, wrote Beaumarchais a discouraging letter in which he suggested they 'give up everything' and that he be left to his career in France. Beaumarchais believed that the Duc de Lorge[3] was behind Coudray's sudden lack of enthusiasm 'for the great cause,' but in reality the overzealous soldier was despairing of ever actually setting out for America. It was also true that Coudray was becoming something of a liability in other ways; always indiscreet, he had told Lorge he had agreed to go to San Domingo, as 'General of Artillery and Ordnance to the American army,' and the duke had then spoken openly about it to others.

Coudray complained of the interminable delays to Vergennes, which also created trouble for Beaumarchais, since Coudray had strong court connections; but Beaumarchais, too, was complaining to Vergennes about needless hold-ups. 'Kindly observe,' he wrote to the minister, 'that if my ships are to go to San Domingo, it is rather useless to transport the artillery from Dunkirk to Brest, when the ship expecting it is bogged down in Le Havre. Is that port less French than Brest?'—

Is it not a waste of money to leave me with a freighted ship that no longer knows what to do? That is, unless you are kind enough to have Monsieur Saint-Germaine send an order for 2,000 quintals of powder to be delivered to me in Le Havre and Nantes, with which my ship can leave under the protection of God and your little fleet.[4] All the warehouses are bursting with goods, and the War Minister is a long way from having taken all the powder that he has coming. If there could be as much waiting in Marseilles, I shall be satisfied, because at least my ships will then be loaded with enough to pay for their outfitting.

'Why can't I be trusted a little more?' he complained. 'Is anyone better intentioned than I am?' He was sick at heart to see how ill everything was going.

Beaumarchais learned he was being fed wrong—if not false—information. He had acquired the most accurate intelligence about the amount of powder in the King's warehouses, where he found that there were 19.2 million quintals in stock; yet the moderate amount that he had asked for was being refused him. 'You must admit that some malevolent devil must be meddling in my affairs,' he grumbled to Vergennes.

When he had computed the quantity of barrels that he wanted to ship, the total mass required six ships, but he had limited himself to five: two at Le Havre, one in Nantes, and two in Marseilles. Following the numerous counter-orders, he had presumed that—in lieu of the artillery 'which prudence is holding back'—powder at least would not be denied him.

He could not, as Vergennes well knew, apply directly to the Administration; but if the war ministry was really short of powder, it meant that Beaumarchais would have to 'see too many people' in order to make up his supplies from elsewhere, 'and be found out by all these suppliers.' Yet with close to twenty million pounds of powder at the minister's disposal, was there the slightest reason to let Beaumarchais's ships stay unloaded in the harbours, imposing enormous outlays on him by way of port taxes? It was inexplicable to him, as a businessman and a patriot, for was not *the King of Our Affair* also the *King of the Artillery*? The exasperation of being passed from one government department to another was very distressing to a man of his resolute cast of mind; he liked to get things done, and if possible to proceed without receiving help from anyone. It was always essential to maintain secrecy about this business, but the way in which things were being mismanaged by civil servants meant he was being continually exposed to his enemies, also the enemies of the 'brave Americans,' and therefore—in his judgement—of France too.

He assured Vergennes and Maurepas that the colonists were not in as bad a shape as was then being reported in the London press (he had just received another letter from America confirming this).[5] Indeed, the Americans were fighting well, and inflicting great losses on their enemies, who had been forced to hide from them. The whole tactic of the British was to deceive France with false news, 'and to make us forget our true interests.'

Beaumarchais was not only concerned to keep his government in line with his own interests; he had also to keep the Americans reassured as to French intentions. He was himself impatient with the delay of ships returning from America; but, trusting to the honour of Congress, he had decided not to wait for the ships 'laden with produce' to arrive in France before sending off his own grim products. Pinning his faith in Deane's contractual promises, Beaumarchais had procured all that he could which might prove useful to the Americans. He took enormous satisfaction in the fact that he had finally started to send supplies to them (beginning with the ship that carried his letter to Congress), however uneasy he felt about the way in which these matters were progressing.

He had decided, perhaps as a security precaution, that the paperwork connected to each shipment should not travel with the cargo. Writing to Congress on 1 December 1776, he informed them that the invoices for the merchandise on his first ship, attested and signed by Silas Deane, would be arriving by a second vessel, which would also be 'laden with munitions.' The invoices for that delivery would be carried on the third ship, et cetera; which was how he intended to proceed with subsequent shipments.

He was, he apologized, unable to increase his financial advances to the Congress; 'For I simply do not have enough friends [that is, backers].' It was therefore absolutely imperative that they fully understood his position: he could not send them further supplies if they did not, in return, send him 'remittances and products of your own country' on the ships that he sent to their ports.

'What I call "my ships," gentlemen,' he explained, 'are actually French vessels that I have hired for freight, according to a contract passed between a ship-owner and myself, in the presence of Mr Deane. I have been forced to this proceeding since the ships that you have promised to send us a long time ago have so far not arrived,' and to underline this particular grievance, he enclosed a copy of the agreement between himself and Deane, implemented in the name of Congress. Once again, he asked the committee for their remittances to be in 'excellent' Virginia tobacco, indigo or rice. 'My advances in this shipment now sent to you must soon be followed by a second one as considerable, which amounts to about one million *livres*.'

On the following day, Beaumarchais wrote to Vergennes to notify him that he had seen the Spanish ambassador—to whom Deane wished to give a printed copy of the Declaration of Independence—and had inquired of him whether or not would it be permitted for Deane to do so in person. Beaumarchais believed that the ambassador himself would wish to consult with Vergennes on this matter, but Deane also wanted to thank the Spanish ambassador personally for the safeguard now guaranteed to American ships in Spanish ports. This, Beaumarchais thought, would be an excellent diplomatic stroke.

In the same letter, he complained about the people who surrounded the all-powerful Maurepas, 'who deliberately pursue and would like to injure me.' This was not delusional, for such suspicions in the over-wrought atmosphere of Versailles were commonplace, although in spite of being constantly humiliated, Beaumarchais took pride in brushing off all petty indignities; 'I attend to the job with self assurance.' Any important papers, he told Vergennes, were safely stored, *and not in his house*. 'But it is not to suppress them that they are hidden. On the contrary, it is that they may be used to defend my conduct when it is attacked.' As always with Beaumarchais, there was a none too subtle hint of blackmail in these lines.

He questioned why Coudray was still hanging around Versailles, and what he could be up to: 'He has been there since Friday … and I have not heard from him in three days.' Everything was ready to go, all was in waiting, and Coudray's ship was at anchor in the harbour—so why the delay? If, as Beaumarchais suspected, Coudray was seeking to take over command of the shipment, it would be better to handle matters personally.

In order to keep Maurepas on his side, he sent particular news to him, surreptitiously extracted from private letters of Lord Germain (the British secretary of state for the American colonies). This secret information was also a sweetener for the chief minister with regard to another problem; for, on 9 December, it had been arranged for Sartine to deliver a memorial. Beaumarchais had written to the King on the subject of his present problems, and Sartine was particularly afraid that Maurepas would not be swayed by the arguments expressed in it. Its author, too, was afraid of this, in spite of the urgent manner in which he had treated the subject; '… Not that I think he will reject the thing for itself, but because of the man [himself] behind it!'

He was afraid that his majesty might be fatigued by its discursiveness, and urged Sartine to try to make him appreciate it 'before the time for objections has arrived.' But if this should fail, Beaumarchais wanted an opportunity to speak to the King in private; '... I believe I know how to get his attention.' He had, in fact, he wrote—inspired by something that Vergennes had said—just had a bright idea!

This was nothing less than to make conclusively sure of Spain, and to convince them to ally their government firmly to France in the American cause; it was, he reasoned, the main problem remaining. This must, of course, be done in the greatest secrecy, yet how could such secrecy be preserved with the growing number of people who were now involved? Above all, how could they negotiate with the intensity of speed required? Beaumarchais, further inspired, had come up with an answer.

'See to it that the King makes up his mind,' he urged Sartine, in a hurried note, 'and I shall handle Spain and England. Have his Majesty but decide and I shall be on my way to London' (to do what, he did not say; but here, for whatever reason, he would stay for fifteen days). On his return, he proposed, he would journey to the south of France, 'stopping over at Aix,' where the pretext of his appearing in court for his lawsuit hearing would bring him closer to his real goal of actually turning up at the Spanish court. 'I shall plead [at Aix], where I shall certainly win,' he boasted; 'After which I shall get on a boat for Barcelona, and from there go on to Madrid, where I can take care of my business within another fifteen days, as I know everyone there.'[6]

The main merit of this proposal was that Vergennes would know, on 'Figaro's' return,—since it was definitely an assignment for him—what to expect about Spain's real intentions. Moreover, the minister would then be able to use Beaumarchais's proposals, based upon what he had learned at Madrid, to object to any of Maurepas's lingering objections to the question of recognizing the new America. 'What can be objected to,' Beaumarchais asked Vergennes, 'if Spain freely adopts a plan that should never have raised one question at Versailles ... and if she joins in with the financing of this inexpensive exercise?' But, because he had explained himself 'too frankly in this matter,' he hoped he could trust Vergennes to burn his letter. If not, he asked for it to be sent back, 'with your answer.'

It had come to his attention, Vergennes informed Le Noir[7] (the Superintendent of Police) on 10 December, that certain individuals claiming to be 'army' officers were spreading a rumour they were being sent to aid the American insurgents, and had been encouraged to enlist for that purpose. He wanted Le Noir's department to arrest the men who claimed to be on their way to America, and he wished to be informed of their arrests. The search for these 'rogues and liars' should, he insisted, be carried out as publicly as possible, 'and severely enough' for the public to see that the government was playing no part in these so-called enrolments for the American cause; '… the publicity of which is supremely disagreeable.'

Coudray was, in fact, the primary source of these rumours, and while waiting for a favourable wind at Le Havre, he had also talked openly about the illegal shipment of arms. Beaumarchais had just returned from that port, where the embarkation problems had greatly multiplied, and he had been working every hour of the day for a week in trying to settle matters (between attending rehearsals for *The Barber of Seville*, his 'cover' perhaps, but where he was identified at the theatre by British agents). The ship *Amphitrite* had been due to set sail 'by the best wind possible,' but the crew suddenly demanded extra money. One officer turned in his commission and headed back for Paris, while many others wanted to be paid above the sixth-month 'gratification' that Beaumarchais had already offered them, and this was to be paid, ahead of time, in letters of exchange, drawn from a San Domingo bank.

Beaumarchais regarded their request as 'not exactly unfair,' and so he yielded to their demand, but this had entailed much paperwork. Afterwards, while still in port, he ensured that no member of the crew carried any incriminating documents in his trunk or pockets, and had sailed out of Le Havre for 'two leagues' just to make certain that the ship carried no dangerous evidence aboard. Certain papers were, of course, indispensable, and Beaumarchais and the captain had worked out, 'under cover of night,' where the best hiding places for these would be. Only the captain and Coudray, whom Beaumarchais still trusted at that point, knew their whereabouts.

Beaumarchais had sent a letter to London from Le Havre, expressing his desire for a secret conference with Arthur Lee and his friends. But he had been warned of the danger to himself should he enter England at this period, and so he decided that another person should go in his stead. A small boat loaded with coal to be sold in England, carrying a courier disguised as a sailor, had been sent from Le Havre, and Beaumarchais believed that he could count on this man.

His decision to visit Lee in London had, however, been unnecessary, since by the end of December 1776, the American was in Paris. For some reason Beaumarchais had not been informed that, in October, the Secret Committee of Congress had appointed Lee to join Deane and Benjamin Franklin as a third commissioner. Lee had taken the place of Thomas Jefferson, who had declined the post, and as Lee had served as the Secret Committee's correspondent in London, he must have struck them as being the ideal replacement. Beaumarchais, when they finally met, early in the New Year, was naturally pleased to have Lee so close to hand—since for one thing it would make communication between himself and the commissioners much easier! But Lee seems to have been antagonistic to him from the first of their meetings in Paris, and he was clearly harbouring some resentment against him.

In January 1777, Beaumarchais had (while still in Le Havre) first heard of Benjamin Franklin's arrival in France as an accredited commissioner. [The American had, in fact, reached France on 4 December 1776.] Afraid that 'in this country of idle gossip,' Franklin would be treated with some indiscretion on his arrival in Paris, he had written to Silas Deane, asking him to 'keep Franklin locked up' until he could return. He himself, although anxious to meet the new commissioner, was forced to stay in Le Havre to meet an 'English accomplice,'[8] whom he then asked to follow him back to Paris with all speed—with Beaumarchais travelling non-stop afterwards, for 'one night and a day, so as not to keep Mr Franklin prisoner for too long.' In the event, he made such good time on the road that he actually arrived in Paris before the American.

At this stage, Beaumarchais was exhausted but 'ebullient,' for his ship had sailed with 130 soldiers and engineers on board, and while the British, who had a royal ship of 60 guns in the Channel, might possibly intercept his vessel, everything was in order. 'To touch it,' he wrote, 'they would have to break glass and declare war. Somehow, I don't think they'll try!'

Yet if Beaumarchais had not gone to Le Havre himself, the ship would not have left for a further fifteen days and, as it was, his secretary had been forced to stay behind to send a second ship, of 250 tons, on its way. The first ship was of 480 tons, but it carried so many passengers, and the gun carriages were so encumbering, that there had been no room left for the rest of the load. This was to leave the following weekend, with another ship from Nantes leaving twelve days later.

A secret envoy had also arrived from England, staying at St Germain-en-Laye, from where he wrote to Beaumarchais, requesting a rendezvous. But Beaumarchais would only meet up with the agent once he had received Vergennes's orders, and he had—with Deane's help—first to settle Benjamin Franklin in new quarters in Paris. He had been extremely put out to learn that the famous American was lodged in splendour at the Comte Le Ray de Chaumont's magnificent house, the Hotel de Valentois on the heights of Passy. The count being a Freemason friend of Franklin's; who, with his stout figure and balding pate, he resembled physically.

Beaumarchais instinctively distrusted Chaumont, but he was also put out because it would have boosted his own standing to have taken charge of Franklin's domestic arrangements while in France. Like most of his contemporaries, he was filled with admiration for this 'courageous old man' (whose reputation had been enhanced by the story currently circulating, that he had bravely allowed the ship he sailed in from America to take two 'purses' from British ships on his voyage—that is, to challenge and board the ships—'despite the risk to his person'). Franklin was to be lionized by the public and society during his stay in Paris, although never openly received by the government. Crowds in the street would cheer him when he passed and fashionable women took to wearing a chic version of his bearskin hat. He was loved for his sober, homespun look, and was seen to be representative of the new Americans. Regarded as a rustic sage from the 'wilds of America,' he played the role with zest, amused and flattered by their attentions.

If Beaumarchais was angry with Deane for not having helped him to secure the person of the most eminent American of his time, he managed to suppress it. When they next met he never mentioned it, but merely apologized for the fact that he had not been able to send the *Amphitrite* on its way before an embargo from the ministry had arrived. Although cannily fearing such a move, he had employed 100 men to work flat out for two nights to fill the ship, yet even so, three quarters of the provisions had to be taken out to the roadstead in small boats. It had, Beaumarchais admitted, been 'an awful mess;' they had worked in too much of a rush to follow any proper plan, or to dispose of goods in a certain order.

The freighting of his other two ships had also been stopped at the instigation of the authorities, and they had been publicly unloaded, despite Beaumarchais appealing to the ministry to reverse their decision; but he still hoped to reload and send the ships to sea once his complaints had been registered and acted upon. He was going to start by having the names of the ships changed, so that they could begin to operate 'with a clean slate,' which might mean less interference from officialdom; the rest 'would be done at night, with little noise.' He lamented, 'What a loss! It's money poured into the sea!'—but he always knew the best way to handle bureaucrats; every blunder, every obstacle, had to be removed by the expenditure of a great many gold *louis*. 'I would be ashamed of my actions,' he confessed 'if I didn't know that we cannot do otherwise.'

He had received a letter from Deane through a 'Monsieur Eyries'[9] who was—according to Deane—'the most finished of villains,' since he chartered vessels to carry goods to America at exorbitant rates. Beaumarchais had long questioned the exact nature of their relationship, but their association was not the only issue to disconcert him; for although he had looked forward to Benjamin Franklin's appearance in Paris, he was also concerned about the change this might bring to Silas Deane's status, on which subject he asked Deane to deal with him frankly. '… Will this mean that your powers as the first agent will alter, and will I have to start all over again with the new commissioner?'

He also wondered if Franklin had brought new funding with him. If so, it could only be a good thing, 'For, believe me, that is going to be essential for us to continue our shipments.'

Beaumarchais received a very formal letter from a secretary in Vergennes's office, and this worried him slightly because it was the first communication to come from the minister through another's hands. He was right to be concerned about the frigid tone of the wording, for the count's attitude towards him would deteriorate from this time onwards. In the letter, Vergennes asked for an 'accounting' of the business dealing of Hortalez & Co, which Beaumarchais naturally found insulting. Such a thing had been prepared for a long time, he assured the minister; and he had it delivered promptly to Versailles.

In this instance, too, Beaumarchais proved to be more scrupulous than his superior when it came to contractual promises. The Americans had earlier been sanctioned to use ships of the French navy, 'having none of their own to spare,' but on 7 January Vergennes, in a letter to Gerard, he refused further permission for Americans to transport their goods on official French vessels. In this way, the minister deceived the trusting Beaumarchais, although he evaded the issue of his personal involvement by putting Sartine in charge of carrying this rejection through. He hoped also, perhaps, to pass his 'troublesome servant' on to him, authorizing Gerard to do the same, 'without throwing off the masks.'

Deane, too, was having his problems. He felt uneasy because 'certain persons' were hinting that the merchandise bound for America was 'neither good, nor well laid in,' and believing this to be false, he proposed having an inspection made of the goods such as would satisfy his critics without making the transactions public. He wanted his colleague Carmichael to travel to Le Havre as an independent witness to examine the state of the arms and stores ready for export. A nephew of Benjamin Franklin named Williams[10]—who was also a merchant, and upon whose judgement Congress could fully rely—should go to Nantes for the same purpose. These men should then make an official report, and both were to remain in the two ports until the stores were safely out to sea, where they should wait upon Beaumarchais for any further orders.

On 11 January 1777, Beaumarchais advised Hughes Eyries (whom he had decided to employ, despite his continuing suspicions) that the ships 'presently loaded' at Le Havre should now go on to San Domingo via Brest, and 'two things are to be noted':

I.   There had so far been no complaints from 'our neighbour' [Great Britain].
II. Their covert operations could reach a deadly stage if they lost any time in putting out to sea. The ship, 'once visited,' should be sent off without delay.

The person who handed Hughes Eyries the letter from Beaumarchais was to be held responsible for bringing back proof that all had been correctly organized, since Beaumarchais believed that 'some rascals of your town' had played a trick on him (although he must have most strongly suspected Hughes Eyries himself). Proof of this trickery should be made as clear as possible to the messenger, to prove that it was not imagined; and Beaumarchais promised, 'we will thereafter do justice to these gentleman,' if his suspicions proved correct. The ship was also to be repacked if necessary, since the first ship had been forced to return to port due to bad packing, 'and the provisions were in a worse condition.'

Aware of the inexplicable chill coming from the Comte de Vergennes, and hearing a rumour of an impending change of political masters, Beaumarchais tried to conduct his business with the various ministries by employing as little contact with them as possible. He explained his reluctance to deal with them directly, saying that he hoped, by so doing, to 'make use of them without compromising them, and not to ask for too much.' Privately, he declared that since the ministers were busy with other business (even if they had a surplus of personnel), 'one wasted a lot of time before gaining their consent to any new development.'

He was further disconcerted to discover that the naval superintendent at Le Havre had received secret orders from his ministry to 'act in agreement with Hughes Eyries' (that is, to the possible exclusion of Beaumarchais). For example, the captain of the ship that Hughes Eyries had chartered was to procure, in whatever way possible, a coastal rather than a river pilot, with everything done in the greatest secrecy—which suggested that further supplies were to be taken on board, the classification of which was to be kept from Beaumarchais. Upon discovering this new deception, he sent secret instructions through a messenger; for as he said, 'When one ministerial embargo is taken off, one must run as to a fire, in fear that another one will take its place!' He also sent his own instructions to Hughes Eyries, telling him to make out that the ship was in fact voyaging no further than Brest (by which means he was able to give Hughes Eyries to understand that he was fully conversant with the ministry of marine's secret orders!).

He offered the outrageous suggestion that, if the captain of the French ship Hughes Eyries had commissioned was to meet a dependable *American* privateer at sea, he should then contrive for his ship to be taken as a 'prize' to the New World. This, he argued, would solve a lot of problems, as the British could not then blame the French government for the loss of a ship destined for other waters. To confuse matters further, he suggested that the name of the ship should be changed 'at the moment of departure.'

To his increasing consternation, Vergennes was again questioning his accounting; this time for the sums 'allocated for England.' True, there were some discrepancies, but Beaumarchais refused to make excuses for them; in a business as complex as this, he argued, there were bound to be some small mistakes made. Vergennes, while he accepted this justification, still astonishingly suggested that the balance due should be paid—either in silver or paper—in London, as it was known that Beaumarchais had considerable sums invested there.[11] Astonishingly, since Beaumarchais had—so far as it is known—never cheated the minister, he agreed to give Vergennes bills drawn on his City of London bank within two months.

In English currency it balanced out at 1685*l*–17s–4d sterling; or—as Beaumarchais explained—'what we call in business "gilt-edged paper,"' which was equivalent to gold in Paris as in London. If that were not convenient, as he further made clear, the sum would then be paid out by his cashier to whomever Vergennes nominated in Paris; 'For I do not have a single *louis d'or* that I can sacrifice to you in gold, and the sum in silver is not portable to Versailles.'

Beaumarchais pointed out, striking back at what he saw as an unjust accusation, that he had made no deduction for his own travel expenses for the past two years, 'whether in this affair or in any other.' This was still, perhaps, not the proper time to pursue such matters, but he hoped that the minister would later solicit the King for a reimbursement of his expenses; although he did not expect a salary, or even a reward, for his efforts in the cause of France. Remembering the shabby way he had been treated in the first year of the King's reign, he must have been dubious about the possibility of receiving any kind of recompense.

Because of some misunderstanding, (never explained), he had been obliged to send his English interpreter to Lorient,[12] so there was now another account outstanding, and Vergennes would receive it on the man's return, 'together with 2,000 pounds relative to it.' Beaumarchais, aware of his reputation as a 'Figaro' character, was always anxious to show that he was completely reliable, in fact the perfect factotum, whether it came to devising plots or adding up accounts.

He was ill with a cold, 'which sticks to my lungs and my back,' and perhaps as a part of the depression this created he was terribly aware that matters were now going badly for him. But despite his despondency on the matter of the accounts, he did not submit a memorial on the subject; there were some things better said than written down. He was, to exacerbate the situation, now receiving serious complaints from the Comte de Le Ray Chaumont, with regard to his interview with Baron Pullecourt. '… His furious resentment against me has caused the raising of other batteries, the mechanics of which you will not mind learning.'

Nevertheless, Beaumarchais believed that he had cleared himself with Vergennes for the 'contemptible indiscretion' in regard to the accounts with which he had been accused. He had not rested, he said, until he found out 'where so much wickedness comes from,' and he heard every day of 'such impossible things concerning the King's ministers that I have to suspect some devil is again cavorting in my business, to ruin everything.' He always knew more about the extent of the machinations at court against him than he dared to acknowledge.

Beaumarchais did, however, warn Vergennes that, far from suspecting such a proven servant as himself, he should look to his own position. 'You cannot see what they are prepared to venture, in trying to remove you from your office, to replace you with one of their friends;' but Vergennes, who at that time must have thought himself irreplaceable, simply thought that Figaro was up to his usual scaremongering. Even the most unimportant courtier was aware that Vergennes's enemies made no secret of their intentions; many people were, indeed, trying to unseat him.

Beaumarchais, meanwhile, unhappily aware that he had lost the confidence of his most influential patron, was back in his bed, suffering, as he said, from 'grief, fever and fatigue.' He hoped to have a meeting with Sartine, 'if I can move', for he could not shake off his chill. '… While evil advances with giant steps, goodness drags on like a tortoise,' he lamented.

By 28 January, the 'devil' was again being very active in his business, largely through Coudray's continuing—and malevolent—influence at Versailles. Coudray had received a letter from his nephew,[13] whom Beaumarchais thought possessed his uncle's gift for making mischief. The nephew, although he also wished to serve in America, had been worried about going on board the *Amphitrite*, since he was fearful of 'adverse encounters with the English,' and the rumour that the ship was incapable of being defended in such a situation was now circulating at Court.

Deane, too, was causing Beaumarchais concern. Normally level-headed and even-tempered, he had been in a foul mood for almost a month; suspecting—and making his suspicions very clear—that there was something 'obscure and inconceivable' in the delays of the ships at Le Havre. Beaumarchais asked him outright for an explanation of his 'offensive tone,' and Deane replied that he was 'tired of not knowing whom to blame.' He had given a memorial written by Arthur Lee on the subject of the delays to Vergennes, and the count had assured Lee that 'for a long time there has been no obstacle from the ministry'—a flagrant untruth, unless the minister was remarkably ignorant of the workings of his own department. He had gone further, saying that if Beaumarchais had informed Lee that obstructions had been put in his way, then it could only be 'some piece of roguery, or some form of swindle, by Beaumarchais or Monsieur de Monthieu.'

Beaumarchais was naturally outraged by this misrepresentation. As he wrote to Deane, he had, in the cause they both served, 'been forced to swallow one disgusting thing after another without complaining, but this one sticks in my throat.' In his defence, he sent Vergennes copies of the four letters written by himself to Sartine throughout the whole of January, which would inform him of how things were really being managed by the ministries, 'if it is possible that you do not already know it.' He wished for his 'whole conduct' to be examined with the 'strictest vigour,' which could only lead to his name being cleared. The naval ministry, as these letters proved, had given orders to stop all activity at Le Havre on 14 December 1776 and again on 30 January 1777; 'Which order has not been changed, despite all my best efforts.'

XIII

Rogue Males

By return, Vergennes assured Beaumarchais that he did not hold him responsible for the manner in which events were developing with regard to the 'American business,' but Beaumarchais was still unhappy. 'I have the strength to stand against everything if you are satisfied with me,' he told the count, 'but do not ever judge me until you have heard me out first.'

He did feel that, despite the obstacles that had been raised against him, he had achieved some small successes. Three of his ships had left within three days of each other, one from Lorient, one from Nantes, and one from Le Havre; the last of these ships being later captured by a British frigate as she left the island of Martinique while heading for America. But he was still despondent, despite his small triumphs against bureaucracy. '… Unless I can send cannons to the colonists, I don't rate any gratitude from them,' he wrote, although Sartine had promised to send him some in the near future. If only Vergennes, 'with a stroke of his pen,' could put a stop to the perpetual and unbearable reproaches 'that I receive without complaining,' his low spirits would be raised. Faint hope; for one of his 'devils' was again tormenting him. Tronson de Coudray, who had supposedly been sent back to his regiment at Metz, 'to stop his noise and punish him for his indiscretions,' had stayed behind in Paris, 'writing memorials and purporting to justify his mischief,' and his 'noise' was doing Beaumarchais great harm. He had been to the Superintendent of Police, Le Noir, to ask him to have the Chevalier de Barberin,[1] a companion of Coudray, put under observation, once he learned that Barbarin was responsible for directing the troublemaker's broadsides against him.

The police were instructed to find Coudrays's secret address in Paris through his friend, and once this was accomplished, Le Noir had promised to send the officer to Vergennes; who would, Beaumarchais hoped, deal severely with the soldier's 'turbulent behaviour.' Already, Coudray's influential friends were 'up in arms' against Beaumarchais, and the various influential clubs with which the officer was associated were busily taking sides. The war ministry had received an avalanche of petitions that were hostile to Beaumarchais, and Gribeauval, the head of artillery and a keen supporter of Coudray, was also 'running around complaining' about him. He was, Beaumarchais believed, 'the intended sacrificial victim.' It would be a big mistake to let Coudray and his friends go on making a commotion in the capital and, more seriously, at Versailles.

He was also disturbed by the increasing hostility of Arthur Lee, whom he had expected to be a natural ally; but Lee appeared to have now taken a strong dislike to him, as well as to his fellow commissioners. His jealousy of Franklin was understandable, for the old man continued to be idolized by French society, and Vergennes had singled out the old man as being the only one of the three commissioners with whom he would deal. The chief burden of the secret negotiations with the French government clearly fell on Franklin, and the rabidly ambitious Lee undoubtedly took exception to this. From the beginning, also, he seems to have been suspicious of Deane's honesty, and in view of the now strong association between Deane and Beaumarchais, he may have begun to suspect the latter's motives.

Within weeks, Lee was making his presence felt, to the increasing consternation of his fellow commissioners, so they very quickly prevailed upon him to take on a mission that would remove him from their company. It would be more useful, they suggested, if he could see what might be done in Spain. Lee, desperate to prove himself everybody's superior, went there in February 1777, and to the astonishment of all, enjoyed a triumph. He soon secured a substantial amount of money from the Spanish government through the intermediary of a commercial contact, even though he was not allowed to enter Madrid. But back in Paris his behaviour became even more intolerable, and once again his colleagues came up with another plan to remove him from their society. He was sent off to Berlin to try to negotiate another deal.

Meanwhile, Beaumarchais continued patiently. He received a delivery of weapons in February, sending an express concerning it to Amsterdam and to Flessinges.[2] Beaumarchais bemoaned the fact that Holland and not France was, at this rate, going to reap the first harvest of all his enterprises.

He then had good news, for Coudray had at last been run to earth. He had been given shelter with friends at Versailles—under the noses of the ministers—and now Vergennes was arranging to have him sent back to Metz in disgrace. But bad news soon followed, for Coudray's arrest created a further problem for Beaumarchais in that fifteen of his fellow officers now refused to set sail for America without him. 'They cannot be swayed unless they know for sure what is to happen to their insane leader,' Beaumarchais told Deane; although he was sure they would become more tractable once they were knew their 'general' was back in the French Artillery Corps, at a lower rank. Coudray certainly felt his demotion keenly, making him even more savage in his denunciations. His relegation, though, was deeply satisfying to Beaumarchais, who pleaded with Vergennes to expedite this matter, so that they could 'move on.'

Deane was himself anxious to help in this affair, since he, too, had long begun to distrust his 'general', although he had added his signature to a letter attesting that Coudray had the reputation of being a good officer and was well recommended (which was meant to help redeem him in the eyes of the authorities). But as Deane explained, he had done this only after being assured that as soon as Coudray had received a new commission, he would depart from Paris.

Deane had been mortified, he told Beaumarchais, by Coudray's 'strange, ungrateful and perfidious conduct,' and he expressed the hope that the man would 'never in his life' see America, and Beaumarchais, of course, wished fervently to keep the man cooped up in Metz. 'His going to America would be the greatest misfortune that can happen to that unhappy nation,' he wrote. But the supremely arrogant Coudray once again ignored the orders to remain in barracks, and was said to have arrived in Nantes in early February, 'fully equipped for service in America.'

Beaumarchais then urgently advised Vergennes that Coudray should never be allowed to set sail, for his very presence threatened the secrecy of the ministry's involvement in the operation. He believed that the 'general' had only decamped to Nantes because his friends at court had led him to hope they could arrange matters in his favour. They were, in fact, petitioning several important people on this question, and had secured the support of many of them, creating further confusion. '… Everyone thinks he is the master here,' Beaumarchais fumed. It was essential the idiot be silenced—whether in Paris, Versailles or Metz—for 'your secret will certainly be compromised as soon as Coudray is able to talk about it;' and it was up to the minister to deal with the man.

Beaumarchais now believed that his enemy's outpourings against him were even more detrimental to his reputation than those of a man who had for some time been his most fanatical detractor. The man, Hopkins,[3] a native of Maryland, but who had served as a brigadier general in the French army, had begun to spread a rumour that Deane was in fact eager to bring about some form of reconciliation with Great Britain (in retaliation against Deane for refusing him permission to return to America as a serving soldier in the rebel army). This rumour also greatly weakened Beaumarchais's position with the procrastinating ministers, but he believed that Hopkins could be contained—if not easily—while Coudray was an altogether different matter.

Indeed Beaumarchais was now so concerned about Coudray's ability to embarrass him in America that he instructed his agent, Francy, to stay on in

Nantes, simply to make sure that the hothead did not manage to slip aboard the ship about to sail, along with some of his cronies. Despite an urgent need for Francy in Paris, it was more important to keep an eye on the troublemaker on the coast; to have let him leave 'would be absolutely inexcusable.'

He was disconcerted to be told, on his agent's eventual return to Paris, that Coudray had never actually been in Nantes, but was believed to have sneaked out of the capital and headed straight to Bordeaux, where he hoped to get a ship by using another name. Moreover, it was not the first time, Francy reported, that Coudray had made such a plan; and so Beaumarchais was now more worried than ever about the rogue officer.

To add to his troubles, a mysterious fire broke out in his house, which he may well have believed to be a calculated act of arson (since by this time his safe and drawers were filled with papers that could prove incriminating to any number of government officials). The fire was contained in time, but the threat nevertheless remained.

Vergennes had passed on the problem of the rogue officer to Sartine, who quickly washed his hands of the responsibility, and advised Beaumarchais to approach Saint-Germaine about the matter—a suggestion that horrified Beaumarchais, since he knew the war minister to be a close friend of Gribauval, the artillery general, and a man of enormous importance to the administration; and who, Beaumarchais firmly believed, was 'the enraged protector of Coudray. Everyone knows how hostile this officer is towards me.'

The situation was also complicated by the fact that Beaumarchais could not reveal any valid reasons for keeping Coudray from leaving for America, where he could have been a potential cause for mayhem. He could only insist the man be prevented from 'talking loosely' while still in France; and, as a result, he was accused of persecuting the very man he had originally helped to promote! Beaumarchais could only answer, 'It is not within my character or principles to take revenge on anyone. ... Otherwise I would have had to spend my life in that despicable occupation!'

Since he achieved nothing with the other government ministers, Beaumarchais was reduced to begging an increasingly indifferent Vergennes to order that Coudray should be stopped from publicly abusing his reputation, and this order could come only from above. At the same time, the minister should inform Saint-Germaine of the reasons to have the man arrested: '... Since that's the only way to avoid future gossip.'

He did, however, find the Foreign Minister hard to persuade, for Vergennes was now very angry with him, accusing Beaumarchais of holding back ship-ments in the hope of obtaining fresh financial assistance, 'which we absolutely do not want to give him!' Vainly, Beaumarchais tried to explain to his patron that *none* of his shipments had been delayed by *his* orders, and that he was in constant conflict with the ministries involved. His fifth ship, larger than all the others, he announced proudly, was due to leave within fifteen days, '*improbo labore*'.[4]

But he was deeply concerned at Vergennes's increasing coldness towards him, as he voiced in a letter: '… If you disapprove of a good servant … then I will have to painfully conclude that it is the labourer who fails to please, and not the work in question.' Almost everybody concerned with this work, he went on to complain, was 'eager to cross the enterprise,' and all of them did it harm 'in their own way,' and the proofs were not wanting. '… They swarm in my papers. I manage the affair alone, painfully, through contradictions and humiliations of all kinds.'

He had demanded a prompt and precise answer from the advisers to King Louis, 'because four shiploads, gathered and paid for in all the manufactories of the Kingdom, cannot remain in suspension for 85 days. They must be promptly shipped away, or the deal will be missed.' On this occasion, Vergennes accused Beaumarchais of having 'chimerical' ideas. But Vergennes was still keen to use his spy, who informed him that 'the goat is returning to France in seven or eight days.' The 'goat' being Monsieur de la Chevre,[5] one of *Mlle* d'Éon's most trusted messengers, who may have been involved in some undercover work on her behalf. 'You can decide at this critical time,' Figaro wrote to his master, 'if you want me to find out for whom he takes such fragrant trips.'

It was now the turn of Beaumarchais to complain about Silas Deane, whom he accused of instigating several 'examinations and inquisitions' regarding their work together, of privately seeking to buy arms and merchandise, and of having visited various depots and stores for secret inspections. '… No doubt they served a useful purpose, since they were thought to be necessary,' Beaumarchais sniffed.

At least Deane's 'examinations and inquisitions' did away with malicious suspicions about the value of his supplies, 'Or, in good English, on the probity of Monsieur Hortalez!' Since matters had been going so well for them both—apart from ministerial interference and the irritations supplied by Coudray—Beaumarchais wished to know 'by what right Deane had become so questioning?' He certainly thought that he could only be praised for his excellent cargoes; and he pointed out that Deane had so far failed to fulfil any of his obligations.

Two more ships had left, and at a season when they could go straight to the coast of North America. But Beaumarchais was now worried that his superiors might discover the true nature of the consignments these ships held, since he had been 'forced' to deceive them about the ships' loads, which were not as set down in the register. He had also been compelled to remain somewhat vague about the exact destination of the vessels. It was a certainty that the ministers would be collectively angered should they learn of the exact make-up of the tonnage.

Apart from this mysterious merchandise, he also had a rich cargo aboard his newest ship, the *Thereze*, which he did not wish to risk, in the 'long days of the season,' by sending directly to America. Beaumarchais told Deane that he was writing to his correspondent, Monsieur Carabasse, at the Cape, with orders to buy three or four Bermudan cutters, the fast sailing vessels for which the islands were famous. These, he explained, 'will act as shuttles between the Cape and your continent, carrying the cargoes in several sections, until such time as Congress will have its own vessels to fetch the goods from the Cape warehouses. Which I will endeavour to keep always full, if acceptable returns are promptly made.'

He was troubled by the fact that he had been lately 'always out of temper,' which was, he knew, a mixture of exasperation and extreme fatigue. As he lamented to Deane, he had exhausted himself for the good of America, 'without being able to know by now if anyone but you appreciates my efforts at all!'

He was certainly alarmed by the Foreign Minister's apparent loss of faith in him; despite the fact that he was in possession of information his employer could never obtain from any other source, and he wrote to remind him of this. He had also begun to believe that Vergennes was in some way now embarrassed by their connection, so he took to arriving at Versailles so late in the evening 'that no one would see him.'

Deane had been anxious for some time about the risk of sending ships so late in the season, all carrying vital cargoes; for if they went directly to the American coast they would arrive in the middle of what was known as the 'cruising season' of British warships, and could easily be picked off. On board the *Thereze* were some 70,000 *livres* worth of goods that had been purchased by the commissioners jointly and, because of this, Deane questioned the course the ship should take. Beaumarchais proposed sending it by way of the West Indies, and they had fully agreed this would be the safest route; but as it would take longer for the goods to arrive, they had insisted upon the utmost dispatch being made.

Beaumarchais could state positively that the utmost dispatch was always made, if not interrupted by outside interference; and now at last, temporarily at least, he could assure them that matters were beginning to get under way.

With absolute confidence, he had written to Congress on 28 February 1777, telling them his ship *Amelie*, loaded with field and ordnance pieces, powder and pigs of lead, had been sent to them by way of Hispaniola. He had charged his representative there to transfer the whole load on to a Bermudan craft, or on to any American ships to be found in the ports on that island.

This was the fourth ship sent by Beaumarchais since December 1776, but the other three had steered a course directly towards the eastern coastline of America, seeking a port at which they could put in safely. The first, of 480 tons, had been loaded with cannon, muskets, tents, entrenching tools, tin, powder and clothing, and it had left Le Havre on 14 December 1776. The second ship, of 350 tons, had contained muskets, tents, mortars, powder, tin, cannon and musket balls. His third ship, of 317 tons, had left from Nantes loaded with 100 thousandths of powder and 12,000 muskets, with the remainder in cloth, caps, shoes, stockings, blankets and most of the articles necessary for the fitting out of troops.[6]

Congress must surely agree that he had done particularly well, Beaumarchais queried in a letter to them, since he was acting as a single individual upon his own initiative; and once again he requested them to arrange a quick turn about, so that his ships might not wait long for the remittances he needed in order to buy new stock, which was essential if he was to sustain the level of the present operation. His plan was to send them an uninterrupted flow of supplies, of such as would be of the greatest use to them, and so he hoped that they would be as prompt as possible in reloading and sending the vessels back to him.

With regard to his own side of the agreement, Beaumarchais now had every cause for personal satisfaction, since he had managed to acquire so much equipment for the Americans that there were not enough ships around to carry it to the New World (although some of the supplies he ordered struck his superiors as being unnecessary, and even eccentric). But the production of nails, for example, as Beaumarchais pointed out to Sartine, was vital for the construction of the many new ships that must be built by the Americans themselves. He had sent the minister a contract for 900,000 'tree' nails, which were partly made of wood, and he had boasted that the best 'tree' nails came from the High Touraine, made by jobbers in the forest of Chinon;[7] luckily for him, as it happened, for this forest had been exploited by a company controlled by him since 1766.

The contract had already been sent to Monsieur Porties in the minister's office, who had sent it back, 'for the reason that he doesn't want to hear about it any more!'—and so Beaumarchais had requested Sartine to pass on the contract to a Monsieur de la Frenaye,[8] another aide, who would then return it to the minister to be signed, 'if my nails please him.' Once this was done—*if* this was done—another contract would be needed from the minister for the wood to be floated, 'at no cost' [to them] on four rivers: the Loire, Cher, Indre and Vienne; all rivers that surrounded Beaumarchais's forest 'exploitation.' The passports were eventually supplied.

In one sense, all was going well, and ministers were even assenting to his requests; but Beaumarchais then received bad news. He at once revealed this to Vergennes in a letter; asking for it to be passed on to Maurepas, 'after you have sealed it.'

Tronson de Coudray, his 'rogue male,' had somehow managed to take ship to the Americas. From Santo Domingo, his first port of call, the scoundrel had written to the American commission in Paris, again denouncing Beaumarchais (who had himself been considerate enough to forward his letter unopened, and in all innocence, since it first came to his door). Coudray's vituperative attack on Beaumarchais was an attempt to persuade the Americans in Paris that it was he, Coudray, acting alone, who had obtained from the French government the supplies that had passed through their 'benefactor's hands;'[9] it was only Beaumarchais's vanity 'as a merchant' that had made him steal the operation from under the noses of his superiors!

Beaumarchais was a prodigious liar, Coudray wrote, and the best example of his endless falsehoods was that only one fifth of the cannon that he 'maintained' he had obtained from the government had actually been taken aboard the *Amphitrite*. The reason that he had stayed on in Paris was because Beaumarchais had callously changed his agents, who were not following his 'corrupt' instructions; and because of this, he had felt that he should stay in the capital for their sake, '… in an affair whose success mattered to him as much as to them.'

On reading Coudray's extraordinary denouncement, Beaumarchais's first thought was that this could only be his justification for not returning to the garrison at Metz, as ordered. But it slowly emerged that Coudray had previously told other people that he alone was the agent of the war ministry, and that Beaumarchais's 'trade' was nothing but a mask. His ultimate purpose, Beaumarchais came to believe, was not only to put paid to his own efforts, but also to destroy Deane's credibility in America; for the madly aggrandizing 'major-general' aspired to appoint himself as the sole 'Saviour of the [American] State,' through his alleged efforts to obtain aid from the French government.

Beaumarchais was incandescent; 'That man is going over to further undermine me!' he raged. 'As a result of this the King's [secret] orders will be eluded in Metz, Paris, Nantes and Santo Domingo. It is infuriating!'

On the other hand, he could only be cheered by the news from America. 'All souls in this country have been uplifted by these successes,' he crowed; 'A surfeit of pleasant things delights the heart.'

What could not have delighted him, though, was that he had recently missed out on profiting from the riches of five ships captured by an American privateer, which had been unloaded in Lorient, for their cargo had been sold by the time his agent arrived at the port. The sale of goods from the five ships had fetched 90,000 pounds sterling, although Beaumarchais believed their true worth nearer to 600,000, and *that* he found additionally maddening.

Because of a government order forbidding American privateers to bring their merchandise to French ports (to appease the British), several of their ships had gone on to northern Spain 'for relief.' This was definitely not the route that Beaumarchais wanted them to travel, for he felt he had a vested interest in any money raised from such an auction, as he had complained to a contact at the ministry, Monsieur Robin.[10] But the Comptroller General had not 'recommended this matter,' and so Robin claimed that he now needed a new order. Beaumarchais requested Vergennes to contrive a private audience with one Taboureau,[11] of the Comptroller-General's office, 'When I will ask him for what is becoming so necessary to obtain, now that my returns are about to arrive.'

The ship that he was now loading, and which was almost ready to leave, bore the name *Comte de Vergennes*, which was not an act of flattery on Beaumarchais's part, since it already bore the name. But although it seemed a good omen to him, he could also see that the minister might take exception to any connection the British might make between the name and the use the ship was being put to. 'Only say one word and I will have it changed,' he said to Vergennes, 'even though it will be hard for me to de-baptize it' (in reality, the ship was not leased by him, and so technically it was not his to rename). Yet when Vergennes did object, in the circumstances, the ship received another name, less challenging to the British.

With that ship departed, Beaumarchais would have six others at sea, along with two Bermudan vessels trading between Santo Domingo and the North American coast, and he was waiting for others to be placed at his disposal. 'Never has a commercial business been carried along with more vigour,' he boasted, 'in spite of all the obstacles standing in our way. May God grant it a successful outcome!'

'Another letter, you will say, he will not quit,' he wrote to Vergennes on 8 March, still sensitive to the minister's coldness towards him. 'But how can

I quit, M. le Comte, when new objectives keep exciting my attention and vigilance? I have to inform you of everything!'

He had learned that a private secretary of Lord Germain[12] had arrived in Paris, via Le Havre, and he had been sent to hold secret discussions with both Silas Deane and Benjamin Franklin. He was, as Beaumarchais reported excitedly, carrying fresh peace proposals to be made between the two countries, and the highest reward awaited him in England if he succeeded, 'Even a dukedom, perhaps!' It was rumoured, Beaumarchais said, that the offers Britain proposed to America were such 'that a commissioner may send them on to Philadelphia in all honour.'

Benjamin Franklin, Beaumarchais also reported, was trying to have Deane sent away from France, but he was doing his best to keep him in place; largely because only Deane could counter the 'insinuations of all kinds' that were still being levelled against himself by Dr Barbeu-Dubourg. It was now becoming apparent to Beaumarchais that Franklin was not well disposed towards him because of the undue influence of Le Ray de Chaumont, the American's landlord; and who, of all Franklin's patrons in Paris, was the most personally opposed towards Beaumarchais.

Another person causing trouble was a certain 'Linguet,'[13] whom he had at first thought of as a decent enough man, but one who had in a very short time become 'embittered and activated by intrigue.' This Linguet, too, was writing the most malicious letters to Maurepas and Vergennes, denunciations in which he detailed the constant excesses of the flamboyant entrepreneur. As Beaumarchais told his employer, 'His disparaging reports will give an unspeakable joy and pleasure to the enemies of the present administration;' since, as he reasoned, these monstrous lies would also reflect upon his masters.

But it was perhaps, by then, too late to do anything positive about it, although he offered to deal with the problem in a way that would not compromise the government. '... Whatever is honest, I can do it!' he said ambiguously, although he had a genuine interest in the case, for it was the *Chevaliere* d'Éon's 'rascal of a goat,' le Chevre, who had been sending out copies of Linguet's letters. Other copies were coming in from Holland; but—if so ordered—Beaumarchais felt he could deal with these critics also.

Beaumarchais knew that Vergennes, or his man Gerard, had conferred with Deane at Versailles, and on a subject that someone he trusted at court had been informing him about. This concerned the most recent British proposals that were thought to be acceptable to Congress, even though—his informant told him—the American people had by now been led to expect an alliance with France. If they were to be disappointed in this respect, and if Vergennes failed in his answer to the question that would be asked of him by the Americans, which Beaumarchais had no doubt would happen, then their peace with Britain could be decided soon, and as quickly concluded. '... Military successes alone cannot suffice, however great the people. The Americans do their best today to subsist, but believe me when I declare that they can go no further without us; or if we spurn them. Without us, they must bring about some form of reconciliation with the English.'

By the end of March he was still distressed to think that his government was going to leave the Americans to perish. He was also aware that, hard as he worked on the behalf of all, his efforts had not pleased Vergennes; even though he had found the one way to back the Americans without having to disburse huge sums. Beaumarchais grew increasingly desperate in his attempts to regain the minister's confidence. 'You have to listen to me today, you've even got to help me, if you are not just to drop a plan which is without risk,' was only one of his many pleas at this time.

Deane, though, was still proving loyal. He had visited Beaumarchais several times to 'treat of this great affair with me,' and he firmly believed that his government would guarantee any loan they would receive from the French. But as long as the French remained on the sidelines this would not be realizable.

Beaumarchais feverishly drew up a new plan, and one that would compromise him more deeply. In it, he planned to incorporate *foreign* merchants, 'many of which have already given me their word that they will participate in this new endeavour,' who would put into the business as much money as he himself would find. He also now requested that he need not contract to replace the armaments in kind, and that his credit with the government should be extended, for he wanted them to give him the means of offering his stockholders 'something with which to attract their interest.'

Even Beaumarchais had to concede that the business deal he had just outlined was only an extension, 'adroitly carried out,' of what he had been doing for a year now. He did not contemplate lending the Americans the two million pounds sterling they were asking for, but he thought that they could be loaned seven to eight millions of French currency, 'biding our time for the rest.'

Beaumarchais also warned Vergennes that other people in Paris were negotiating covertly with Benjamin Franklin, of which he thought the minister might not be aware. He was convinced that Silas Deane had not confided this information to Vergennes, 'convinced as he is that his colleague will not be swayed, and not wishing to hurt his good reputation':

> ... But I, whose long experience of treachery has made me suspicious, and who
> am accustomed to drawing conjectures from what strikes me, have concluded,

from the news I have received from London, that M. Deane is looked upon as a formidable obstacle to any reconciliation plan. As a consequence, he is, I am sure, to be withdrawn from this country, whatever the cost may be.

He believed that this possibility was behind an attempt to compromise Deane in what came to be recognized as the first terrorist attack in modern times. An English enthusiast for the American cause, John Aitkins—'John the Painter'—accused of setting fire to a rope-factory in Portsmouth, England, in an attempt to burn down the docks, had alleged at his trial that Silas Deane had *paid* him to commit this act of arson. Beaumarchais himself believed 'this farce' to have been devised by two English lords, not only to make Deane hateful to the British but also loathed by the French; although Deane had, it turned out, and as he eventually admitted, twice met the arsonist in Paris (in his home) and given the man a small amount of money, but only because he was almost penniless. He had also, Atkins later insisted, given his blessing to the destruction of not only the dockyards at Portsmouth, but for a later attack upon those at Bristol. Mysteriously, Deane had also procured a passport for him to travel back to England, a document signed by Vergennes in King Louis's name, dated 13 November 1776, and it is difficult to believe that Beaumarchais was unaware of this singular development:

Yet, [he reported], our news services carry such a categorical statement of the ministry's intentions that all my previous guesses have now become facts. They [the British] are planning to have Deane removed from France and make him the scapegoat for their insane undertaking in America. I have reassured him, however, and indeed promised him that his safety will be secured such as to prevent any action against him [for example, kidnapping].

He should, [Beaumarchais pleaded his superiors], be able to sleep peacefully in this protective and neutral country.

XIV

'A Way with Words'

Beaumarchais was again to be frustrated by the reaction of the ministers to his 'new' idea, and he wondered if it was perhaps because he had expressed it poorly. The truth was that he was afraid of wearying the elderly Maurepas, and so he often discarded more detailed explanations, which might then have left his 'concise' expositions too obscure. He was always oddly convinced that 'nothing is done through writing,' and it was necessary for him to be heard in person if he was to be fully understood.

'This critical time calls for putting the head and the arms together,' he wrote to Maurepas, 'for a meeting between the leaders and the workers!' He wanted, he said, to bring the minister's attention to two 'very different' documents: one from England and the other from the American commissioner.

The first was a political essay in an 'insulting' English pamphlet printed under government sanction.[1] In it, the writer sardonically instructed the French in what they could best do about the Anglo-American situation (which was astonishingly close to what Beaumarchais himself had earlier recommended), and the writer then further insulted the French by castigating them for not following that course of action! The other letter, from Silas Deane, expressed much the same viewpoint, but was couched in more respectful tones, and Beaumarchais, of course, entirely concurred with the sentiments expressed by both writers (they were, after all, his own!).

'M. le Comte,' he pleaded, 'spare your servants the sorrow of seeing your memory reproached some day. You could have unyoked America from the English master and bound her to us through trade; and you neglected to do it!'

Beaumarchais was actually of the opinion that Maurepas, despite his vast political experience, in some way distrusted his own powers as a minister; he had, after all, spent twenty-five years in exile for being too outspoken.[2] But Beaumarchais stressed that the count's age and wisdom gave him a great influence over a young king, 'whose heart is well-formed, but whose politics are still in the cradle.' He also reminded the minister that King Louis XVI, as an absolute monarch, was capable of taking innovative measures denied to other European rulers, but his *thoughts* could be changed by the persuasion of others. Yes, King Louis would, Beaumarchais assured Maurepas, be amenable to whatever a wise man suggested.

But time was running out fast, and Deane waited upon Beaumarchais's answer before he could himself dispatch his messenger—'who will carry encouragement or desolation to Congress'—depending upon the decision of the French government. Depressingly, Beaumarchais could only again stress that his proposals were good, and acceptable to all high-minded parties. '... Do not make my efforts fruitless for want of cooperation on your part, and let my reward be the honour of having obtained your approval.'

He also wrote to Vergennes having 'let the week go to the cares of the other world': a long time to let elapse in view of his anxiety. Impishly, he could, he said, discern the minister's 'patriotic zeal through the veil of circumspection that always enshrouds your style.' The insolent English paper, he wrote, was 'spitting in their faces,' but one did have to admit that there was some 'force and truth' in what was said. Did not the minister agree?—and should they not answer this charge with resolute action?

Vergennes's answer was to draw the 'veil of circumspection' even more heavily across his majestic features, but Maurepas did at least agree to grant Beaumarchais an appointment in his office at Versailles, which the inspired word-spinner turned into a sizeable victory; for the chief minister, 'carried away' by his reasoning, or rhetoric, did allow that the matter should be discussed with Vergennes.[3] But Maurepas was anxious to know what the government could expect if it were to fully commit itself to such a huge commercial undertaking; it might be impossible to enter into such a commitment without the financial 'freedom' of a public bank, and could they hope to raise the funds required from such a quarter?

There would be no need to depend upon banks, Beaumarchais assured him. In fact, little ready money would actually be required if the minister could give him the means of extending his credit; but, as he carefully explained, a lot of funding would be needed from other—less public—sources, if the government should reject his 'thrifty' plan. He managed to convince Maurepas that Vergennes approved of his project, however 'circumspectly' the minister may have felt it necessary to express himself on the subject; and certainly, by the end of Beaumarchais's summing-up, which was apparently masterly, the chief minister was in full agreement that they must see Vergennes, to make a final decision. 'Only support me, M. le Comte,' Beaumarchais pleaded. 'Only back me up.'

The offensive English paper was the *Westminster Gazette*, and Beaumarchais decided to have the article copied and translated, with the idea perhaps of circulating it around the court[4]—a judgement that would rebound upon him, for it quickly became apparent that the article in question was politically enigmatic, and Vergennes's adverse comments on it certainly caused

Beaumarchais to have his translator check its phraseology. He was assured that, while the style and vocabulary were subject to misunderstanding, some paragraphs had been taken almost verbatim from Tom Paine's political pamphlet *Common Sense*[5] (which, while it contained little in the way of original thinking, still put into words what a great many patriots had been forming in their own minds). Apart from the article's hostile and accusatory tone, however, not all of its assertions against the French were correct. Three of the ships that Beaumarchais had chartered were wrongly identified, and a banker that he had used was named, but 'poorly indicated,' while Le Ray de Chaumont was mentioned only in connection with a contract for gunpowder. Most astonishingly of all, and to his undoubted relief, Beaumarchais's name did not, 'thankfully,' appear. 'It all rather looks as though the ideas expressed have been taken at random, and the "facts" are based on hearsay,' he decided; but whichever anonymous hack had written it, he concluded, the article had certainly been published at the instigation of Lord Germain.

Germain was also at work nearer to hand, for Beaumarchais received word that his secretary, a 'Mr Schmitz,'[6] was presently staying in Paris at Lord Stormont's house, 'where he executes the secret orders of his master, relative to the conciliation proposals with the American commissioners.' Mr Schmitz was, apparently, 'disguised under a chaplain's wig, while little Mallory, a real chaplain, pretends to be giving up his place to the newcomer, if his stay in Paris is not injurious to him.' Beaumarchais knew Schmitz to be a spy, for he had something of a dossier on him. '… I am on the right track,' he wrote, 'he won't escape me.'

But others *were* managing to avoid his scrutiny, most particularly Tronson de Coudray's old friends. Beaumarchais agreed with Vergennes that all the 'commotions,' as the minister described them, then being occasioned by Coudray's admirers, only served to 'ruin everything.' If they could only *extract* that 'tribe who call themselves artillery officers' from the scene, the turmoil they created could then be avoided. Secrecy was absolutely essential to any future success, he urged; for the article published in the *Westminster Gazette* showed only too clearly that the British were aware that something was astir. Even if they could not—as yet—pin these clandestine movements firmly on any decision reached by the French government. But if the present covert system was continued, Beaumarchais assured Vergennes, he could guarantee there would be no danger of further compromising his Majesty.

He also concluded that it was essential for the rest of Britain's armed forces to be kept in Europe, 'out of respect for our own presence'—without, that is, precipitating any direct confrontation between their two countries; and so he came up with an artful solution. The French, he suggested, should embark on a policy of destroying Britain's sense of security in European waters by the simple act of deploying French vessels in 'mysterious manoeuvres.' That is, in exercises that would *appear* to be threatening without actually being directly confrontational. In this way, they could 'neutralize' a section of the British fleet, which would then free vessels of the French navy to 'lavish their help upon the American patriots.' Beaumarchais also pointed out that, by giving all French ships access to these hitherto British dominated sea-routes, they could be 'taught the high road to America, and a new way for French trade to operate.'

Whether he succeeded in re-convincing Vergennes of his usefulness to the minister and the 'great cause,' it would seem that Maurepas, having once recovered from the onslaught of the playwright's way with words, was now relapsing. Beaumarchais hoped that Vergennes could 'excite a little movement in Maurepas's soul,' and he counted on the minister's 'great wisdom' to achieve this. He pointed out that Silas Deane was growing increasingly discouraged, and even believed that France was on the edge of making a great blunder by *refusing to do as he suggested.*

But if Beaumarchais had hoped to elicit some positive response from either minister, he was to receive no satisfactory reply.

He did, however, meet with the Spanish ambassador, Count Aranda, and he lost no time in 'painting for him the truest picture of the American scene.' He again suggested that the French and Spanish fleets should make 'mysterious and continual moves' in European waters, to keep part of the British navy confined there, if only to keep the activities of their fleets under surveillance.

This would, he also pointed out, prevent the King of England from completing the raising of a loan that he was then seeking from his parliament, and as a result, the shrinking of private funds in Britain would lead to a satisfying fall in the stock market. In turn, this would create renewed hope for the Americans, and would cause them to believe that these financial moves had been made solely for their benefit, 'thus increasing their courage.' In the meantime, once extra supplies had arrived in the United States, Beaumarchais could absolutely vouch for the British campaign failing there again.

He was planning, if the Spanish ambassador approved of it, to travel to Madrid in order to talk the Spanish government into providing some *real—* financial—assistance which, joined together with whatever he could 'filch' from France, would supply the means of sustaining the American effort until the following December, and would prevent any reconciliation between them and the British.

He wrote down a part of his conversation with Aranda, which could have sprung from the pages of his own satires:

AMBASSADOR: Personally, you know what I think, and what I want. But as the Spanish ambassador, I cannot tell you either black or white.

BEAU: Why is that, your Excellency?

AMB: Because the [Foreign] Minister has not yet publicly mentioned a word to me concerning it, and so I am officially ignorant of this matter.

BEAU: But, Sir, it is with his consent that I am talking with you about it now.

AMB: Perhaps. But in an affair as important as this, I must learn from the mouth of the minister himself that he approves of your views before I may reply to him officially.

BEAU: Sir, the minister will talk to you whenever you wish it, because I shall send an account of this conversation to him.

The ambassador agreed to attend the court at Versailles on the following day, even though it was not strictly a day for diplomatic attendance. 'Your ministers are friends of mine, and they are at ease with me on any matter,' he said. 'But you must have them talk with me about this subject, otherwise I won't say a word about it. They know very well that we are asking for nothing better than to act in concert against British tyranny.'

Aranda gave Beaumarchais a further appointment the following Wednesday morning, after the ambassador had spoken with the ministers, thus initiating the new proceedings. Encouraged by this, Beaumarchais—in his usual manner—took over, suggesting to Vergennes that he be entrusted with a 'light' mission to Madrid, to provide the minister with 'accurate information, such as only I can procure,' on the disposition of the Spanish cabinet.

If he could gain no assistance from the Spanish government for the American cause, Vergennes would know 'once and for all' to what extent he could 'count on, or mistrust' whatever suggestions came out of Spain. Beaumarchais had, in fact, little faith in that country, but he assured Vergennes that just 'two serious conversations' with the new prime minister, Floridablanca,[7] or even two or three private dinners with the Prime Minister's favourite butler would tell him all that he needed to know. A few meetings with the French ambassador to Spain, Monsieur d'Ossun,[8] would also be enlightening.

Beaumarchais wrote that he had other things to impart to Vergennes after a three-hour long exchange with Silas Deane, but as he was writing from a 'strange' house, he would not commit himself to paper. He did, however, want the minister to receive this report, so that he could use it as the *punctum vitae*[9] for their conversation on Tuesday (always supposing, of course, that the Spanish ambassador had been allowed to enter the palace in an unofficial capacity).

In the event, Beaumarchais's next meeting with Aranda turned out to be as lacking in purpose as had that of Aranda's meeting with Vergennes, since the Spaniard was given no opportunity to broach the matter with the minister. Apologetically, he later told the exasperated Beaumarchais that he planned to see Vergennes again on Friday morning, but that, as always, Vergennes would have to officially 'break the ice, or it will remain unbroken.' '… Nothing,' Beaumarchais wrote despairingly, 'is more detrimental to business than protocol!'

When it came to the bottom line, he was also suspicious of the Spaniard's true motives. Was he being diplomatically discreet, or was this nothing more than 'an ambassador's parade?'[10] He begged Vergennes to set aside ceremony for once, and to speak with Aranda 'off the record;' for the Spaniard, he insisted, was eager to know if the Americans had proposed any further political advantages, besides those already offered to both crowns. Aranda had solemnly assured Beaumarchais that any information he could provide on the subject 'would not pass his lips.'

As Beaumarchais said, 'Everyone is looking out for number one, and in the jungle of politics the prey are often no better than the predators!'—but it was essential that France knew where it stood with Spain, and so one must play the game according to the diplomatic rules, however absurd. He did not himself say whether he had fully confided in the Spanish ambassador; Beaumarchais, when he deemed it necessary, also knew how to play the political tactician.

Parker Forth,[11] a friend of Lord Mansfield[12] and an undercover agent employed at the British Embassy was back in Paris. Astonishingly, he carried an urgent letter to Beaumarchais's agent, begging to be allowed to be 'corrupted' in the British cause. But the ever-loyal Francy, instead of approaching Parker Forth—if only to see in which way he could expect to be bribed, and how substantial the bribe would be—showed the letter to his employer.

Parker Forth said in his letter that he would meet Francy on that same day, April 11, but Beaumarchais decided to meet him in his agent's place, to ask why he himself had not been approached directly 'with this noble offer.' Lord Mansfield was Stormont's uncle, and Beaumarchais could only assume that the offer of corruption had come initially from the British embassy in Paris; how flattering it was that they should seek to place an informant in his office.

All teasing apart, though, Beaumarchais was really not in the mood for this kind of development, since he was trying to cope with an increasingly

despondent Deane, 'writhing with anxiety.' Deane was extremely keen on
Beaumarchais's proposal for deploying French and Spanish fleets in a bid to
split the British navy, saying that such a rupture would 'uplift everyone in
America;' but, so far, the plan had failed to raise any enthusiasm at Versailles.
'... Oh what hateful thrift, which can thwart such high purpose, for so little money!' Beaumarchais protested; believing that money—or the supposed
lack of it—was all that lay at the root of the matter.

He was even more frustrated to learn from Aranda that his second official
meeting with Vergennes had been no more successful than the first; and the
matter had still not been broached. '... You must understand,' the ambassador told him, 'that as long as the question is not mentioned to me, I can
utter no word about it.' Beaumarchais, in fact, perceived no such thing,
but he told Aranda tactfully that he had to concur with 'such a powerful
reason.'

In private he protested sardonically that future generations, reading the history of these negotiations, would mock the idiocy of the etiquette involved.
How could they possibly believe that *for twelve days* a decision on such an
important issue had been postponed solely on the grounds that the first word
spoken about it should come out of 'this' rather than 'that' mouth? '... May
God help the Americans, and the Commerce of France!' He tried to persuade
the Spanish ambassador to tell Vergennes that the two of them had spoken
about it together, and that the minister himself had, at some time previously,
privately authorized Beaumarchais to speak up about it. If this failed, he suggested that Aranda could explain to Vergennes that Beaumarchais had become
so pressing on the matter that the ambassador now felt obliged to bring the
matter up with the minister unofficially.

But Aranda still demurred, protesting that he must continue to play 'within
the rules.' Finally losing patience, Beaumarchais briskly informed Vergennes
that if he did not deal incisively with this 'puerile obstacle' of protocol, and
speak plainly with the Spanish ambassador, the three of them would be hanging about for three months or more on the 'thread of such a grave difficulty.'
To waste so much time was far worse than to come straight out with an outright 'No.' When a government refused to act then one knew where one was,
and what to do about it; but to prolong such diplomatic delicacy 'produces
nothing but nothingness.'

As he also pointed out, British ministers—who claimed to be 'well
acquainted with the collective mentality of the French administration'—had
ordered their ambassador to 'speak loudly and proudly in Paris; telling us how
well the English were doing in America.' According to Lord Stormont, it was
already too late for the French to aid the American insurgents further, for

the reconciliation between the two countries was in fact now firmly resolved, fixed—'he almost says signed!'

One of Beaumarchais's merchant backers, in fact, alarmed by this news, had written to Silas Deane to discover if it was true, and Deane had boldly replied, 'Untrue. It is pure Stormont.' But even so, Beaumarchais insisted Vergennes be warned that Lord Stormont's message had got through to the Comte de Maurepas, who was again telling others that it was 'too late.' The always irresolute first minister must be reminded, Beaumarchais told Vergennes, of how many times in the past eight months he had been convinced that it was 'too late;' for how many useful decisions had been delayed because of that mistaken notion, when all along there had been plenty of time? If Maurepas could be re-convinced that there was still plenty of time to forge a lasting bond between France and the Americans he would—perhaps—change his mind again, and even stick to a decision this time. Was it not farcical to switch so constantly from 'It's too early' to 'It's too late'? The more time that one wasted, the less of it remained to make up for the harm done in wasting it in the first place!

But Beaumarchais could at least congratulate himself on having prevented the Spanish ambassador from sending 'distressful' news, via the diplomatic mail, to his government in Madrid; and he continued to give what courage he could to his merchant associates by making a great display of it himself at all their meetings; he thought it essential to keep all involved 'up to the mark.'

He knew that even those most closely connected to him supposed him to have other, secret, resources at his disposal, a conclusion they had reached only because of the massive calm that he continued to display at their conferences. If only they could know the effort that these performances demanded from him! Every morning he received letters from people concerned by the delay, and every afternoon somebody called upon him to ask the same question: '… What news from Versailles?'

Silas Deane, by now in a deep despondency about their unceasing frustrations, asked him if he thought the two of them should go on with this mad pretence of 'trying to fool my unfortunate countrymen any longer, letting them entertain a hope that we ourselves no longer share.' All Beaumarchais could say was 'Wait,' but Deane believed that his people could no longer afford the luxury of misguided hope; and, indeed, his orders from his superiors, or so he said, were 'so very positive in that respect.'

Beaumarchais could only suppose that *his* superiors had completely turned against his arguments; or, rather, from their fear of his creating an international scandal if he followed these arguments through, as was beginning to be voiced. He pleaded with them to judge him on his actions alone and, recognizing their long distrust of the wily 'Figaro' in his character, he supposed that they thought he should work under closer supervision, and so he suggested this possibility; even though they must surely know that the 'secret' could only be truly safe with him for as long as he worked alone. Had not the indiscreet behaviour of his chief persecutor, Coudray—more insane than the rest of them put together—shown the government how easily shared information could be leaked?

But even as he put forward the idea of working under closer scrutiny, he almost immediately retreated from it; for he knew that his own arrangements were models of secrecy, and he would challenge anyone to quote under what name, what cargo, in which port, and for what destination, he had expedited all his ships. Surely, he argued, if despite all the spies that surrounded him, who had vainly sought to learn his secrets, wasn't it unfair to hold him responsible for other's wrongdoing? Even worse, to use it as a pretext for refusing his modest requests for assistance, 'with such deadly consequences.'

Questions were beginning to be asked that he knew he could not possibly answer; as he explained, he had only made himself a merchant in order to conceal his work as a negotiator. Certainly, if ministers or their friends sought to know where he had found the capital for his spurious business deals, he could not oblige them since it would put others at risk. He cannily pointed out that if 'mistrustful people' thought him capable of deceiving the public while setting up his business, might they not equally question the part secretly taken by the ministry in his affairs? These had been equally well masked by the covert associations that he had created with these other merchants—merchants who had taken a personal gamble 'on all of our (so-called) illegal shipments to America,' as he never ceased to point out.

In view of this, when he could answer 'for the happy consequences of an enterprise so well combined,' why was the all-powerful minister again refusing to cooperate with him? What, for example, lay behind the delay of the mission to Spain? Why, when Vergennes and the Comte d'Aranda had privately agreed with him that his plan was a good move, did they not even speak to each other concerning it? For the honour and financial interests of France, the decision could surely no longer be postponed. M. de Vergennes must bring all the power of his authority to bear on the almighty Comte de Maurepas.

But even as Beaumarchais closed his latest letter to the minister to raise these valid points, news came of yet another of his ships being held back on the point of departure. In this case he had been specifically ordered to obtain a special licence from the naval ministry, for a 'covert and secret permission' to employ ten sailors selected for their particular 'expertise'—a skill that was never fully explained to him. The rest of the crew was to be comprised of ordinary seamen, but the ship could not sail without these 'experts.' For some reason this singular order had not been officially complied with, and the men were not aboard, which meant that the ship could not set sail. An urgent note was sent to Vergennes, requesting him to arrange a top-priority command with the Minister of Marine to have the requisite men transferred to his ship, so that it could depart.

Shortly afterwards, Beaumarchais was again the victim of yet more bureaucratic obstruction, and he was compelled to write to the marine commissary in Nantes, requesting that the ship *Thereze* should be allowed to take on another ten leading seamen (to make up the body of junior ratings, now held to be the mandatory number permitted to sail on these particular voyages to America). This ship had already been detained in Painboeuf[13] for twelve days, for one petty reason after another, and Beaumarchais felt beaten down by these continual obstacles so inexplicably placed in his way; but he was not, and never would be, 'the man to be refused, and harshly refused at that,' and so he kept on plugging away at his masters. He was also not, as he repeatedly pointed out to them, a 'pestering protégé who asked only for personal preferment, but rather a useful worker employed in the common cause.'

But while all may not have been well with that cause, neither was everything all bad with his enterprises. For 'Lady Luck' had brought into his hands a piece of news that immediately 'revived his hopes.' The *Amphitrite* and the *Seine*, his first two ships to be sent directly to the eastern coast of America, had arrived safely in Charleston, South Carolina, and he was not particularly worried about his other, lesser, vessels; for only the two larger ships carried heavy munitions. Beaumarchais was sourly amused to learn from a secret source that he had been described by ministers as a 'corsair,' thanks to the activities of his crews, carried out in his name on the Spanish Main.

The *Thereze*, richly loaded, finally set sail 'by the best wind' from Mindin on April 26th; but, as a result of the constantly contradictory instructions from Versailles, a package of letters—intended for transportation—was delayed by two mail deliveries at the main Paris post office, despite all Beaumarchais's precautions. He had no doubt that the packages and letters had been opened up and copied, but he regarded this as 'a small evil' because the ministry had not been compromised in any way. It was nevertheless a scandal that an important package could be 'shamelessly' delayed from Monday to Friday, and that a ship should have to leave without its mail, having waited for four days, during which there had been good winds.

More harmfully, what this also meant was that the people who received the ship in America would not know of the proper use to make of its valuable cargo. The ship that had carried the papers of the first vessel could be delayed by as much as three months, or could even 'go under,' and the 'silly curiosity of the gentlemen of the Post Office' had put at risk more than one million *livres* of precious goods. To prevent any such similar abuse in the future, Beaumarchais requested Vergennes or Maurepas to give him a royal order to rectify the situation, allowing any important package to be sent without post office interference—otherwise he would have to dispatch a messenger with each voyage, in order to convey instructions verbally.

Beaumarchais was disheartened but, as always, he philosophically shrugged his shoulders; but then his correspondent in Nantes wrote to say that *every* letter sent to him was now being delayed by one or two mail deliveries. He did not know why this was so, he wrote; but Beaumarchais did: '… Curious people who want to know all in order to divulge all are behind these manoeuvres.'

Beaumarchais also warned Vergennes that 'the traitor you are looking for is closer than you think. There are many plots against myself,' he wrote, 'but there are even more against you.' Vergennes, though, could hardly have been ignorant of this; conspiracy and intrigue were still the two great pastimes at Versailles—nothing had really changed since the time of Louis XV.

XV

Following the Fleet

Beaumarchais wrote jubilantly to Deane, informing him that the *Thereze* had sailed for America and that another ship would soon be on its way. Deane was not to concern himself about the possibility of these vessels being intercepted by the British, for as Beaumarchais advised him complacently, 'They will either have to inspect it or else to open fire on it, which will trigger a war between France and England.'

The *Heureux* was still berthed at Marseilles, but Beaumarchais had ordered it to sail up to Dunkirk—where, he promised Deane—it would be loaded with the best freight he could find. He would cram in the goods then on their way to the port from the 'heart of our manufactories.'[1] However, his elation was still tempered with a touch of despondency for he was, he wrote, now 'at the end of my rope to find more money,' adding slyly that he had been told of a commissioner who was now in receipt of cash from the secret fund in America. He did not (as yet) know from what source, and neither did he know the name of the commissioner in question; but there was, he wrote, even the suggestion that it might be Deane himself! If this was true, then Deane must surely appreciate that he himself could make better use of such money, and it was a hard fact that a serious lack of funding was beginning to affect his own operations.

More disturbingly, he had also heard that the American commissioners had selected a banking house in Paris to manage their funding, and he was insulted to find that the 'gentlemen from Passy' were giving their business to an 'outsider,' instead of to somebody who had already proved his worth. He assured Deane he would not cease to serve his fellow Americans in Paris because he was convinced that their compatriots at home were as ignorant of 'this incredible step' as he had been until recently;[2] but he did intend to now distance himself from people he had previously thought very highly of, who were—as he could now see—'doing their best to do their country a disservice.' He did not for a moment, he hastened to add, include Deane among their number, although he did accuse him of not being energetic enough 'in checking all the wrong these people are doing me.'

Deane did not respond to this letter, which was galling enough; but that no money came to Beaumarchais from his American colleagues was even more aggravating, since he was by now experiencing great financial difficulties.

The only person to come to his aid was Vergennes, who could hardly have done otherwise since Beaumarchais's financial quandary stemmed largely from the government's lack of action. The minister undoubtedly dreaded Beaumarchais's ability to retaliate publicly if nothing was done to relieve him; Beaumarchais, the much-publicized writer, was always an adversary to be feared.

An unofficial interim payment was made, for which Beaumarchais wrote to thank the minister for his 'kindness,' saying that he could now 'breathe until the 15th;' but adding that a percentage of his resources would need replacing after that date, or 'I will be strangled again.' Yet Beaumarchais now felt sufficiently 'unburdened' by Vergennes's generosity to set out to the country, '… to finish a job I could not have finished in the city's noise'—which presumably meant that he was engaged in writing; the first stirrings of *The Marriage of Figaro*,[3] no doubt, since his next move was definitely in keeping with the servant's wiliness.

Certainly—in a stratagem worthy of Figaro—he was, he informed Vergennes, about to pull off a considerable *coup de theatre*. He was going to 'feign' fitting out a ship in Dunkirk, as he knew that nothing could be done in this particular port without the English learning about it, and so they would concentrate on any open activity there; but all the goods that he had secretly amassed in Dunkirk would actually be sent, also in secret, to Brest, while his workmen were filling up the ships in Dunkirk with 'safe' merchandise. The compromising cargo would also have to be transferred in secret to his ship in Brest, since it, too, was under surveillance by the British. British spies were all too aware that the movement of munitions to areas in the French dominions would be 'more frequent and natural' from Brest, as the country's main naval base—a fact that Beaumarchais used greatly to his advantage , taking, in turn, the necessary steps to hide his own involvement in the transportation of armaments. Unknown to him, however, British spies were not the only people keeping an eye on his movements; he had also attracted the interest of government opponents.

In fact he was in trouble with the naval ministry for overriding their orders; at one point being forced to send Vaillant, his secretary, out in the middle of the night to change his instructions, since they conflicted with a directive he had received at the very last moment. An exchange of letters between Beaumarchais and Francy, his invaluable assistant, also had a farcical outcome, due to each communication arriving too late to be properly acted upon—and a ship left before the arrival of Beaumarchais's messenger, who carried orders contrary to the ones with which its captain had been issued.

To add to his difficulties, Arthur Lee was now back from Berlin, having made a fruitless journey there. He had been away from May to July 1777, and had managed to make himself as unpopular in Germany as he was in France;

the problem being that Franklin found nothing constructive for him to do, whereas he had entrusted Deane (whom he rather liked) with much more important work, letting him handle the business of secret aid. As a result of this, Franklin suffered Arthur Lee's 'magisterial snubbings and rebukes,' as he put it, and there can be no doubt that Lee, always neurotic, had by now—believing himself to be superior in ability to both his partners—become seriously disturbed. Distorting every situation, and with nothing else to occupy him, Lee began to look more deeply into Deane's methods of business. Distrusting both Deane and Bancroft, he quickly grew convinced that Beaumarchais, too, was involved in whatever he suspected of his fellow Americans!

Beaumarchais by this time was extremely downhearted, and he called upon Deane, to whom he tried to make clear the difficulty that his loyalty to their cause had placed him in (hampered as always by the fact that Deane's French had not improved and that Beaumarchais's English remained idiosyncratic). He now proposed that Deane should take more responsibility in the administration of the business by running his own account, and to his astonishment, perhaps, Deane agreed to this, after thinking things through. It may be that Bancroft acted as interpreter during this important conversation and later advised Deane to take on this responsibility, with consequences that would bode ill for both men; though, as a result of this meeting, the two men decided to set up a new compact between them, and it is perhaps from this time that they began to speculate on the war news revealed to them.

Yet almost at once, Beaumarchais reproached Deane, despite having given him permission to do so, for making arrangements that conflicted with his own plans. For the American, after learning that Beaumarchais had given positive orders for a ship leaving Brest to head straight for the American shore, had then countermanded this and had the ship re-loaded, directing that it should head for the island of Martinique. His explanation for this was that he had been instructed by his superiors to forward any express orders to one William Hodge Junior,[4] who had been sent to France by the Secret Committee of Congress in October 1776—and Hodge, who owned a privateer based in Dunkirk, had decided upon Martinique, which was 'as much a French harbour as any other.'

Deane, in trying to defend his own actions, complained to Vergennes that although Beaumarchais claimed to be their friend, he often delayed vital shipments needed for various campaigns, a flagrantly unfair accusation. Beaumarchais, deeply offended, wrote to Vergennes to complain about Deane's criticism, but at the same time asking that the minister mediate between himself and the American, since he realized that any sort of rupture at this stage would be critical. Deane was his only ally in the American commission, and had he not been conspicuously, perplexingly, and *humiliat-ingly* unsuccessful in his efforts to involve Deane's compatriots?

In the middle of this petty—and yet highly significant—controversy, his secretary Vaillant[5] arrived; and Beaumarchais immediately sent him to Francy with new orders. The dependable agent was charged to proceed along the lines that he was by now conversant with—the original method as laid down by Beaumarchais—but Deane was to be held responsible for its performance (successful or otherwise) from now on. Upon learning about this resolution, Deane himself wrote to Francy saying that he was 'in complete agreement with his employer about this decision'—perhaps because he only anticipated triumph and not disaster.

Triumph, however, was not to be smoothly anticipated, for there were many concealed hazards to be encountered in this 'great undertaking;' but Deane, who 'except for his whining and scolding' was less to be dreaded 'than the disgrace of falling foul of our masters,' could still be made use of, and then set aside (in much the same way, perhaps, that the ship *Marie Catherine*, a privateer not under Beaumarchais's control, 'may go get fucked at Martinique').[6]

Yet Beaumarchais could not hide his fears about Deane's contemplated use of an armed American vessel to protect his own shipping, and advice received from on high hardly reassured him. 'I hope that you have had no part in that beautiful expedition,' he was warned, for 'Those who are behind it need not embark victuals, for their ship won't go very far.'[7] To add to his anxieties, it was rumoured that Captain Hodge was not simply in the business of conveying goods across the Atlantic; he was hoping to capture a prize. Beaumarchais was also on edge because the British were, at that time, cruising in front of the harbour at Nantes, and he feared that his ship there would be taken and lost to them 'without recourse.' If the privateer had not already left, he requested Francy to check the papers secretly to see if anything could be changed, 'so that it will not risk any danger en route.'

If Hodge's ship was still in port, he suggested that unloading it was a possibility, and its cargo laden on to the next one due to leave. 'Don't address it to one place or another until I tell you to,' he ordered apprehensively; for Beaumarchais may well have surrendered temporary control of shipments to Deane, but he was still hard at work on the protection of his investment. It was he alone that could arrange things to be done 'obscurely,' because he knew that the Post Office would be handling the packaging side of matters, but he also needed to be sure that there would be no ministerial outcry if the British navy seized this minor vessel and discovered its controversial cargo. This was his main concern, for any imprudence 'at this stage of the game' would cause difficulties later for his major ship, the *Seine*.

By now Beaumarchais was in poor health, largely due to the state of his nerves, for the constant frustrations were beginning to wear him down. To increase his depression, he knew that he was running out of stock, and he knew that he could not rely upon Vergennes to supply more goods for his newly acquired ship. They must either obtain a smaller vessel or load the hold of the present ship only half way. He came up with the solution that 'old copper' might make up the freight, and he duly informed Francy to collect the requisite amount. Meanwhile his assistant was to try to find out what goods were still being held in Dunkirk, through a Monsieur d'Ostalis,[8] so that Beaumarchais could check up if their statement was consistent with what he thought to be the facts. It was also important that no one knew his secretary—Vaillant—had made two secret trips to Nantes.

'To summarize,' he instructed Francy, trying to clarify the conflicting situation created by his decision to allow Deane to believe that he was *actually in charge*: 'You [must say that you] received an order from Deane, and you acted in consequence of it, as you thought he and I were in agreement. My counter-order arrived too late for you to change the situation.' This was the story that Beaumarchais would tell the ministers at Versailles if he had to defend his actions on this occasion. Francy, however, had actually been instructed to ship the goods away in secret, or to do so in great haste at least, so that by the time Vaillant reached him, it would not seem the secretary's arrival had actually activated him. '… For the rest, may God watch over it!'

As he was about to let the *Anonymous* leave port, Beaumarchais realised that the ship was in reality a worthless derelict. He gave the order for her to be unloaded, reserving for later the question of the damages he would claim for being fobbed off with this hulk. He decided to leave the boat by the dock in the exact condition that it was in when purchased and refitted, and he meant to embarrass those who were involved, since it had cost him 35,000 *livres* to have the ship refitted, before learning of its complete unsuitability.

Even more distressing news now reached him. Bonill,[9] the new commander at Martinique, had notified his merchants that 'the courts of England and France had together agreed that the English navy has a right to search all vessels coming from the French islands'—which meant that they could seize every kind of merchandise coming 'from the American continent' into the Franco-Spanish Caribbean. This had been startling news for all concerned, but Beaumarchais was temporarily floored by it, since he had planned to re-route his cargoes from America through these very ports.

From this time on it seemed that all was over for him, since American ships had now no place in French waters, and the British were empowered to be 'the exclusive customs agents on the ocean.' No commercial companies in France had been given previous notice of this arrangement between the two countries, although many fortunes had already been affected by previous seizures. From now on, no sane merchant could possibly expose himself to this new danger; indeed, ships would never have been dispatched at all had it been possible to guess at such a one-sided understanding being reached between Britain and France.

Beaumarchais did not blame Vergennes (or at least not to his face), for he realized that the minister must have been seriously compromised in some way to have signed such an agreement. Nevertheless, he was in despair, for he had only managed to make his June 10th repayment by selling at a loss all the commercial bills that he held. It was such a bad moment for him 'that had a million *livres* arrived the next day it could not have repaired the harm done the day before for the lack of only 30,000.' He had paid out the 184,328 *livres* as required, with 21,864 *livres*, eight *sols*, four *deniers* left in arrears from his payment of the 15th, on which he had cashed in only 200,000 instead of 221,304.8.3. He therefore lacked 490,168 *livres*, 16 *sols*, 7 *deniers*, along with the loss of his paper resources, for his three last payments, which he must find some means of repairing if he was to remain in business.

He requested Vergennes to let him have a warrant for 500,000 *livres*; 'after which I'll take a trip.' He did not specify where this would be, or what would be the reason for it, although he agreed to discuss this later with the minister.

His spirits revived somewhat when he received the good news that the *Amphitrite*, 'after a tiresome crossing of eighty-five days,' had arrived at Portsmouth, seventeen leagues north of Boston, with 'the whole crew at the end of their strength and courage.' They had now recovered, and Captain Heraut, commander of the *Mercury*, back from Boston in a passage of only twenty-three days, marked the good news after his arrival at Nantes.

More good news followed. The *Marquis de la Charolais* managed to steal into Charleston, Carolina, accompanied by three other ships, on 4 May 1777. It was encouraging to hear that, despite the new agreement, the British were—as yet, anyway—proving inept at intercepting French vessels. The *Amelie's* cargo had arrived at the Cape and had already left from there, its merchandise having been divided between several American and Bermudian ships. He was able to report that the army officers who were at the Cape had also left on the schooner *Catherine*, bound for Boston, Massachusetts. The men had been expedited without artillery, he noted dryly, 'but with a load of 100 casks of rum, to shield them from danger!'

Beaumarchais carried his good news to Vergennes, along with a report he had received concerning the condition of the American armies as of June 4th. All in all, it could be agreed that everything was going well for the Americans; and there had been no more activity on the part of General Howe.[10]

But Beaumarchais was distressed to receive confirmation of the fatal announcement made by Bonill at Martinique. It was now certain that the French government had conceded to Britain the right to stop and search any French vessel coming from the islands, and to seize them should they be loaded with any kind of merchandise from North America. By now, Beaumarchais had got over his shock sufficiently to boldly question Vergennes's motives in allowing this perplexing compact. '… What extremity could possibly have led you to sign such a convention?' he asked—without receiving a satisfactory answer.

He also pointed out at this meeting that British merchants often went themselves to French colonies to carry out clandestine deals, and to take goods from the islands. He suggested that, if armed French ships were to meet up with British vessels, carrying cargoes recognizable as coming from French sources, could they not, by way of reprisal, be able to seize them in return? They could look upon these seizures as 'prizes,' legitimately stopped on the high seas.

This proposition had actually come from a group of disgruntled French merchants, and Beaumarchais was only their spokesman, passing the motion on to his superior while 'deploring the bad news'—which he could not, in any case, he said, believe until he had heard it confirmed from the minister's own mouth. To his mortification, it was confirmed.

As a result of this disastrous decision, Beaumarchais was convinced that gunshots would inevitably be fired between the protectors of the merchant vessels of both Britain and France, 'who are [ostensibly] at peace with each other;' since, while the British claimed to be authorized to cut the throat of the other's foreign trade, the French would be in no mood to comply with the 'kindness' of their own administration to the British, at the expense of all French commerce.

Beaumarchais received a brief from Dunkirk, containing a woman's complaints about a memorial that had been printed there dealing with the government's lack of concern for French interests in the American affair. The publishers of this paper, which had originated with a consortium of local merchants, intended also to start a suit against the ministers they felt were responsible for abandoning their interests. A 'prudent person' in the port had sent a copy on to Beaumarchais, asking for his advice, as one who was heavily involved in the trade. In turn, Beaumarchais advised Vergennes that the paper was serious enough to reverse many a government statement, 'and even to cause a great noise.'

He sent the count a crude poster, from the same source, which proclaimed that the French government wished to make the merchants and ship-owners pay for all the blunders that the ministers themselves were making overseas by their inability to reach a decision concerning the War of Independence. '… Oh, if the British could make peace with America today, how they would make war on us tomorrow!' Beaumarchais cried, in total agreement with the advertisers. It was, he urged, essential to neglect nothing that would keep that peace from happening.

Otherwise, everything was reported to be in good shape 'over there,' with one exception in his view; the detested Tronson de Coudray had arrived in May 1777, accompanied by no fewer than eighteen officers and ten sergeants. To Beaumarchais's astonishment, he learned that General Washington had sent the Frenchman on to Ticonderoga, to defend the fort there. Generous as ever, after thinking the thing through, he gave it as his opinion that, 'Although this man is crack-brained and mean-hearted, I believe he will do a great job. He errs not out of military ignorance, but only out of reckless ambition'—even though, during the summer of 1777, Coudray would repay his faith in him with a twenty-seven-page statement to Congress restating the old canard that he, Coudray, had been the sole instigator of French secret aid to America. A copy of this treacherous declaration had been given to Francy by James Lovell,[11] who was French interpreter for Congress, and Francy forwarded it to Beaumarchais inside his letter of 31 July 1778.

The receipt of this could only add to his tribulations, since he was still at the mercy of various ministers, as they sent out one maddening order and counter-order after another—all of which were meant primarily to delay, or even stop, his ships from sailing. But with some crews instructed to unload the vessels, leaving their cargoes unprotected on the dockside, their actions went deeper than mere bureaucratic mismanagement. There was, it seemed, at the heart of government, a decided policy against assisting him in his scheme; and he could only retaliate against this political malice through his talented pen. Two letters to the navy minister sharply reminded him of his duty to protect French trade and of the rights of France as a *neutral* state, while two of his letters to Congress encouraged the Americans to fight on. This last letter curiously echoed the sentiments of the Declaration of Independence.

Meanwhile, the American commissioners in Paris were still creating problems for him. Silas Deane wrote on 9 August to say that he had paid Hughes Eyries a sum of money drawn from the account of Messieurs Morris and others in Philadelphia, which was to be employed in the purchase of a vessel.[12] At the same time, he reminded Beaumarchais that Eyries required a speedy settlement, asking if this could be done as soon as possible. He hoped that Beaumarchais would conduct the transaction himself, and he enclosed the necessary papers, saying that he had written to Eyries to acquaint him of Beaumarchais's personal involvement. So much for Deane's gratitude after being given 'full control'!

But apart from being once again saddled with problems that he had hoped to pass on to others, Beaumarchais's difficulties with the various ministries also rumbled on. On 28 August he complained to Sartine that one of his most trusted agents, a Monsieur Chevalier in Rochefort, had been questioned by the port authority at great length, a result of which another ship had been hindered from departing on time. Beaumarchais considered that 'only one of those prowling and prying Englishmen, who are all over our ports, could have sounded the alarm in such an untimely fashion, and caused your highness, by ways most familiar to them, to plan an unprecedented inquisition into the affairs of French merchants.'

It was inexplicable to him that his government should have allowed the British to infiltrate their ports to the extent they had; every move he made in the cause of the Americans had to be camouflaged.

One of the King's warships, the *Hippopotamus* came up for sale, and even though its condition now seemed beyond repair, Beaumarchais decided upon buying it, since he saw immediately to what use an armed vessel could be put in the service of his little fleet. 'We are,' he wrote to Vergennes, 'having it repaired at great expense. Moreover, we do not think it contrary to the laws of commerce to do so. Neither will it make us suspect of wanting to thwart the pacific views of the government.'

Yet he freely conceded that many of his enemies suspected his motives in making such a purchase, since 'a vessel of such high calibre can only be intended for great adventures':

> But is it not natural, milord, [he contended], that we should use such a ship to prevent us, in a time of peace, from being shot at, boarded, searched, looted, perhaps seized and confiscated, in spite of the regularity of our papers, (as has happened to many others)? Even when there is not to be found among all our cargo an ell of cloth whose colour or quality happens to displease the first Englishman who runs into us?

The maritime merchant was, of all the King's subjects, Beaumarchais insisted, the one who most needed immediate protection. The English, for example, by attacking a French vessel could cause a French merchant to 'lose the fruit of a good mission,' but their actions could afterwards be explained away by simply claiming that 'the captain was drunk' during this unfortunate episode, or that it had been 'a misunderstanding'—which would incur neither loss nor penalty. Such a trite or banal excuse might—at the diplomatic level—appease the wrath of the French government, but the useful merchant, 'whose role it is to entrust his fortune to the waves, even on the faith of unbiased treaties, would remain nevertheless ruined. In spite of the compensation he has been promised, but which can always be easily set aside.'

The purchase of the *Hippopotamus* was, of course, a complicated procedure, in view of the 'infamous' identity of the real purchaser, and one that had to be kept secret throughout. At no time could even certain members of the government be made aware of the identity of the true buyer, let alone the British spies who were in the port at the time, and may even have attended the auction. But the transaction seems to have been carried out without attracting undue attention, with Beaumarchais's agent, Chevalier,[13] becoming the highest bidder, under his own name, and therefore—nominally—the new owner of the King's ex-warship. As such, Vergennes assured him that he would be granted the first royal freight for the colonies, *but he did this by telling him through Beaumarchais*, who, in turn, begged the count to keep his promise, since this would be the best way to ensure the 'true' destination of the ship: the American colonies.

In September, Beaumarchais informed Silas Deane that he had allowed a certain 'Mr Williams' to do 'what he pleased' in the loading of such a 'puny' vessel as the *Monsieur le Bobi*. This was a ship that seems to have acted under independent control, although Beaumarchais included some of his own merchandise among its cargo—largely because, as he said, he must lend himself to everything that facilitated the transport to America of so many objects that were then being 'tossed about from one port to another.' He was outraged to learn that the war ministry had sent their men to have the boat unloaded 'in full view of the public,' and under the watchful gaze of British spies.

Fortunately, Beaumarchais had cleverly contrived to have Mr Williams's harmless containers made up in such a way as to completely hide anything that his own people had already packed, and which might have caught the attention of the minister's officials during the unloading and reloading. 'I will try fortune once more, or perhaps misfortune,' he wrote caustically, 'For the latter seldom fails to come when one seeks the former.'

He had sent another ship, the *Hardi* to Carolina from Marseilles, although he had initially been unwilling to do so, and he had done it only at Deane's request. As an agent of the General Congress, Deane himself was not involved with this particular shipment, but he had told Beaumarchais that the troops in Carolina were in dire need of it, the appeal having come from the president of the Carolina Congress himself.[14] Although he could expect little—if any—commercial profit from the voyage of the *Hardi*, Beaumarchais nonetheless decided to make this 'new sacrifice.'

The *Heureux*, the Marseilles ship that he was anxious to send to sea, but which had been held back by the authorities, was now also on its way. Beaumarchais had ordered it to be loaded at night and then only a little at a time to deflect interest in the operation, but even this subterfuge had been futile. The British ambassador, then visiting Marseilles, had been secretly informed of the operation, and had once again insisted upon the ship being unloaded. This had been done in the full glare of noon, 'causing a great uproar;' and yet despite what could have been a tremendous setback, Beaumarchais had cleverly managed to get the boat re-freighted, and it was now at sea.

A part of this new load was some old artillery that the war ministry had scheduled to be melted down for scrap, but the bulk of which Beaumarchais had managed to get smuggled aboard in its original form, in the nightly reloading of the *Flamand* (the new name for the *Heureux*—a name that he considered totally unfitting after the strains of the past two months). The ship was thought—by the ministry—to be 'free of artillery,' and so it was sent off to Santo Domingo.

Beaumarchais sent more than unauthorized armaments across the ocean, on this occasion, for he had decided upon dispatching his assistant, Francy, to America, in order to make direct contact with the various committees attached to Congress, and to plead his case before them. Francy set sail on the *Flamand* on 17 September 1777, and he arrived at Portsmouth, New Hampshire, some time in December.

Above all, Beaumarchais wanted Francy to uncover the reasons that lay behind Congress's curious neglect of him, for he had not heard from the American legislature for a whole year. At the same time, Francy was to complain to Congress about the 'infernal obscurity' in the way that his master had been treated by 'the gentlemen of Passy,' who were still ignoring him. Unable to deal with this matter in any other way, Beaumarchais gave his agent full powers of attorney in the matter, apart from being his mouthpiece; but, as such, he was to tell the Americans of Beaumarchais's actions on their behalf. Beaumarchais knew that this drastic action would displease a few people at the French court, but he felt that he now had no alternative; he had, he declared, no option but to 'henceforth disregard all the small considerations for which I have so far had too much regard.'

He wanted Francy to carry the strongest recommendation from Silas Deane; in fact he was relying upon it, as he wrote to Deane: '... As you can count on the true feelings with which I am, for life, Monsieur, your most humble and obedient servant.'

In the meantime, his troubles continued with the various ministries, particularly with that of the Comte de Sartine. A 'sail embargo' had been planned for his Rochefort ship, and Beaumarchais challenged the minister with regard to this, gently insinuating that—as he was now planning to do in America— he might go public in France if he was to be again frustrated in this new restriction. 'Nobody must dissimulate anything, since this affair concerns the interests of the State as much as it does mine.'

Lord Stormont had complained to Vergennes, upon having learned that a warship the King had lately sold was now destined 'for service in America' (which he may have thought was on loan to the newly emergent American navy). Beaumarchais at once demanded to know how the ambassador had managed to come into possession of this knowledge, since he himself had managed it 'in all secrecy.' Was Stormont simply 'making an assumption, based on uncertain inferences'? In any case, it was surely the height of audacity for Stormont to dare make this assertion before the King's ministers, 'who know, because I secretly told them, that this ship was *never* destined for service *with* the Americans. It is designed for purely mercantile purposes only. That is, it has been outfitted against the British only in defence of my commercial fleet. I planned for it to go and fetch me such returns as have been kept away from me for too long, either by my debtors' indolence, or by their penury.'

He gave Vergennes the 'facts' as he saw them. The Americans, as of that date, owed him five million *livres*, which he now saw would take a long time to be repaid. An ordinary ship could only bring back, at the most, 300 hogsheads of tobacco; which, all outfitting and other expenses deducted, would barely yield in France 150,000 *livres*. According to their exact computation, in order to recover the sum of five million spent, Beaumarchais would have to outfit *thirty-two* ships, and so run the risk of being taken by the British that number of times on the way there and back. Not to mention the three months wasted in waiting for these shipments to appear, and without counting the 1,001 contradictions he would experience while outfitting the ships.

He had been forced, therefore, to look for other means of honourably fulfilling his obligations to his backers. Too many enemies were conspiring to ruin him, and his few successes had already attracted envy, even though he had contrived to disguise these successes in the very nature of the operation. Yet success alone would demolish his enemies. This he was attempting to do by outfitting a vessel of 1,000 tons; with which, in one trip, he intended to bring back a fifth of a third of what was due to him, without fearing for the ship to be taken en route.

This was the King's old warship, which, by virtue of its size alone, would warrant respect. '... Even a brutal Englishman would look at it twice before insulting it!'

His commercial officer was already on his way to purchase and store in either the port of Williamsburg or Annapolis as much tobacco as his ship would be able to hold. The order had already been given at the Cape to detain any of his other ships until the arrival of the ex-warship, in order that they could be loaded at the same time and be accompanied by it on the way back. He had learned this lesson with the loss of the *Seine* and the seizure of the *Anna* by the British, on their way from Santo Domingo; these ships, once captured, had been taken to the British possession, Jamaica. Beaumarchais said that he had not complained of this earlier since he knew complaint to be useless, finding 'little consolation coming to me from Versailles.'

Once the ships had rendezvoused at Chesapeake Bay, and as soon as the ocean crossing ceased to be physically dangerous, his ex-warship would take the lead in bringing back *all* his ships under its protection. Since he had purchased the man-of-war, the *Hippopotamus* had been renamed *Proud Rodrigue*, in tribute to Hortalez & Cie. Whether Beaumarchais could follow up on a plan that he had been carefully thinking out for the past six months would depend upon the goodwill of the King's ministers. This plan could, he was aware, be ruined by a simple stroke of a pen; and if this happened, it would mean his total failure.

But *partial* failure was also imminent. If his main vessel were to be laid up, as Lord Stormont demanded, where would he find the means of outfitting others? Who would repay him the 10,000 *louis* that this ship had cost him? Who would reimburse him for the goods he had already loaded it with, and who would give him back the 15,000 *louis* he had paid for the 15,000 guns he had just sent? Not to mention the cost of his last outfitting, or his tobacco and sugar purchases from Virginia, which would spoil on the docks if they were not picked up on time. Moreover, without the protection of the *Proud Rodrigue*, his ships would be defenceless against the harrying of the British, to be easily picked off if they were not in convoy; one million *livres* would not repair such disorder. Would the British ambassador be willing to recompense him for the damage he had personally inflicted upon a legitimate financial enterprise, carried out in what was still, as far as the French were concerned, *peacetime*?

Beaumarchais stressed that the Americans themselves were in no way implicated with these particular problems of his, (except in so far as they were proving singularly slow to send him adequate returns). But he himself was so deeply involved that if his ships were to be stopped from sailing he would be ruined and dishonoured; 'Good only to hang or drown—the choice to be made on the throw of a coin!'

1 Portrait of Beaumarchais (1732–1739)

Charles Gravier Comte de Vergennes
Conseiller d'État Ordinaire, Ministre et Secrétaire d'État
et Chef du Conseil Royal des Finances

2 Charles Gravier comte de Vergennes, three-quarter-length portrait engraving, created in Paris between 1774 and 1789

3 Silas Deane, drawn from the life by Du Simitier in Philadelphia, engraved by B. L. Prevost at Paris in 1781

4 Benjamin Franklin, half-length portrait by artist Benjamin Wilson, 1761

5 Madame d'Éon alias Chevalier d'Éon. Caricature of Charles Éon de Beaumont dressed as a woman, 1791

6 John Jay (1745–1829)

7 De La Fayette
Engraving originally published by
J. Fielding, Paternoster Row, 1785

8 Lt. Gen. Burgoyne (1722–1792)

9 General Sir William Howe.
Engraving originally published in 1778 for T.
Robson

10 Lord Richard Howe.
Engraving first published by J. Fielding in
Paternoster Row in March 1785

11 Infantry of the Continental army, 1779–1783.
The illustration depicts uniforms and weapons used during this period of the American Revolution

A Real American Rifle Man

12 Engraving of an American rifleman in military uniform, created in 1780

He was aware that he was now speaking openly about secret affairs, but he felt he had no choice in the matter, for he must—*solely in his capacity as a French merchant*—seek reassurance from his government. He, in turn, promised them that if they released his newest ship, then its reputable outfitters would give their assurance, 'if need be,' to return to a French port within six months carrying only the merchandise duly expected from Santo Domingo (where the ship was, in fact, carrying French troops that had been pledged to the Americans).

Again, Beaumarchais stressed that the secret connection between his maritime trade and the political situation was so well masked that one could very well disregard it, 'and have no concern for the false alarms of the most indiscreet of ambassadors.' Moreover, the members of the crew would be so much on their guard that if, during the crossing, the ship was obliged to give a 'good beating to those who come to insult it,' it would be done with every legal *punctilio*. So much so, in fact, that the outfitters would feel entitled to ask their government to avenge them for the insults they had received at sea.

How shameful it was for France that the royal tobacco farm had to pay up to 120 *livres* per quintal for tobacco, or else to do without, due to the present shortage in France, even while there was a glut of it in America! If only the King's ministers could realize this. Should the War of Independence last another two years, King Louis XVI would see a catastrophic lowering on the profits from taxation on tobacco. It was only because his Majesty was 'honest enough to remain neutral,' and because it pleased the English—who could no longer supply the French with this produce—to insolently forbid them to buy it from the only country in the world where it was grown. How could the French remain neutral in the face of such opposition? Beaumarchais assured Sartine that 'everyone in London is joking about our lack of spine.' There was, he insisted, a strong connection between the right of the French to trade freely with America and 'the greatest political event to occupy our government in this century.'

XVI

News from America

By 30 September news had come from America that Admiral Howe's fleet had been encountered on August 7, at 35 degrees latitude, which might prove a threat to Beaumarchais's own little fleet[1]—though this seemed impossible to him.

The next day he was able to give Vergennes further news from America in one of the few letters to reach him (many compromising letters had been thrown into the sea, to stop them falling into British hands). The only interesting bits of the letter confirmed Beaumarchais's suspicions—also held by the foreign minister—regarding military and naval action in the Gulf of Mexico, which was temporarily interrupting local business.[2] British operations in that area were, both men believed, further evidence of the lunacy of King George III's council!

But Beaumarchais had other news to reveal, which was of more importance in the short term, since he was able to inform Vergennes that the American commissioners in Paris had been empowered by their Congress to deal with *all* European powers, and this included Britain. He had also learned that Benjamin Franklin was waiting for a directive from America as to whether he should stay in Paris or leave. Beaumarchais believed that the British were urging the commissioners to reach an agreement, and he thought that instructions would come to Franklin from London, although he thought him to be incapable of double-crossing the French.

Franklin had been saddened by the loss of his friend, Doctor Samuel Johnson,[3] Beaumarchais wrote, and by the loss of the *Lexington*, but what tormented him most was his uncertainty about what he must do following the reply he was expecting from America. Franklin, who had so far steered clear of Beaumarchais, now asked him—through a member of his staff—many questions regarding Vergennes's disposition with regard to the 'American question,' and Beaumarchais, always the 'eternal conciliator,' tried to maintain the old man's courage with hope. He dealt with him, he wrote, 'as the [chief] commissioner of Congress, and who, as the latter, [dealt] with the American people.' It was a chain of hope of which Beaumarchais held the first link, or so he believed. He could only trust that the Comte de Vergennes did also, which would make the chain stronger.

The ship *Independence*, under Captain Young, arrived at Lorient with two British prizes in tow. The ship had left America on August 10, even though the English fleet had been sighted on the 7th, sailing south in spite of a contrary south-southwest wind. The audacious Captain Young bore dispatches from Congress, dated July 14, and he also carried American newspapers up to August 1st, which contained strong criticism of the officers in charge of the defence of Ticonderoga, captured by the British on 5 July 1777.

Another vessel left from Delaware on 16 August, and this also arrived at Lorient. The captain had been in charge of grave news from Congress, but while being chased by the British and believing his ship about to be captured, he had thrown the papers overboard. He asserted that a part of Admiral Howe's fleet was now back in New York after showing up in Delaware for three days (from 2nd to 5th August), and that the remainder of the fleet had sailed south. If it had entered Chesapeake Bay, as it was believed that it would, Congress in Philadelphia would have heard from them three days later.

The only real news of British activities came from a French captain, arriving from Martinique, who swore that he had met a British fleet 'of 200 sails' more than 100 miles off the American coast, again sailing in spite of a contrary wind. This agreed with Captain Young's report, except that he had estimated the British force at more than 300 sails.[4] Below Virginia, there was not a single port, nor a navigable bay, at which war ships could put in, Figaro concluded that this fleet was headed not for Charleston but for the French islands. This was supported by their position 100 miles off the coast, which they were seeking only in order to avoid the current that drove ships north.

The Philadelphia newspapers of 30 July reported that the British had not yet left Skenesboro,[5] their first encampment after capturing Ticonderoga fort, and that the Americans were at Fort Edward, where they received considerable reinforcements. By 16 August there was no news of any further British movement in the north, but it was claimed that the Hessian troops of George III had arrived in New York with the fleet, and had been set to working on the ships. The British army was believed to be in a state of near-rebellion.

The *Lexington*, under its American captain, had been on its way from Morlaix to America when it was captured, at about 45 degrees of latitude, by a British cutter. All the officers, including the captain, had been killed during the encounter, except for one who suffered only a broken leg. Again, the dispatch for Congress had been thrown overboard during the fight for the ship.

On October 11, Beaumarchais wrote to Vergennes to say that he would be absent from Paris for a month. He had at last received news that two American frigates, of 32 and 20 cannons, had arrived at Lorient. They had left Portsmouth, Virginia, on 22 August, in order to cruise, but without intending to cross to France, although what it was that had brought them across the ocean was never made clear. To Beaumarchais's considerable annoyance, when he interviewed the captain, the only news they brought was that a corps of 2,000 men—Indians, Canadians and English—had left from Montreal and sailed down Lake Ontario under Sir John Johnson,[6] an American loyalist who had fled to Canada the year before. Johnson's mission had failed at their first engagement, however, when his makeshift regiment had been roundly beaten at Fort Stanwix by an American force, with 300 men and their leader killed, and the rest fled. Johnson's party had been planning to get to Albany from the West, while General Burgoyne[7] marched down from the north. It was to be hoped that these failures, as well as that of Benedict Arnold's[8] imminent arrival to join the Ticonderoga troops, would stop Burgoyne's plans.

Private news from London confirmed that General Howe had finally arrived at Chesapeake Bay and *had* gone up to Nottingham, from where he was sending troops to North Pennsylvania to try and destroy the large stores at Carlisle. It would appear that his army was trying to stretch a formidable line from the fleet in Chesapeake Bay to those men who were to go up to Newcastle and Delaware, so as to separate Maryland from Pennsylvania, where he hoped to obtain his provisions for the winter. General Washington had gone down to cover the country and defend Philadelphia, and the action would therefore take place in that area.

Back in Paris by the middle of November, Beaumarchais wrote to Robert Morris,[9] the 'financier of the Revolution,' the letter to be delivered to him by one Perrier, sailing on a ship sent to America by Messieurs Ricard and Merle, merchant friends of Beaumarchais. In it, he advised the American that the *Flamand*, out of Marseilles, would shortly arrive in Boston, and Francy, who would be on board, had the task of going over every detail of the arrangements between Hortalez & Cie and Morris, as well as the Secret Committee of Foreign Correspondence. Francy was to 'update these gentlemen on a lot of things that are impossible to put into writing.'

The French people, Beaumarchais wrote, had been led to believe that the British had captured Philadelphia, and that Washington had been defeated. It was not believed—at least by himself—who recognized it as a rumour spread by the English parliament to calm their people and to counter the attacks of their opposition. But, Beaumarchais added gallantly, even if the American capital *had* been taken, it would only be a matter of time before Morris's countrymen recovered it.

*   *   *

'Milord Stormont,' Sartine wrote to Vergennes, 'was wrong about the quality of the munitions sent to America, but he was not badly informed nevertheless.'[10] The British ambassador had complained about one ship in particular, the *Anna Suzanna*, and Sartine had promised to look into his allegations.

Fortunately, Beaumarchais was not in Paris at that time, but was once again on his travels. He had arrived in Marseilles only to learn about the *Amphitrite*'s arrival in Lorient; where, he was astonished to hear, its cargo had been disputed—not by French officials, but by the American commissioners in Paris! He was told that Benjamin Franklin and Arthur Lee had written to the harbourmaster demanding that it should not be turned over to Beaumarchais, stating that its cargo was addressed and consigned expressly to them, for the discharge of their mounting debts in Europe. The news completely stunned Beaumarchais, who might have expected such a move from the troublemaker Lee, but not from the wise old philosopher Franklin.

As he was not in direct communication with the two men, he felt that he could not immediately answer them, but instead could only ask them to speak with Silas Deane, who would surely set them right. He wrote to Deane, asking him to inform his fellow commissioners that the *Amphitrite*'s 'meagre cargo' belonged exclusively to him; and he wished Deane also to remind Franklin that it was *he*, Beaumarchais, who had paid for the freight on the ship that had brought him to Europe. It had been, in fact, the first payment on a huge debt that had accumulated over the past eighteen months, and which was *supposed* to have been paid off within a year.

This was an extraordinary development, and he wanted an explanation for this insulting and injurious behaviour by the Americans. Could it possibly be that they were unaware of his prior claims, or were they simply indifferent to his financial problems? Such were the complications created by his loyal adherence to their cause.

Beaumarchais, the courtier, may have been inclined to act diplomatically over this unexpected setback, but the merchant in him quickly decided otherwise. If they could not give prompt satisfaction for their outrageous decision, he would not only have this particular cargo seized, he would see to it that the contents of all the ships that came into French ports from America were similarly treated. If Messrs. Franklin and Lee thought that they could insult him publicly in Europe, they would find they had chosen to take on the wrong man. Not only would he denounce them to their own Congress, he would reveal all the wretched schemes they had employed to try to stop him from serving them—in his own country!

Beaumarchais was always aware of the conspiracies against him, but had 'Figaro' the arch-schemer even then been alerted to an incipient form of corruption among the 'upright' Americans he had been dealing with? It was certain that their scheming against him must have been very deep, for he had not heard one word from Congress in answer to all his letters—save one response by a minor official, enclosing a receipt for the cargo of one ship. It was always possible, of course, that whatever messages sent to him from America, via the commissioner's 'packets,' had probably been intercepted by the British, (or, more hopefully, been thrown overboard)—though this could hardly apply to *every* answer to his constant queries.

Beaumarchais felt sure that the truth would inevitably be revealed, and he would be vindicated. Meanwhile, he was claiming the *Amphitrite*'s cargo, and since even this would not realize enough to get him out of his present financial difficulties, he further asked Deane and his colleagues to make him an additional sizeable payment. He had no doubt that they were in a position to grant his request, since he well knew that they had been making payments for equipment well after his own advances, 'and certainly on less generous terms.'

Captain Fantrell,[11] captain of the *Amphitrite*, who had obeyed Beaumarchais against ministerial orders, had just been jailed for his loyalty. In compensation, the grateful Beaumarchais had assigned him 2,000 *ecus* as a bonus for his trip, and he was now planning to add this sum to the money he expected to receive from Franklin and Lee to further compensate him. Should this money not be forthcoming, he planned to write to the 'Gentlemen Commissioners' in America, and he told Deane that he expected him to back him up to the best of his ability; '... For the sake of your country, your honour, my needs, and for justice!'

Deane replied to him immediately, saying that he totally sympathized with poor Captain Fantrell, who had suffered imprisonment instead of being properly rewarded for the services that he had rendered both their countries—and it was still harder upon Beaumarchais, for being deprived of so trifling a remittance after the immense sums that he had expended in the cause of the United States. The cargo must be restored to him, and he was sure that it would be, once the case had been fairly stated to his fellow commissioners. They could not, however, he regretted, assist him by other payments, since it was not in their power to make them; the money at their disposal being greatly inadequate for the purpose for which it was originally advanced, and for which they 'stood engaged.' He himself was equally powerless to make any financial return that was in any way 'proportionate to your great disbursements of money.' Until his poor country's affairs took on a 'more prosperous turn,' Deane felt that he dared not make any further financial commitments on his own authority.

*   *   *

After the victory of the Americans at the Battle of Saratoga on 7 October 1777, the political context was changed. In an action lasting only 52 minutes, the Americans had demonstrated their ability to sustain their declared aims by the force of arms. It was now time for France to recognize the new nation before a compromise was reached between the Americans and the British. In a masterful political paper addressed to the ministers on 27 November 1777, Beaumarchais 'prepared the way' for the regulations of the French alliance with the new United States of America; and the procedure he then suggested was to be later adopted by the French government. Indeed, some of his 'less vigorous' language was actually repeated in Vergennes's official declaration to the British of 14 March 1778.

As always, the ministers took their time about responding to his proposal, and in the meantime he suffered a fall caused by a runaway horse in the Passage de la Chapelle, as he was leaving Maurepas's house. He had travelled into Versailles with a messenger just arrived from Congress, and had spent the morning there, comforted by the excellent news from the States; news that was simultaneously received by Vergennes at the palace. Returning to Paris in a light two-horse carriage, the postillion had carelessly run over some large stones and the vehicle was overturned 'so outrageously' that his companion, Monsieur Grand,[12] had suffered a broken shoulder. Beaumarchais had bled profusely from the nose and mouth, while a piece of jagged glass had jabbed into his right arm. He did not imagine himself to be as injured as he in fact was, and he showed more concern for his fellow travellers; his black servant having broken his back.

After having been 'bled from the foot,' he was now laid up, 'sicker in my mind than my body,' for it was not his postillion who was 'killing him,' he insisted, but rather the dilatory Maurepas. The good news from America spread some balm on his wound, and the rumours that reached him of the King's decision not to let such auspicious events 'be marred by a total desertion of their American friends' was also some comfort. 'I am, therefore, the voice that cries out from my bed to them.'

He knew that Vergennes had received a copy of the *Boston Gazette*, which had described the Battle of Saratoga in swaggering detail, but he also sent him an abstract from it that he had made himself and wished to pass on to the *Courrier de l'Europe*; this, however, did not appear. It was only fair, Beaumarchais believed, that he should respond 'with my sentences' to the verbal 'stabbing' he had received from the British ambassador in Paris. He signed his article with his wounded arm; he was spitting blood, but he had no fever.

There was very positive confirmation from America, too. A ship dispatched from Boston by Congress on 8 November arrived in Nantes, with packages bearing the great news in more detail. On October 17, General Burgoyne had surrendered at Saratoga, with an army of 5,752 men. The very generous terms of capitulation granted to him by the American General Gates included the honour of war, the delivery of their artillery to a nearby fort, and their being escorted by the militia to Boston (to save Burgoyne from being tarred and feathered by the New Englanders!). From Boston they were expected to embark for Britain, after pledging never to bear arms against America again, *in any country*. The number of the royalists killed, wounded, made prisoners, deserted, or lost, from September up to and including the capitulation of October 17, amounted to 9,213 soldiers. At last, after this spectacular victory over the British, Louis XVI finally assured the deputies of the new 'United States of America' of his 'affection and interest' in their cause.

But nearer to home, the news was again not so good; in fact it was such as to make Beaumarchais try to rise from his sickbed to attend to it. He had heard that Franklin and Lee had, despite his warnings, taken over the modest cargo of the *Amphitrite*, and had given orders for the monies from it to be given to them alone. Lee took as his pretext for this 'injustice' that he had been informed by Vergennes that Beaumarchais had taken, on his own account, all the matters of his shipments, and that the minister would 'make a deal' with Beaumarchais, who would never require *any payment* from them. 'Revolted' by this absurd excuse for robbing him of his cargo, the invalid immediately ordered his correspondents at Lorient to stop the handling of the goods.

He sent a copy of the letter he had written to the Berard Brothers[13] to all three American commissioners, although he exempted Silas Deane—'the most honest man I know'—from any participation in this outright swindle. He also wrote to Vergennes, whom he felt should be told of this nasty 'little trick of theirs,' which in his opinion also deeply compromised the minister. Somewhat nervously, in case Vergennes *had* given his permission for what he saw as an outright robbery, he hoped that the minister would not disapprove of the 'noble and proud' manner in which he had countered the Americans' claims. The only cheerful intelligence to reach him came from his physician; he had nothing broken in his body from his two falls, and so he could hope to be up and about very soon.

In his letter to the Americans, Beaumarchais boldly stated that the cargo on the *Amphitrite* belonged solely to him, and he claimed it entirely. He suggested that John Dorsius, a commercial agent of Congress,[14] had perhaps addressed it to the commissioners in error, but it was an even greater error on their part to imagine that they could dispose of it to his loss. Langton of Boston,[15] in acknowledging receipt of the *Amphitrite*, had informed him that he had an order from Congress to send the ship back to France—that is, to him—with 'suitable returns.'

The munitions and merchandise that Beaumarchais had sent by this ship were in themselves one of the least of his claims upon the new Republic. Deane had assured him from the beginning that returns from America would 'cross his ships' on their passage across the Atlantic, and that they would arrive shortly. Yet a year had passed, and nothing had been sent, although Beaumarchais had continued dispatching all kinds of shipments, and had spent much time and energy in the service of their country, 'the budding republic.'

Beaumarchais summarily rejected the idea that 'such a wise minister' as Vergennes would have suggested to anyone that he would take these matters to his own personal account, or that he would make such a deal with himself, and ask the Americans for no payment. How could they believe that he was wealthy enough to turn himself into a charity, and on such a huge scale? These matters were actually no concern of the ministry, except for the covert protection they had agreed to offer Beaumarchais, and which, having often been denied him, had caused him immense losses.

Therefore, when the 'totality' of his claims against their countrymen now amounted to several millions, invoices of which had been sent to the Congress, it was peculiarly indecent of the commissioners to wrangle about such a modest return has had been brought to him by the *Amphitrite*—especially at a moment when his zeal for the Republic, and his trust in its honesty, had caused him to go well beyond his means, creating much straitened circumstances for both himself and his backers.

While waiting for their answer, he had stopped the unloading of the ship and made the Berards guarantors 'for the least appropriation in favour of anyone.' He hoped that the commissioners would write to them immediately, informing them that the cargo or the sales money was to be held at his disposal:

> For which I will give you a receipt on account of what is due to me. I will not insult you by fearing that, when the armies of the Congress deal so generously with their enemies in America, their commissioners in France are tempted to do a flagrant injustice to the man most dedicated to the interests of the Republic.

Beaumarchais hoped that Deane would arrange to send him their reply, at the earliest, for he greatly relied upon him. In fact he had always drawn a clear distinction between the 'honest' Deane, the insidious Lee, and the strangely mute Dr Franklin, (whose behaviour towards Beaumarchais was 'impossible to comprehend'). He suffered the psychotic Lee, along with everybody else, but he got along well enough with Deane to expect him to plead his cause to the old man.

The news from America had 'set in motion all the idle heads of this country,' as Beaumarchais wrote to Vergennes. The 'English' (by whom he meant those rare Frenchmen who were partial to Britain), 'don't know where to hide themselves' now that their arrogant accomplices were facing their just retribution. He was waiting with pleasure to receive the details from London on how the British were receiving the unwelcome information from America; '… My pleasure in their grief will match the grief they have inflicted upon me!'

He had got out of bed for the first time since his accident on 7 December. On the following day, despite contusions, pain and weakness, he planned to start going about his business 'outside.' Four days later, even though he could only use his right arm with difficulty, he forced himself to write to Vergennes; indeed, he could barely suppress his elation at the news he had received from London. English people were in such ferment at the impending loss of America that it had created a crisis which threatened to sweep away the 'deceived King,' his insolent ministry, and the 'most corrupt of Parliaments.' The opposition had triumphed and secret meetings were on the increase. Ireland was ready to rise up against their oppressors if the French—inspired by Vergennes—gave them the word. He was prepared to travel to Versailles, ignoring his weak condition, to give Vergennes greater details, if a meeting could be arranged on that day or the next; '… My poor aching body can stand the tossing.'

It could always be said that, while Beaumarchais's news was swiftly received, that received by his master was 'sluggish,' and the servant could not help crowing. 'An energetic individual often finds a way where official policy only finds obstacles,' he wrote. Furthermore, the count might recall that 'Figaro's mail, and even my person,' always managed to convey the latest news to him, 'while the ambassador's packets were held back.' All those people, he reported, that he had sent to London to speculate on the Stock Market and sell, based on the possibility of a Burgoyne defeat, already knew that, even before their agents arrived in the capital, the news was known in London (and to himself). As a result, annuities had fallen to 77 pounds sterling.

Beaumarchais now tried to interest Vergennes in the idea of a French packet boat, which would free the minister of reliance upon English news. 'It would not cost the King anything,' he urged, for he had set it up so that it would be able to operate without outside help, and Vergennes indicated that he approved of the scheme. But the Boulogne expert whom Beaumarchais had requested to visit Versailles to follow up the business had been so badly treated by the court intermediary that he had fled from the palace before he could confer with the minister. 'Disconcerting to see such a patriotic project being so rudely rebuffed,' Beaumarchais complained; 'What a country, when the slightest private interest can thwart the most important public enterprise!'

He then sent an abstract of his views concerning the political situation in London, where Lord Temple[16] and the Duke of Marlborough[17] had returned to the House in order to reinforce the ministry; Temple had stopped attending and Marlborough was for the King. Forty men of the King's party had been 'debauched' from the Commons, while John Wilkes promised to subvert twenty-eight others. He and men from the city undertook to have the mob assemble at Westminster, to join in as soon as opposition voices were raised against the King's party. Several lords had set their wives to recruit the Queen[18] into the league against her husband's ministry! Lord North had twice offered his resignation to King George III, '... who, as yet, did not want to accept it.'

Lord Chatham, after having made a proposal in the House, had received through a Mr Sayer[19] two very important letters from the King of Prussia,[20] at that time allied to Britain. Lord Shelburne and Mr Townsend had told Chatham that nothing would be so easy as to burn the French port of Brest, and that was where they must start. Indeed, their means appeared to Beaumarchais to be as easy as they were simple, or so he reported to Vergennes.

Mr Smith, Lord Germain's secretary, had written to Mr 'Heinsen'[21] an American spying for the British in Paris, to say that he was about to cross to France in order to broach a 'certain matter' with the American commissioners in Paris. George III had little faith in the man, saying acerbically that he would perform 'as well as any other North American spy' in this delicate matter, believing that 'Heinsen' was actually encouraged by Deane and Franklin, 'and only gives intelligence in order to deceive.' John Wilkes, who knew about this matter, said that he would denounce this step in parliament. Most people in London were convinced that Vergennes's severity towards the Americans at Versailles was a sham, and that he had, in truth, rewarded the captains of the American privateers for the two British ships they had taken to Nantes.

It was also being rumoured in London that Beaumarchais would be the only victim to be publicly sacrificed to the British. 'Let it be!' was his reply. Vergennes and Sartine were said to have come to an understanding with the American commissioners on this point, and Lee had written to Lord Shelburne confirming it. Beaumarchais did not, he assured his master, believe it for one moment to be true. Nevertheless, he thought it might be useful 'to the King's affair' if he himself were to confess to his involvement in advance. 'This consent would let all Europe know that my sacrifice [by the ministers] could have entered into my [own] plans!'

The rest of his news, 'all detail,' was good to hear, he said, but boring to read. This glorious news apart, though, Beaumarchais was at a loss, having received orders from both Maurepas and Sartine that cancelled each other out. 'My mind is at sea, on an ocean without shores!' His continued mistreatment by the 'Passy Americans' also added to his confusion. They had left his last letter unanswered, and Lee's conduct in particular—he had been told—was attributed to Vergennes's encouragement. He could not believe that he was being asked by the King of France to submit to what offended all sense of honour and fairness in a Frenchman, let alone the question of common sense. He asked for a 'cold and methodical' conference with Sartine, to discuss the matter; he had seen Vergennes, and all he now wanted was to be given 'uncontradictory orders.'

This piece of news was so important that Beaumarchais sent it by postillion on 15 December:

> An express messenger has left St James for America at full speed, [he reported to Vergennes excitedly]. At the same time an Englishman has been sent to France, (he arrived two days ago). Upon his secret arrival in Paris, he immediately sought a meeting with Deane, whom he has, in fact, seen yesterday. They conferred a long time together, had a secret dinner together, and around 7pm Deane's valet went into the street to check if anyone was watching the house. He saw a carriage standing thirty paces from the house, about which he asked questions. (It was actually the carriage of 'our' spy, whose driver said he was waiting for two ladies.) Then the Englishman left on foot and our man followed him discreetly. He went into several cafes and then wandered about as though familiar with the town, finally walking up the rue Richelieu to the Boulevard. There, he strolled about as if to make sure he had not been followed, and he finally returned to the Royal Bath Hotel, after a thousand detours. Our spy managed to ascertain that this was where the mysterious Englishman is staying.

Beaumarchais thought that the spy was Smith, Lord Germain's secretary, for he knew from a good source that Mr Heinsen was expecting him the previous night; but, as Heinsen 'talks too much' it was obvious that the Englishman had decided to 'do what he had to do,' before advising Heinsen of his arrival. Beaumarchais then decided to have this Englishman 'tailed,' and he was coolly amused when Deane asked him that morning if 'a certain person' [Vergennes] had heard of the arrival of this Englishman. Beaumarchais affected ignorance, saying that he had no knowledge of it; '… What a lot of mystery!' But from this date he began to regard Deane more warily.

XVII

Spies and Prophecies

A Hessian officer had arrived in London, Beaumarchais learned,[1] and he was complaining bitterly about the way his men were being sacrificed in place of British troops; he was himself threatening to leave the King's service.[2] The Germans had lost 782 men during an assault on Fort Mercer, a large earth-work on the Delaware River, mounting fourteen cannon, protected by a ditch and a rampart of felled trees on the land-ward side. Two thousand Hessians had been detached to capture the fort, and among the dead were twenty-eight officers and two generals. It was, Beaumarchais recorded jubilantly, 'sure news about their dissatisfaction.' Even better, the British had lost 195 men in Augusta, Georgia, and the entire crew of a frigate of twenty-six cannons, 'which they called a sloop.'[3]

The British loss was reflected in the prices of the London financial markets, which Beaumarchais also exultantly recorded. Stock of the West Indies was at 163 and a quarter, the Bank of England was at 126 and a half; the market fell with each reported disaster. If France could only seize this moment of funk and uncertainty among the British, all the forces of that nation, and all their formidable energy, would not suffice to sustain their markets!—everything would be off-centre, and at once.

Despite still being sick, Beaumarchais assured Vergennes that he kept an eye on everyone, particularly the mysterious Englishman, still at large in Paris. Sartine, once Beaumarchais was partially recovered, agreed to see him, but at his house in Paris rather than at his office in Versailles. Beaumarchais had actually asked for a conference with Sartine and with Vergennes at Versailles, but this had been refused; '… It's not the same thing for me,' the frustrated invalid recorded philosophically, 'but I'll go anyway.'

He had no intentions of changing his operations; wishing only to demonstrate to all the ministers that the contradictions between the orders given and decisions made must be straightened out. It was impossible to have both 'pro and con' at the same time; what had already been decided must not later be prevented.

The name of the mysterious Englishman at large in Paris was Paul Wentworth; a man used by all British ministers in difficult missions, by the opposition party as well as by that of the King, since he was always 'ready to live at the expense of both.' His particular mission on this occasion was to determine the state of relations between America and France, that is, 'to feel out the commissioners.' Whether Deane had satisfied him in this regard, or whether—having been fully informed of the American position—he was looking for evidence of further plots, Wentworth moved into a grander hotel, the 'Vauban,' where two other suspect men were also staying: a Captain Nicholson,[4] who had an English address; and the American, Carmichael. Wentworth had to wait almost four weeks in Paris before a highly suspicious Benjamin Franklin agreed to a meeting, on 6 January 1778. William Eden,[5] nominally head of the Board and Trade, but also a manager of the British Secret Service, had given his messenger a letter to show Franklin, with the assurance that it was from a source close to the throne. The letter stated unequivocally that Britain would fight another ten years to prevent American independence. Franklin replied that the Americans would fight another *fifty* years to *win* it, and that both countries would be better off when they were bound to each other only by peaceful commerce. Wentworth's mission failed totally.[6]

Wentworth, Beaumarchais said sarcastically, spoke French better than he did; and he had to admit that he was one of the most skilful spies in England. Beaumarchais also knew that another two Americans—one of them being Carmichael—were about to leave for America, carrying with them important letters, possibly from Franklin, whom Beaumarchais had now come to totally distrust. Such a letter was exactly the sort of intelligence the French should know about, but how could they get hold of it? Vergennes could, of course, 'throw some money through the window' to obtain this information, but Beaumarchais had other ideas. Could a meeting be fixed up with Sartine as soon as possible, day or night, to discuss this matter?

There was rumour of a riot in London, where many people had died, although Beaumarchais had no direct news of it. There was, however, a popular demand throughout Britain for a war with France, 'which in good French,' he wrote, 'means peace with America!' The moment seemed supreme to Beaumarchais, and he begged Vergennes to listen to his newest proposals, about Ireland, on which the minister had failed to comment so far. The Spanish ambassador had a saying, Beaumarchais wrote, 'God is a Bourbon; it is only the Bourbons who don't wish to behave like Bourbons!'—a reflection upon the King's patent timorousness.

Maurepas, meanwhile, had a new use for Beaumarchais. He wished him to 'help out' with Prince Ferdinand of Prussia,[7] a remarkable general and one of Frederick II's most 'intimate' friends. The prince was said to hold a sentimental regard for the Americans, and he also wished to injure the British, whom he greatly despised, along with the little German states that hired out mercenaries. He was said to be ready to openly expand Prussia's trade with the Americans, which had so far been *sub rosa*. Quite how Maurepas wanted his 'Figaro' to deal with the prince was never made clear, although Beaumarchais later boasted that he had a 'sure way to do it,' which hints at blackmail.

Francy was in Portsmouth, Virginia, having left from Marseilles on September 26 1777. Beaumarchais's biggest ship had not yet left for America, but when it did, all of his fleet would be at sea. The naval ministry now feared that such expansive commerce would take away too many seamen at a time when they may suddenly be needed for their own ships. (So they did believe that a British peace with the colonists would mean an outbreak of hostilities at sea with France.) All vessels returning to their home harbours were to be held until further notice, and the most rigorous orders were given on this matter in every port, but especially in the ones where Beaumarchais operated.

It seemed that the 'force and speed' of his operations had caused Lord Stormont to 'raise a few shields' at Versailles, and the ministry was afraid of being suspected of encouraging this trade, whereas in fact it was mostly done without their help, and often in defiance of their objections—as, with a ship ready to sail, the artillery that it was due to transport was suddenly confiscated. Beaumarchais spent fruitless days in negotiating to get it returned (or replaced), and this held him back at the port. The huge losses that these seizures entailed for him left others unmoved; as he said, 'the ministry is inflexible.'

Even more aggravating was the fact that the American commissioners were still trying to cheat him of the *Amphitrite*'s modest cargo. They had still not replied to his letter, even though the cargo was worth only 150,000 *livres*; 'a long way from this drop of water to the ocean of my claims!' He could only hope that Francy had obtained a reasonable payment 'on account' from the Congress, and he believed that his man was still buying up tobacco. He was, it turns out, wrong about the latter, since inflation was then running wild in America and tobacco merchants were extremely reluctant to sell their merchandise in such circumstances. Most of their crops were being hoarded in the warehouses of Robert Morris.

Beaumarchais still clung to the idea that his ships would find their cargo waiting on the docks, ready for hoisting into the holds, as soon as his ships arrived where Francy was waiting to greet them. If events continued to delay his ships from leaving France, then Francy was to follow other advice. He was to send the bulk of the goods on the *Flamand*, by using the additional quantity of munitions loaded on to that ship by Landais, another of Beaumarchais's many agents in the French ports. This extra cargo, Beaumarchais thought, would help him out 'of the straits where I presently find myself'—that is, becalmed.

Beaumarchais counted on the honesty and fairness of Congress. Even though the commissioners in Paris were treating him so unethically, he still held to a belief in their 'American integrity;' he knew that they lacked funds and he believed that 'need often makes the most unlikely people unscrupulous'—or that, at least, was how he preferred to interpret their recent behaviour. He had not lost hope of redeeming their friendship, 'by reasoning, calmly and fairly,' and he thought that his problems with them arose from the fact that the 'interests of this great cause' had been entrusted to several people at the same time; 'One alone would have succeeded much better'—with that man preferably being Silas Deane, who was, he believed, 'sorry and ashamed of his colleagues' behaviour.'

It was all Lee's fault; there was no question about that. Lee was undeniably furious at being left out of something that he thought he had helped to bring into being, and his reaction was to accuse Beaumarchais, and all who were involved with him, of being dishonest. At this stage, the Congress of South Carolina was also acting 'unpleasantly' toward him, and Beaumarchais wrote to President Rutledge[8] (via one of his captains) to complain about their treatment, and to demand justice. The captain was to contact Francy and report on the outcome of his presentation. Yet despite his troubles, the news of American successes continued to delight him, 'Brave, brave people!' By their military conduct they had justified his esteem, and the 'beautiful enthusiasm' the French held for them. He only wanted a proper return for his outlay in order to serve them in new ways; 'To cope with my own debts, so that I can continue to borrow in their favour.'

The French troops that he had helped to send across the Atlantic had, 'if one can believe the news,' done marvels in the battles of Pennsylvania.[9] He was proud of the way they had conducted themselves, and of the reputation of their corps, and for the part that he had played in procuring such employment for them. In fact, the Americans had long become wary of 'foreign adventurers;' the arrogant Tronson de Coudray in particular, who had to be treated with exaggerated respect for fear of jeopardizing the whole programme of French aid. At least three American soldiers had threatened to resign if Coudray were made senior to them, and violent rivalry and jealousy had developed between this latest French import and the French engineers who had arrived before him. It was a relief to them (and to Beaumarchais) when the troublemaker inadvertently rode his high-spirited young mare onto the Schuylkill Ferry, instead of leading her onto it, and was drowned 'like a schoolboy' when the horse leapt into the river.

The City of London was in financial turmoil, Beaumarchais learned, with the King's ministers at bay while the opposition triumphed, if somewhat harshly. The King of France, however, he wrote in despair, 'like a powerful eagle gliding over these events, still preserves for himself the pleasure of *watching* the two parties floating between fear and hope, as to what he will decide. ... Which must be carrying great weight in the quarrel between the two hemispheres.'

He was also growing increasingly aware of the absurdity of trying to dictate action to Francy from 2,000 leagues away. All he could really ask, he wrote to Francy, was that he serve him from so far away to the best of his ability, and it was entirely up to him to involve the Americans in their mutual cause. He now realized that recovering the money owed to him depended upon the 'concurrence of many events,' but his good reputation still belonged to him, 'just as yours is presently being made by you.'

He then had second thoughts about the eventual destination of his 'big' ship, the *Proud Rodrigue*, since he had compromised himself with the ministry. He had given his word to Maurepas that it should carry no more than 800 men to Santo Domingo, and that it would return to France without travelling to the American mainland; which was a promise he could not break, but one that he could not keep either! He knew that its cargo would be of particular interest to Congress, and that it should go directly to them, since it consisted of ready-made uniforms, cloth and blankets, of which the Americans were in great need, since the army still faced the end of a hard winter. The ship also carried artillery and 60 brass cannons.

He now needed a plan to controvert his promise to the minister; so he swiftly conceived one. Francy was to arrange with the Secret Committee in Philadelphia to send one or two American privateers away from Santo Domingo at the time the *Proud Rodrigue* was scheduled to arrive, and the American ships were to then send their shallops[10] to the French Cape. There, his agent Carabasse would arrange to 'capture' the *Proud Rodrigue*, under whatever pretext, and so take it to an American port.

His captain, Montaud, would righteously protest to Congress, who would publicly disown the 'brutal Corsair,' free the captured ship, and apologize to the French. In the meantime, the cargo would have been unloaded, the hold filled with tobacco, and the ship would be sent back to France, in company with whatever other ships were ready for the return crossing. The details of this plot were to be conveyed aboard the *Carmichael*, a very fast vessel, so that Francy would have plenty of time in which to arrange the business, either with Congress or with two friendly privateers. In this way Maurepas would be no longer held to his word, or Beaumarchais by his, and the operation would be successful in spite of all the obstacles!

The *Proud Rodrigue* was to sail before 15 January, and it would be waiting to hear from Francy at the Cape; but for Beaumarchais, hope was, as usual, deferred, for according to a postscript to this letter, the *Proud Rodrigue* was detained in port. It was still there on 20 January 1778.

Beaumarchais continued his work of keeping the King's ministers up to the mark. In a private memorial, written on 27 December 1777, he outlined twenty-five points which covered everything he thought relevant. They ranged from his concerns about the information he had received about British intentions to fund a militia for a war against France, to his suggestions for saving French ships against British fury. The best retaliations, in this case, would be for France, Spain and an *independent America* to combine to 'tame that arrogant nation;' but most of his 'new' points were a reworking of the many suggestions that he had been proposing for the past two years. His most radical proposition being to not conclude a treaty with America in France, through the commissioners, but to send a faithful agent directly to America, specifically entrusted with the mission of presenting and finalizing conditions. Beaumarchais would then start 'garnishing' the Atlantic Ocean with upwards of 80,000 men, and he would give 'his' fleet the most 'formidable air and tone, so that the English may not doubt that I am in earnest.' (Beaumarchais writes of 'my' fleet as though he were a monarch himself! It is also clear that he envisions himself as being the emissary to America, which would be a perfect revenge upon the commissioners in Paris!) A war must also be fostered in Turkey against Russia, he suggests, in order to keep British soldiers 'busy in the East,' in support of the Russians.

This was Beaumarchais's manifesto to the King's council, and Figaro's cry from the heart. Seemingly ignored at the time he sent it, the gist of this project is to be found in the official French declaration to King George III of March 13, 1778.

XVIII

'The Fruits of his Labours'

In the last days of December 1777, Lord North had openly sent a new envoy to the American commissioners in Paris. Bypassing the usual diplomatic channels, (although his presence was undoubtedly known to the British embassy), the man—probably William Pulteney, M.P.[1]—soon visited Benjamin Franklin, and was empowered to offer him a peace proposal. Beaumarchais, however, who had earlier received information from London concerning this new move, had not lost track of the man since he had left England. Pulteney's mission, he believed, was to 'unsettle' the American commission at any cost; but the man was a diplomatic courier, and he may even have had a safe conduct from King George III. As such, he was untouchable.

King George III, Beaumarchais had been reliably informed, had promised Lord Germain, the Secretary of State for the American Colonies, that he would sacrifice the unsuccessful General Burgoyne and give his support to Germain—one of the King's most unpopular, and one of his least competent, ministers. If it were true that Germain was to be entrusted with the operations in America despite his lack of ability,[2] Beaumarchais believed that Germain's next appearance at the opening session of the new Parliament would 'decide everything that was previously undecided.'

The question of peace in America, however, seemed to have already been absolutely resolved, perhaps as a result of Burgoyne's failures. Beaumarchais's agents in London had told him this explicitly; and the settlement seemed to be connected with the arrival of a new British agent in America, who would treat directly with the Congress—and who was, apparently, the opposite number of the emissary to France.

Beaumarchais had also been told that his own government had granted assistance in cash to the American commissioners, 'through the pockets' of Monsieur Grand; the 'gentlemen of Passy' were, it seemed, almost out of funds. Interestingly, he had been given this information, not by a Parisian connection, but by a London 'contact,' and it was said to come from a good source—that of a certain highly-placed British minister. He was grimly amused to learn, from this report, that he himself was 'out of favour, which displeases no one in England.' Beaumarchais also understood by this that he had 'lost the fruit of his labours'—and apparently by the very efforts that had led others to glory! Although he had, for some time, suspected as much;

largely because of the strange way the Americans behaved towards him, and by the frigidity of Vergennes—though he counted upon the minister's sense of fairness to treat him with the respect that he felt he deserved. 'Before I perish as a businessman,' he pleaded ironically, 'I request to be fully validated as an agent and negotiator.' He now also wished to turn in his ledgers, so that he could prove how no other man could have done as much as he had with so little means; '… And in spite of so many vexations!'

Maurepas had at last permitted Beaumarchais to acquire guns from the arsenals and send them to America, assuring the bureaucrats in the office of Saint-Germaine that when they had been dispatched, he would have the *buyer* 'replace the weapons in kind'—although where Beaumarchais was expected to find these replacements was never disclosed. As it was, having done his work well, he gave 'notes in payment' for the acquisition of the weapons, notes that were guaranteed by the bank to mature. Maurepas, however, then appeared to forget their arrangement and insisted upon Beaumarchais paying the armaments manufacturers with ready money. As a result of this, and by the delay in loading his armoured ship, Beaumarchais fell behind in his receipts by the equivalent of more than 800,000 pounds sterling.

Another result of the *Proud Rodrigue* being held back in port, 'for some official reason,' was that many people were starting to regard Beaumarchais as a ruined man. Without warning, his many creditors all suddenly clamoured for the money he owed them, and it seemed almost certain that he was about to go under, since he had not the funds to meet their demands. '… Yet I have not yet lost my mind!' he insisted with his usual bravura.

He *was*, however, running out of energy and boldness, and his self-confidence dipped even further when he learned that his business rivals, the Grand brothers, had now gained the full trust of the ministry. Vergennes had granted them two million *livres* in 1777, to be spent in the American cause, and another million would be loaned to them in 1778. Beaumarchais began to believe that he might have to declare bankruptcy, or even leave the country; although his accounts would reveal the true picture. 'May God lead me on my way! It will be proved that the King has lost a good servant, but neither events nor the actions of men will have the power to dishonour me.'

Beaumarchais was downhearted, but his alter ego remained as resourceful as ever, and 'Figaro' tried to capture the fickle attention of his master. On the 4th of January 1778, he begged Vergennes for 'a moment of your attention tomorrow, after you have dined.' He also wanted his moment with Maurepas—if the minister was at liberty—for he had some 'novelties' that he wished to present. When both ministers ostentatiously ignored his request, he wrote again, saying that he knew Vergennes had been 'snowed under yesterday,' but that he hoped the minister would be free the following day. It was an urgent matter that he wished to reveal to him, which could only keep 'for a few hours.'

In the event, it kept for three more days, since he was unable to see either man; although he was ordered to attend a commercial tribunal on the night of 8 January, to account for his inability to repay his creditors (as though his masters could possibly be ignorant of the cause!). He was convinced by this time that there was no way out; he was about to perish for the lack of 400,000 *livres*. It was not, he wrote, his commercial interests, but 'politics' that was strangling him; he hoped to die with honour, by working harder than ever, *and by proving he was right.*

With regard to this, he bombarded Maurepas with his thoughts on the situation. Referring to his private memorial of 27 December 1777, he stressed his anxiety at the decision France would take. He was more convinced than ever that the British and the Americans were on the verge of reconciliation; it had, after all, not been a war between two nations, but solely between a colony and the British administration. Even at the height of the war, he argued, the Americans had always shown great courtesy to the English. General Burgoyne had written to friends in England, saying that his officers had been moved to tears by the 'noble way they were treated in America.' The British public was aware of this, 'and their hearts had been softened.' The King of England knew very well that he could solve everything just by appearing to have been disarmed by his people's tears, 'and he is ready to surrender.'

How could the Americans refuse an offer of peace when they saw that the English people themselves were driving their sovereign to propose it? It could even be argued that King George himself had been misled by the absurd and barbarous policies of his ministers. With peace restored, could not a simple and free confederation, founded on the principles of the Magna Carta, unite in one nation two warring sections of the British dominions? The British certainly felt they had no reason to feel humiliated by their defeat, since the results of the quarrel had shown that 'only an Englishman can defeat an Englishman!' (even when he called himself American). It had all been no more than a glorious insurrection against unfair parliamentarians, and Beaumarchais begged Maurepas to reflect on this.

What he wished to stress at this very crucial moment was that France simply could not count on the two countries continuing to be at odds with each other. Yet it would seem that certain French ministers held on to the belief that there was still time for them to make up their minds. On the contrary, it was *essential* to bind America to a treaty, so they could say that France was the first to honour their success and treat them on an equal footing.

If Monsieur de Maurepas feared that the American delegates might fail to keep the secrecy needed for this important development between their two countries, and would divulge it precipitately to the British, he need have no fears. Arthur Lee, the person most likely to disclose such information, was to be excluded from all negotiations, and to be forcibly kept away if necessary. Beaumarchais had a plan already worked out to keep the troublemaker from Paris while the alliance was concluded; neither should Monsieur be worried about the political dispositions of European neighbours if France was openly seen to side with the Americans. Nothing the French might lose in Europe could balance the advantages to be gained in America.

The only danger lay in Britain and America coming together; 'but once let the Americans be allied to the House of Bourbon, and even the most ferocious war the English could make on us would still leave us with a greater advantage.'

Sir Henry Clinton,[3] the new commander of the British forces in America, was said to have ordered the evacuation of Philadelphia and had retreated to New York. This was false news, for the new British Commander-in-Chief, having failed to defeat General Lafayette in Pennsylvania, had executed a difficult retreat to New Jersey. It was, however, taken for a fact at that time, and Beaumarchais ended his appeal to Maurepas by pointing out the immense benefit this situation possessed for France. 'If General Clinton is a prisoner with his army, and if New York is back in the charge of the Americans, as has been suggested, this is tremendous news [since the British would now be forced to make a deal with the triumphant Americans]. And when it is known in London there will no longer be years, months, or even weeks, but days and hours in which our laggard ministers have left to make up their minds!'

Beaumarchais was determined to make his protests heard by the ministers before he would finally concede defeat, and so he wrote another, more 'painful,' memorandum—one that took him eight days to complete, since he was, he wrote, so 'engrossed with the awful muddle of the matter it contains.'

For four days he had thought that his efforts were in vain, for it already seemed to be too late; yet to complete it he gave up working on his petition for bankruptcy, and with his usual physical resilience he managed to get back on his feet within fifteen days. He was, however, growing increasingly angry at the 'silent' treatment wielded by the ministers and by the difficulties their procrastination had already placed him in. Looking through his papers to check his statements, he was struck afresh by the obstacles he had managed to overcome in the past two years, to achieve all that he had done; but if he was to be rescued now, Vergennes could not do it too soon or too secretly; 'Letters of exchange, like death, wait for no one!' It was, he thought, particularly important to keep the details of his present crisis hidden from certain people; the banker Baron Necker,[4] then Finance Minister, especially. The Swiss financier—a genius, certainly—was too busy trying to reform the fiscal system to encourage 'foreign adventures,' and such a man would always regard 'this great matter' in such a light. Troublesome details must therefore be kept from him, and yet people had to be made aware of Beaumarchais's present difficulties. If he was not to be helped, then 'Amen,' he had done what he could.

On the plus side, he had heard that two of his ships from Marseilles had now reached Charleston, South Carolina—and this in spite of British interference (and that of his own people!). Sixty-six cannons, 22 mortars, bombs and balls in proportion, 80,000 quintals of powder, cloth, tin, sulphur, and '… my poor guns,' *for which he had not yet been reimbursed*! —all were now in America, an achievement for which he had been forced to deceive everyone, and to take frightful losses in order to do so in secret. 'Ah, Monsieur le Comte,' he chided, 'my bankruptcy statement will show what an active man you have let be undone and dishonoured if you fail to prevent this horrible misfortune!'

He had not the heart, he said, to talk further, but three days later he was telling Vergennes that he had 'not the heart' to leave him in the dark regarding the latest American news. He had just received a letter on the subject, and he was sending it to the minister by express post. He thought it important enough to be handed in to the King's council; it was news of such interest that it 'could not be delayed, even for one minute.'

But back to his accounts. He had been working since the previous evening, and had tabulated his present financial situation at approximately 60,000 *livres* 'in hand;' on more than the nine millions he had balanced, in yet to be realized assets and existing liabilities, he thought that was exact enough. Taking the long view, his prospects were superb; it was only his present predicament that was worrisome. If Vergennes could come to his rescue temporarily, he could 'vouch for the future.' He was sending his financial statement by the next day's mail.

To his consternation, he learned that Franco-American treaties were to be signed on 6 February, but he was not to be called into the negotiations, and he was not even informed officially that they were taking place. It had been left to his spies to uncover that piece of information, so injurious to Beaumarchais's pride. On the other hand, there had been a lessening of bureaucratic interference, and many of his ships had left for America, although the safeguard of the fleet, the *Proud Rodrigue* was still held back. While he could not overlook the insult to him as the originator of the Franco-American commercial pact, he was more concerned with the present difficulties of himself as the merchant-adventurer. Despite his assurances, he knew that his company was now in deep financial trouble.

Once again, Beaumarchais sent off a memorial to Vergennes, this time concerning the economic difficulties of Hortalez & Cie, hoping that he could shame the minister into a personal intervention on the company's behalf, or at least persuade him to mediate for him with the most pressing creditors. Since he knew that he could no longer depend upon the goodwill of the count, he was simultaneously soliciting aid from other, lesser men of influence, 'flinging myself about incredibly,' seeking to parry the awful blow. As the days went by without any positive response from any source, he knew that he was struggling in vain, for he was 'going under.' Seeing his work so horribly repaid, he said, 'drove him insane.'

When he asked for the return of his flagship, the *Proud Rodrigue*, and also to be reimbursed for the loss of the guns which had been taken back into the 'protection' of the war-ministry, he was, as he wrote, asking for no favours. He had acquired the guns in good faith (and they were now, in fact, strictly the property of his creditors); it was a matter of simple justice that both ship and guns be returned to him. Apart from this outrage to him 'as a merchant and a patriot,' could any sane person conceive that the ministry would let such a valuable agent go under, risking everything just for the want of fulfilling, in all fairness, their obligations to him?

If Vergennes now refused to help, Beaumarchais assured him that he would not regard it as a denial of his favours, 'since you are the master of it.' There spoke the pragmatic factotum. Surely it was only on the basis of his 'superior' views regarding the American situation that Vergennes should still assist him? It must have been apparent to many that Beaumarchais, a natural plotter, had a much better understanding of the ramifications of the tangled state of affairs between Britain and America than King Louis's ministers, even habituated as they were to the world of intrigue.

But an increasingly disillusioned Beaumarchais grew to see that he had little hope of help from this quarter. He had, perhaps, no 'right', as he put it, to force the Foreign Minister's hand; yet he must have had every belief in his right to be protected by his most powerful political patron. Moreover, it made no sense to let him perish for want of official aid. It was surely a 'nonsense' to deprive him of his means of credit, whereby he could keep his creditors' trust; it was, in fact, inconceivable.

Vergennes did, in time, take an 'obliging' interest in his best agent's predicament, and he came to his aid, however reluctantly. Even as Beaumarchais closed his register, and decided against paying a large settlement—since it was the Sabbath, although the bill had been due the day before—word came from Versailles. Vergennes had saved him, at least for the time being.

But the government had also been saved, at least from embarrassment; for, as Beaumarchais quite sensibly reasoned, if he was to be exposed to the disgrace of a bankruptcy hearing, how could he not have publicly explained the circumstances of his inability to meet his debts, without 'an involuntary and deadly indiscretion?'—which was obviously the reason the government, on reflection, bailed him out. Maurepas had received him, at their interview, as if he had been 'an English corsair, who would have insulted our flag of convenience,' said Beaumarchais, outraged. For once, however, he kept his own counsel on this occasion, barely opening his mouth; 'I would have had too much to say!'

He now knew that America's interests had not been abandoned, for he learned that Silas Deane's brother[5] had left Paris secretly to carry the news to America of the treaty of commerce that had just been signed between France and the new United States. Beaumarchais, however, decided to keep this a 'deep secret' until after the American's ship had left from Bordeaux. Keeping silent about his knowledge of the secret negotiations would be the best proof he could give of his resignation 'in bearing with the aloofness and scorn of those who had kept me from being a part of these discussions.'

The main thing was that he was saved financially, at least for the moment, and he abjectly 'gave a million thanks' for what Vergennes had done for him. Once more he was 'up and doing' (quite literally, since he had abandoned his sickbed), and he sent off new instructions to his agent in Holland, covering his back by sending a copy of these orders to Vergennes, 'for his comments.'

Throughout all his recent difficulties, Beaumarchais had thought it prudent not to admit that—via his secret informers—he had been aware of everything the ministers were doing. He had managed to see and read most of their papers, or transcripts of them, and he had pretended ignorance on the matter in order to sustain his reputation for 'discretion and faithfulness,' which should have pleased Vergennes, 'since they relate to the basic principles of honour.' He would, he wrote to the count, never forget his very generous efforts to save him from 'going under'—though he must have asked himself, 'How much exactly has Vergennes actually *done*?'

Vergennes apparently found Beaumarchais's letter of thanks 'extremely garrulous,' and Maurepas, of course, seemed now to have written him off. Beaumarchais tried to find additional ways to prove his 'discretion' to the latter minister, although surely nothing could have proved it more than the way he daily demonstrated his ability to 'swallow everything, including my own losses, which are due almost entirely to the actions of Monsieur de Maurepas'—or, more precisely, his *in*actions. At the same time, with the hint of blackmail still hanging in the air, Beaumarchais promised to 'keep silent.'

Beaumarchais suddenly found himself in possession of £40,000 in gold bullion, from some unnamed source; but what pleased him more was the fact that he was now also back in control of the *Proud Rodrigue*, and he wrote to Maurepas, saying that, by returning the ship to him, the minister had shown a 'meritorious fairness.' He could not, however, help adding a threatening note; for if the minister would be kind enough to add a *reimbursement* for the temporary loss of this important vessel, 'upon which my very existence depends,' he would still keep silent. 'Only remember,' he wrote, that he had suffered greatly, although he could now thank the minister 'that I no longer do.'

He sent his letter of gratitude to Maurepas via Vergennes, doing so 'less for the letter than for the accompanying abstract'—and, as usual, since the subject matter of this latter was secret, he asked Vergennes to put a little wax under the envelope, once the abstract had been removed, so that his letter of thanks would be sent on to Maurepas sealed.

The abstract, in fact, contained two pieces that should have been of concern to the minister, though the second was of more importance than the first. The first was a satirical poem of '50 lines of bad verse, though a virtual diatribe' written by 'Anon', although the unknown writer must have been somebody close to the seat of power since it reported a highly indiscreet conversation between Vergennes and Maurepas, and it was inflammable stuff. 'But really it is so bad that it cannot be called wicked,' Beaumarchais sneered, but he was concerned that Vergennes might not know of it and that was his reason for delivering it to him.

However, this was not the gist of his abstract, which concerned news that Beaumarchais had received from London. An express from Jamaica had arrived, bringing to King George III the news that two English frigates, while pursuing an American ship in the area of Santo Domingo, had rammed the latter into the shore, near a French fort [the name is too poorly written to be decipherable]. The fort had raised its flag and blasted the English ships with their cannon, but this had not stopped the frigates, which came after the American vessel right under the walls of the fort. The gunners on shore had fired twice to warn them, whereupon the English ships then raked the fort with their own gunfire, thoroughly destroying it. Finally, they had set the American ship ablaze.

This news had led people in London to fear that the French would move against the British in retaliation, hastening the crisis for the ministry. As a result of this panic, it was very likely that Lord Chatham would be back in power within eight days, with Lord North deprived of it; the members in parliament were only waiting for him to present his bill before they struck. The aging Lord Chatham, although physically weak, was still working with surprising energy to supplant the present ministry, and his friends did not doubt for a moment that he would succeed. All in opposition were waiting impatiently for that moment and it appeared that Lord North had walked into a trap set for him, and would not have the courage to get out of it. 'He will either resign willingly, or be forced to; you may take that for certain.'

'What a time we live in!' Beaumarchais cried, half-exulting; for no matter how King Louis's ministers tried, he said, it seemed there was no longer a way to back out from a confrontation between Britain and France (although he well knew that the treaty of alliance with America, which had been secretly signed in Paris on the 6th of that month, had yet to be ratified by Congress;[6] neither had it been notified in London).

The poem that Beaumarchais mentioned in his abstract in fact lampooned many other courtiers beyond Maurepas and Vergennes. In the style of the time, it described a sort of interchange, both political and sexual—frequently the same thing—between the people it pilloried: Baron Necker's financial relationship with Maurepas; the Queen's supposed sexual liaison with the King's younger brother; the Comte de Provence's[7] lack of sexual relations with his wife; even Louis's seeming inability to breed from Queen Marie Antoinette. The aged Voltaire was connected to the Marquise de la Villette, and Beaumarchais himself was coupled with Mademoiselle d'Éon! 'There is no point in paying attention to things as silly as they are reprehensible,' he advised Vergennes in the letter that accompanied the offensive poem. The minister, in fact, treated the whole business with superb nonchalance.

Beaumarchais had taken a briefcase to Maurepas, filled with papers he considered to be very important; but he could tell from the ambiguous answers he received to the matters they dealt with that he was still under suspicion. He welcomed this, however, 'for it will also prove a time of vindication.' Still, there were bureaucratic comments expressed in the reports dealing with his papers that were so absurd it surprised him that a man 'as enlightened' as the minister should respond to them. He must, he wrote in his defence, be able to speak freely to the ministers, and at least reassure them that he was judged 'by enmity,' with the little good he had done being misunderstood, or hidden.

Beaumarchais was working overtime in an effort to reinstate himself with the minister. He sent Vergennes another abstract from London, 'which deserves some attention.' He also sent a report on 'some of the silliness being done in this country;' among which was the matter of the person recruiting

French soldiers to send on to Georgia and Virginia. Beaumarchais had been asked to give them passage on one of his ships, but he thought the project would not benefit the Americans, and would do nothing but create a scandal with England. If Vergennes agreed with him, he would like to be sent the list of all those 'volunteer bandits,' for he knew what was to be done to stop this useless outburst of manly bravado, and he also knew how 'to do it quietly.'

By 9 March, Beaumarchais had received only one reply from England with regard to the 'liberty' taken by the editor of the *Courrier de l'Europe* in one of its most slanderous articles, although he thought that Vergennes must have been informed about this scandalous piece of trouble-making. If the minister hadn't read it, he would send him a copy, since he did not wish 'to turn away any opportunity to serve Monsieur de Vergennes.'

He did have more agreeable news, however. It was being reported that General Howe had evacuated Philadelphia on 12 January,[8] and that John Adams, the patriot statesman, was on his way to France, to bring an answer on the treaty ratification. Beaumarchais insisted that 'The last item was only to be whispered;' but he could hardly have supposed that Vergennes was unaware of it. It was, though, just as important to let the minister know that he, too, was as well informed as the various ministries on such matters of importance; or, indeed, as well informed as the entire cabinet put together!

XIX

Congress and Commissioners

Silas Deane had been recalled to America, the news arriving in Paris on 4 March 1778. Officially, he had been called back to report to Congress on affairs in Europe, but it was also rumoured—as Deane himself also suspected—that he had been summoned back to answer charges laid against him by Arthur Lee. He had been attacked in Congress for showing poor judgement in letting so many foreign adventurers enter America—a mistake that Deane had certainly made, since he had gone far beyond his authority in making contracts with French and other European officers who wanted commissions in the Continental Army, and he had no qualifications for sorting out the real soldiers from the mere opportunists. Henry Laurens[1] was to write later that Deane 'would not say nay to any Frenchman who called himself a Count or Chevalier.'

Beaumarchais was deeply shocked, both by the charges and by Deane's imminent departure, since Deane was the only contact with his fellow commissioners. He at once wrote to Congress on the inadvisability of this move, and made suggestions for the diplomatic steps to be taken to retain—or detain—Deane in France. When these efforts failed, his proposal for providing Deane with testimonials for a 'job well done' soon followed. Congress must be made fully aware of the vital role that Deane had played on their behalf.

Beaumarchais was at Versailles on 10 March, there solely to make ministers aware of a few facts about the continuing usefulness of the American. He thought the matter so important that he sent a special messenger to Vergennes, instructed to bring back a time for his appointment, and he begged the minister to make no decisions until he had heard what he had to say. He had information about the American set-up in Paris that was 'of major importance,' he said; but since it could only be a reiteration of his constant complaint about being overlooked by the commissioners, it is unlikely that he got a hearing. Deane, who would undoubtedly have backed up his fault finding, was also supposed to have been with him at the palace that night, but there is no record of his appearing there.

Three days later Beaumarchais was even more deeply shocked to learn of the true reason for the American's recall, and of his disgrace. He at once sent Vergennes his views on this matter, enclosing a statement on the shape of British finances that he had revised, but which were, in fact, incorrect, and even fanciful. These accounts covered more than three legal-sized sheets of parchment, entitled, 'The Incontestable Proofs of the Enormous Expense of the War between America and England, and of the Total Ruin which there-fore threatens the Financial Resources of that Kingdom.' What a pleasure it had been to write out such a *resounding* title!

His secret memorial for the King's ministers on the matter of the continu-ing feud between Silas Deane and Arthur Lee was rather more accurate than his accounts of British expenditure, but it was naturally biased in favour of his protégé:

> By character and by ambition, M. Arthur Lee has been, from the first, extremely jealous of M. Deane's successes in France, [he affirmed], and he has finally become his open enemy, as happens when small minds are more concerned with supplanting their rivals than in surpassing them in merit. M. Lee's con-nections in England and his two American brothers, who are members of the Congress,[2] have made him a prominent and dangerous man. His design has always been to choose between England and France, whichever power could more surely promote his fortune. As he often made clear to me at the libertine suppers I attended with him in London …

In order to succeed, Beaumarchais wrote, Lee needed to get rid of his rivals, and so he had succeeded in making Silas Deane out as an object of suspi-cion, largely by managing to put the worst construction on Deane's (perhaps misguided) zeal in sending volunteers to join the continental ranks. As some foreigners undoubtedly behaved badly upon arrival in America, Lee had seized this opportunity to assure Congress that Deane himself had sent, in spite of advice to the contrary, men who would prove useless to the emergent repub-lic—a decision made by Deane simply to gratify his own sense of power.

And so it continued, with a fairly accurate, if prejudiced, account of Lee's career from their first meeting in London to Lee's temerity in writing to friends in Congress, suggesting that he alone should be made sole 'Minister to France.' When this presumptuous request had been rejected as a matter of course, Lee had straightaway turned to the 'what might be called guerrilla or sniping diplomacy' he had engaged in against Deane (and also the 'irre-proachable' Franklin). This lamentable business, Beaumarchais insisted, was simply a result of Lee's frustrated ambition.

He could well have been correct in his assessment; but the 'ever distrustful' Lee, whose suspicions did indeed verge upon the paranoid, in fact had very good reason to suspect the 'honest American' that Beaumarchais so fiercely defended—as would be proved later, to his further astonishment.

France concluded an 'offensive and defensive' alliance with the Americans in February 1778, and this inevitably precipitated another crisis between France and Britain. Cries of joy from the courtiers greeted the news of the Alliance when it was broken to them by the Comte de Provence at a pre-Lenten *bal à la Reine*, where he had come fresh from the King's council.

The 'Treaty of Amity and Commerce' between France and America was notified on 13 March 1778, the contract being, in fact, two treaties—the first, of commerce and amity (in which France recognized American independence), and the second a treaty of alliance to become effective in the event of war between France and Great Britain. Despite having been completely excluded from an outcome that, almost alone, he had set in motion, Beaumarchais regarded this as the best reward for his hard work. France, however, once having made America her ally, could not entirely trust to the attitude of Britain—technically still a friendly neighbour—towards this pivotal decision.

Beaumarchais, though, could not believe that the British government would be rash enough to declare war on France while they still had hopes of overturning the situation in America; although such news could come at any time.

For the next few weeks he kept up a busy correspondence with his agents in London. Everyone around him, it seemed, was making 'campaign plans,' but Beaumarchais had calculated one that he believed would be 'as safe as it was certain,' and one which involved as much political involvement as it did martial. The sketch was already on paper, and he planned to offer it to Vergennes as soon as he could have a fair copy made. (there is no adequate record of the amounts of money that Beaumarchais expended upon having his ideas transferred to paper by copyists.)

Meanwhile 'Figaro' could inform his master, 'as a sure thing,' that there were some fourteen English 'corsairs,' armed with between 16–30 cannons, around the Channel Islands of Jersey and Guernsey, ready to bear down on France, 'as soon as the whistle blows.' It was important for the minister to know about this 'pirate den' before they could attack inoffensive ships. In the past three months he had heard of forty-four French merchant vessels leaving for North America, with five of them captured and only two arriving at Chesapeake Bay, while the fate of the other thirty-seven were completely unaccounted for. Furthermore, the British had seized two American ships, one destined for Nantes and the other for Bordeaux, with the ships so close to the French coast that pilots had been aboard. He had received this information from agents in Nantes and St Malo.

He also sent Vergennes a particular letter that he had received from America, which must have been from his agent Francy, although the contents are not known; but between his arrival in Portsmouth, South Virginia, on 1 December 1777, and January 11 1778, Francy wrote three letters to his employer. In one of them he reported that most of the French officers were anxious to return home, since the fighting was not coming up to their expectations of 'gentlemanly warfare.' He had also heard about Deane's recall, more openly said to be 'in disgrace' in America, and even though he had heard a different side to the story, he absolutely concurred with Beaumarchais's judgement, as stated in his last paper. The contents of the other two letters, including the one that Beaumarchais thought important enough to send on to Vergennes, remain a matter of conjecture.

But regarding the Deane affair, Beaumarchais again wrote to Congress on March 28, expressing his deep concern. Having first congratulated the members on their 'useful and noble alliance' with France, he said that he owed it to the truth, as well as to the honour, of himself and Deane, to make the following declaration to them—which Deane would carry with him to America. In this letter, Beaumarchais astonishingly revealed his true identity to the members of Congress.

He also gave them a detailed account of his involvement with the American cause, from his meeting with Arthur Lee in London to his association with Deane in Paris, where they worked together to fulfil the explicit orders of the secret commissioners. Beaumarchais reiterated the promises that Deane had made in the name of his American employers, saying that it was only because of this particular understanding that he had been able to gain the trust of his co-investors in the scheme, along with sufficient funds for his first disbursements.

He insisted that the Americans owed his own early successes to Deane alone; he had done all the work necessary to overcome the difficulties they had faced together. But the fact remained that, without the reliance Beaumarchais had placed upon Deane's promises, he would never have succeeded in putting the enterprise into action.

When the returns that Deane had solemnly pledged on behalf of his employers had not arrived within the time agreed, it had caused considerable difficulties, and these returns were still awaited, while Deane had lost the confidence of French colleagues in the enterprise against the slowness of their remittances. Indeed, these colleagues would have abandoned the undertaking, which then seemed to present only hard work, risks, and little hope of profit.

Beaumarchais could not resist complaining about Deane's fellow commissioners in Paris, who had 'denied me even the most basic courtesies;' but he was now certifying that his personal money advances, and the shipments of munitions and merchandise, owed everything to the indefatigable exertions of Mr Deane. He hoped, therefore, that Congress would reject any insinuations by which others might try to take credit for the success of his business, and would, instead, take the word of the man most capable of informing them of the true facts.:

Who is the undersigned,
        Caron de Beaumarchais: your most humble and obedient servant.

To add gravitas to this letter—and to let Congress see they were not dealing with a nonentity—he added, truthfully, that he was 'Secretary to the King' and 'Lieutenant-General of his Hunts.' The gentlemen of Congress were not to know that these positions were purely honorary in nature.

Deane, alarmed by his imperative recall, resentfully decided not to return to America until Congress had sent him a description of the charges against him. He was naturally unwilling to deliver himself up to his personal enemies back home without having with him the proofs capable of refuting them, but it was Beaumarchais who, having got over his own state of shock, had persuaded him to change his mind.

In fact, he now thought that Deane's departure might be a 'lucky event,' since the American could explain his particular situation more coherently in person than any amount of letters could do, and so too much trouble could not be taken in order to accomplish Deane's return to America:

Your complete defence [he reassured him], is in my portfolio. Arthur Lee accuses you of having sent officers to America without the proper author-ization, but I have in hand a coded letter from him, begging me to send engineering officers and other men to help the American army. He claims he has received assurances that all my shipments were the gifts of France, and that everything else was the result of your greed. But, again, I have in the coded correspondence between Lee and myself, proofs that my shipments were established by him in the form of an active and reciprocal trade, and not otherwise.

It could be easily proved, therefore, that Deane had simply extended an enter-prise already instigated by Lee, his 'false accuser.'

Beaumarchais in this way succeeded in restoring Deane's courage, and he persuaded him to face 'this brief tempest' bravely, promising to supply him with a memorial for the Congress that would vindicate his probity and patri-otism. His enemies, confronted by such written evidence, would 'come to repent their imprudence in charging him.'

Since Beaumarchais had by now convinced himself that Deane's appearance before Congress could only further his own cause, the man's departure seemed a matter of pressing necessity; but he also realized that a recommendation from himself alone would not be enough, so he proposed that various French ministries should add their commendations to his, with regard to Deane's 'wisdom and efficiency.' He even decided that he could risk asking for a royal token, such as a portrait of the King, or some other remarkable present, to assure his countrymen that Deane was much honoured in France. Deane did, as a result, receive a snuffbox, decorated with a portrait of Louis XVI, studded with diamonds.

Emboldened by Beaumarchais, Deane himself also made the extraordinary request to be taken to Boston by a ship of the French fleet, believing that this would counter charges that he had been acting against the interests of France; and this request, too, was granted. It was decided that Deane, properly armed with citations, but giving the appearance of a man suffering disgrace, should sail for America. In this way, his enemies in America and France, anticipating an easy victory, would be encouraged to relax their precautions.

To add flavour to this ploy, Beaumarchais suggested that he, too, should leave Paris, seemingly also under suspicion, and his lawsuit at Aix would furnish him with an excellent pretext for his departure. Beaumarchais also prudently proposed that a reliable *Frenchman* should leave with Deane in order to bring back a verbatim report of the results of Deane's actions in Congress. He hoped his own views would be seen as sensible to the members, and therefore approved; but he would not rest until he had soundly established Deane's vindication.

As it was, Beaumarchais did not go to Aix, but instead was forced to travel to Rochefort on urgent business, where he was delayed, and so it proved impossible for Silas Deane to wait for his return from there before setting out for America. It was also unfortunate that the short time permitted Deane to prepare for his voyage did not allow him to settle his accounts with Beaumarchais, and the 'absolute necessity of setting sail' also obliged him to leave other transactions in the same unsettled state.

Because Deane had managed to convince himself, by the time he set sail, that he was only being sent for in order to more fully inform Congress of the state of their affairs in Europe, he hoped to return to France 'by as early as the Fall'—at which time, he wrote in a parting letter to Beaumarchais, he would make a final settlement of the accounts. While in America, he promised to do all that he could to bring his staunchest French friend the justice that he so richly merited, and—he flattered himself—he would also be able to remove 'any ill impressions made by designing persons;' although he felt sure that Francy would already have succeeded in a great measure in this matter, and had perhaps by now even procured a large remittance for his employer. If this were the case, bolstered by his own commendations, Congress could no longer delay in doing justice to Beaumarchais's important services in the cause of American liberty.

A French fleet, under its admiral, the Comte d'Estaing,[3] arrived in Delaware Bay on 9 July 1778 with Deane on board, along with the first French ambassador to the United States, C.A. Gerard.[4] Yet two vital months had already been lost, since Deane, who had first set sail from Bordeaux, had then been forced to disembark at Brest fifteen days after leaving, and had been kept waiting while some matter was settled in Paris.

Meanwhile, he had requested his friend Doctor Edward Bancroft to wait upon Beaumarchais in Paris, (possibly with the intention of keeping an eye on their mutual interests). There is no greater irony in the life of the creator of the arch-manipulator 'Figaro' than that he had put his trust in these two hugely deceitful men; but even when Deane's duplicity had been explained to him, Beaumarchais could never bring himself to see the American—whom he described as a poor 'militia diplomat'—as any sort of accomplice. Had Deane been that crafty the man would have taken greater care of his own interests, he later reasoned; but when Beaumarchais wrote a farewell letter to Deane, saying that he felt sure 'his friend' would inform the Congress of his devoted service in their cause of a free America, he had no reason to doubt Deane's integrity.

He wrote this letter while on board the *Proud Rodrigue*, then anchored in the Rochefort roadstead; and whose cargo he had consigned to a local merchant, Monsieur Chevalier,[5] in a new stratagem to recover the funds he needed; for this shipment was to be *sold* in a cash transaction directly to commercial dealers upon the ship's arrival in America, instead of being sent on to the brokers for Congress, as had been the case with most of his other cargoes. He had, all the same, recommended Chevalier to give priority to the Committee of Commerce for the items they wished to acquire. He also wrote to ask Deane to take care of Chevalier, the captain, and Francy, and 'all that pertains to my business, as I have taken care of yours and those of your Congress in Europe.'

In the same letter, he requested that if some 'unforeseen impediment' had delayed the 50,000 pounds sterling he had charged his agent to obtain from Congress in order to purchase tobacco, he counted on Deane's friendship and gratitude to do whatever he could to expedite the matter right away. Chevalier, 'the bearer of this letter,' had received an express order to solicit Deane's 'good offices for all the occasions' in which the American might be useful to him, and Beaumarchais had no doubt that Deane would gladly oblige.

At that time he still had only an inkling of the true reason for the American's recall; to answer charges raised up by Arthur Lee, in the many officious letters written by that troublemaker to Congress—mostly to the effect that all the merchandise and munitions shipped by Hortalez & Co to America were an outright gift from France, and therefore required no commercial return. Lee had, he declared, been so informed by 'Hortalez' himself. The fact that Congress had now been made aware that this 'merchant' was no more than a fabricated character did not stop many of its members from looking with a jaundiced eye on the invoices and various requests for immediate payment from the company that bore Deane's signature—even though they came from a 'commercial' house that functioned under a strict condition of remittances to be made as soon as possible.

In fact it had been very easy for Lee to blacken Deane's conduct, and to accuse him of dishonest dealings. He simply repeated stories, that were based on no real evidence, of Deane's alleged underhand manoeuvres in which he contrived to demand money from Congress, to be sent to France 'in the cause,' and in which he expected to share. This alone, perhaps, explains the astonishing silence that Congress observed, even after receiving *ten* detailed letters from Beaumarchais on the subject.

Swinton, the London-based publisher, wrote to Beaumarchais, saying that the Lords of the Exchequer had forbidden the exportation of goods from England that was not accompanied by a specific permit; as a consequence, the current issue of the *Courrier de l'Europe* had been stopped at the customs in Dover and sent back to him in London. He believed that this prohibition would not be lifted for a long while, and he wondered if it would be appropriate to have the paper reprinted in Paris, asking whether or not Beaumarchais could promptly secure a minister's order to this effect.

For Swinton this presented some drawbacks, as he explained to Beaumarchais:

I.   The people who refused to believe that the *Courrier* was printed in London would now be confirmed in their belief.

II.   If up to only ten sheets were being reprinted, wouldn't people ask: 'Why not the *whole* paper? In that case, what stock could be taken in a sheet revised, corrected and *castrated* by the Paris censors? Such might be the reactions to be expected in that event, and the *Courrier* would thus come to be regarded as a run-of-the-mill paper, deprived of the originality, energy and liveliness, which had made its reputation.

III. On the other hand, the public was getting very tired of the long delays suffered by this paper as a result of it being published so far away from its point of sales. Subscribers had complained and would-be contributors did not come forward as a result of the long time lapses between committing themselves to paper and seeing their efforts in print. Meanwhile, the editors of other periodicals had begun to spread unfavourable rumours about world events, which ought to be checked, and this could only be done in the pages of the *Courrier*.

Swinton therefore requested Beaumarchais to let him know what decision should be taken in this critical situation. The playwright's extensive knowledge of the ministerial world in France would suggest to him, Swinton hoped, some means by which he could best reflect the intent of a government 'whose orders it will always be my duty to comply with.'

Beaumarchais immediately sought to carry out Swinton's request to have the paper printed in France, although he thought that Boulogne would be a more sensible place than Paris to set up his presses, as there would be less interference from meddling officials.

On 20 April, Vergennes informed Maurepas that the American mission had just made representations to him with regard to the discouragement then being shown to them by the maritime merchants of Nantes and Bordeaux who were involved in trade with America. These merchants were now also asking for armed convoys, (such as the one that Beaumarchais had fitted out), to be provided for the security of their cargoes.

The American commissioners may have been experiencing difficulties with their suppliers on the coast, but Beaumarchais himself was also having problems with the remaining Americans at Passy, where Franklin and Lee were, he complained, still mistreating 'America's Best Friend.' They were now trying to take back from him the value of the cargoes brought back on other ships, even though his agent had succeeded in getting a proper contract drawn up between Hortalez & Co and Congress, which was up for ratification by the commission in Paris. The Deane-Lee controversy, however, was still very much alive, and there were embarrassing new questions for Vergennes and Maurepas to try to answer. The three trickiest being:

(a) Had not King Louis XVI agreed to furnish secret aid to his new ally?

(b) Did the commissioners *have* to pay off Hortalez & Co.?

(c) Who was Hortalez anyway? He seemed not to exist.

In the opinion of the very much alive 'Hortalez,' Vergennes's answer to these three questions amounted to no less than a betrayal of a state secret, a breach of faith, and the abandonment of his most loyal agent. In short, the cover that Beaumarchais had worked so hard to protect had now been blown wide open!

He wrote once more to Benjamin Franklin, now in possession of these three facts:

> Monsieur de Beaumarchais is honoured to present his very humble homage to Mr. Franklin. He begs him to kindly let him know, by the postillion delivering this letter, upon what day he will be able to confer with himself and Mr Lee, with regard to the ship *Thereze*. Letters from merchants in Nantes require M. de Beaumarchais to give prompt orders for the sale of the cargo in its hold. Time being of the essence.

Yet despite the urgency, it took the commissioners five days to reply to him. They were waiting, it seemed, for further, more confirming, news from America, or so Beaumarchais convinced himself; but if this was so, it was dire news for him, when it came:

> In a letter we have received from the Committee of Commerce, of 16 May [the commissioners wrote], we are informed that they had ordered several vessels to South Carolina, to be laden with rice. The Committee has directed the agents in that State to consign these cargoes to our address.
>
> In a letter from Mr Livingston[6] to us, dated 'Charleston, S.C. 10th June 1778,' he has subjected the cargo of the *Thereze* expressly to our orders. In your letter to us, dated '8th September 1778,' you demand that the cargo received on your own vessel should be sold, and the money remitted to you, in part of what is due to you by Congress. But we are at a loss to know how you claim the *Thereze* as your proper vessel, because M. Monthieu claims her as his. He has produced a written contract for the hire of her, part of which we have paid, and the remainder he now demands of us. However, Sir, we beg leave to state to you the powers and the instructions we have received from Congress, and to request your attention to them as soon as possible. For which purpose we are ready to enter into a discussion of these matters at any time and place that you please.
>
> But until the accounts of the company of Rodrigue Hortalez & Co are settled, and the contracts either ratified by you and ourselves, or rejected by one party or the other, we cannot think that we should be justified in remitting to you the proceeds of the cargo of the *Thereze*. We will, however, give orders to

our agents for the sale of the cargo. So that the proceeds of this sale may be put in reserve, to be paid to the House of Hortalez & Co, or their representatives, as soon as the accounts shall be settled, or the contract ratified.

By a copy of the contract between a committee of Congress and a M. Theveneau de Francy, dated 16 April last, we perceive that the 17th article in it, respecting the annual supply of 24 millions of *livres*, shall not be binding upon either of the parties. That is, unless this same clause shall be formally approved by Rodrigue Hortalez & Co, and by the Commissioners of the United States at Paris. We take this opportunity to inform you, Sir, that we are now ready to confer with the representatives of Hortalez & Co, or with any other person authorized for this purpose, at any time or place that they, or you, shall appoint.

It took another six months for the question to be resolved. On 10th September, the American commissioners informed Vergennes they had received certain powers from Congress, which they wished to 'lay before his Excellency.' On 13 April, they reported, Congress had resolved 'that the Commission of the United States in France be authorized to determine and settle with the house of Rodrigue Hortalez & Co.' Any compensation was to be allowed them on all warlike stores shipped by them for the use of the United States, *prior* to 14 April 1778—and this was to be over and above the compensation allowed them in the sixth article of the proposed contract between the Commission of Commerce [in Congress] and John [sic] Baptiste Lazarus Theveneau de Francy.'

In the official letter to Franklin, in which the foregoing resolution was enclosed, the congressional committee had noted that a contract was to be entered into between J.B.L Thevenau de Francy, agent of *P-A Caron de Beaumarchais*, and the Committee of Commerce:

You will observe that their accounts are to be fairly settled, and what is justly due is paid for, as on the one hand, Congress would be unwilling to evidence a disregard for, and contemptuous refusal of, the spontaneous friendship of His Most Christian Majesty. But on the other hand they are unwilling to put into the private pockets of individuals what was graciously designed for the public benefit. You will have the accounts liquidated, and to direct in the liquidation thereof that particular care be taken to distinguish the property of the Crown of France from the private property of Hortalez & Cie, and to transmit to us the accounts so stated and distinguished. You will accompany this by an invoice of all articles imported from France into America and the resolves of Congress relative thereto. You will appoint, if you should judge it proper, an agent to inspect the quality of such goods as you may apply for to the House of Hortalez & Co before they are shipped, to prevent any impositions.

On 16 May 1778, Congress resolved 'that the invoice and articles to be imported from France, together with the list of medicines approved by Congress, to be signed by the Committee of Commerce and transmitted to the Commissioners of the U.S. at Paris. Who are authorized and directed to apply to the house of Rodrigue Hortalez & Co for such articles as they have previously purchased or contracted for.' Copies of the invoices were to be delivered to 'Mr de Francy,' together with a copy of the foregoing resolution. The articles to be shipped by the House of Hortalez & Co were not to be insured, but prior notice was to be given to the commissioners in France, 'so that they may endeavour to obtain convoy for the protection thereof.'

The American commissioners sent Vergennes a copy of this contract made between the U.S. committee and Francy, plus a copy of Francy's new 'powers' and a copy of the list of articles to be furnished according to the contract. The foreign minister 'had before him all the papers relative to the subject,' but they particularly wanted his advice about the firm of Hortalez & Co, which really meant that they wanted him to disclose the identities of the persons who had built up the business of this mysterious company. Arthur Lee, of course, was particularly keen to learn the names, for he was convinced that everybody involved with it was now acting dishonestly (from which he did not exclude his superior, Benjamin Franklin. '... I am more and more satisfied that the old doctor is concerned in the plunder,' he wrote to his brother Richard Henry Lee on 12 September 1778, 'and that in time we shall collect the proofs').

As with so many of Lee's denunciations, the proofs were to be 'collected in time,' which never prevented him from making an accusation simply on suspicion; but he well understood—as indeed did Franklin and Congress—that they were under a direct obligation to King Louis XVI's goodwill for the greater part of the merchandise and the 'warlike stores' that had been furnished by this cloak and dagger enterprise.

Yet they could not, the 'Gentlemen of Passy' still insisted, discover any *written contract* made between Congress and the company of Hortalez & Co. Nor did they know of any living witness, or any other evidence, 'whose testimony can ascertain to us' the true identities of the personnel of Hortalez & Co. Neither could they discover the terms upon which the merchandise and munitions of war were to be supplied; whether as to the price, or the time, or conditions of payment. As they had said before, they understood that the United States was obliged only to the King of France for all the supplies, and they wished to discharge their obligation to his Majesty as soon as 'Providence shall put it in their power.' In the meantime, they were ready to settle and liquidate the accounts according to their instructions, at any time and manner that *the King and the Comte de Vergennes* would point out to them.

They also wished for Vergennes's advice on the subject of further ratifying—or *not*—a contract for future supplies with 'Hortalez & Co.' 'Would it be prudent,' they asked, to 'depend upon supplies from this quarter?' (ignoring the fact that the suspect company had already contributed enough supplies to have radically altered the military fortunes of their countrymen)—'And would it be safe?' If they should be disappointed, 'the consequences could be fatal for their country' (again disregarding the fact that, without the help of Hortalez & Co, the consequences for their country might already have been far more fatal than they were at present).

As a result, Vergennes wrote to Gerard—the new French ambassador to the U.S.—informing him that the commissioners in Paris were now asking for verification of the Hortalez account, and for ratification of the contract between the Committee of Commerce and Beaumarchais's agent Francy. Franklin was especially interested in the matter of which specific 'articles of war' had been officially furnished 'by the King's command,' and which by 'Hortalez' on their private account. Seeking to protect King Louis XVI, Vergennes now said that he was going to tell the Americans that the King had personally furnished *nothing*, he had simply allowed Beaumarchais to help himself from the royal arsenals, simply stipulating that the financier replace the stores 'at a later date.' Moreover, he assured Ambassador Gerard, who must in turn assure the Congress, his Majesty would be pleased if the Americans should not be pressed for reimbursement for the military stores—a total betrayal of Beaumarchais.

As for the contract that Congress had entered into with Beaumarchais's agent, the commissioners in Paris were now saying that they were empowered either to ratify or reject it, but they were asking for the minister's advice on this (when, surely, the advice they should have sought, if they really needed it, was that of their colleagues in America). But Vergennes, by this time trying to extricate himself from a situation he had begun to see could rapidly become a source of international embarrassment, betrayed his most faithful operator even further, telling the commissioners that *he did not know* of the House of Rodrigue Hortalez (despite having earlier revealed that he knew of its existence). He could not, therefore, answer for the company, and it was impossible for him to have an opinion upon the firm's financial soundness, or it's faithfulness in fulfilling its obligations.

Even more astonishingly, Vergennes then asked his ambassador in America to communicate these two answers to Congress, (which Gerard did on 9 February 1779). Beaumarchais had been away from Paris, and was therefore unable to meet Vergennes as ordered to do so (when the minister probably wished to explain his reasons for his extraordinary treachery). Since Beaumarchais's return to the capital he had made the trip to Versailles, but he had been kept so late in discussion with the Comte de Sartine that Vergennes had already retired to bed before he was free to meet him. He now asked, still ignorant of Vergennes's actions, for the minister's orders, 'since your head is freed of more important affairs.'

Beaumarchais had been in Provence, to try to settle the legal business that still ate up his time and energy, and afterwards he had been in London for twelve days (even *he* asked himself if this was not 'the highest imprudence' since he was *persona non grata* there). He did, however, have a typical explanation for making such a dangerous journey; he had, he said, been forced to answer an insult, 'of the silliest sort,' from the British Under-Secretary of State, by way of a vigorous reply to be *made in person* to the spy known as 'La Francaise' (the possible code name of William Eden, who was in charge of espionage in France).

Beaumarchais, having returned to France 'with honour satisfied' (although never explained), was also happy to report that he was now ready to put to sea a fleet of more than twelve sails, under the guardianship of *Proud Rodrigue*, (which had returned to Rochefort on 1st October, in remarkably good condition). This fleet might contain up to 6,000 tons, 'outfitted absolutely in war.' He had already sent instructions to Francy in America, by the corsair ship *Zephir*, which was to distribute its merchandise there.

The instructions were fairly simple. When the ship *Ferragus*, out of Rochefort last September, made land in America, Francy was to hold it from returning to France until the new fleet arrived. The loading of these ships had been arranged between Monthieu and Beaumarchais, and they had largely freighted it according to a list provided by Francy from America. Since Beaumarchais was by this time trying to get back his outlay rather than to accumulate claims upon Congress, most of the return cargo was therefore to be made up of tafia, sugar and a little coffee; not from North America, but from the French Islands.[7]

He had also, as per instructions, switched many of his exports to America, which were now composed of *English* hardware, cloth, gauze, ribbons, silk, nails, canvas, gear, samples of several types of paint, paper, books and brushes; along with other articles that Francy had 'preferred' (commercial materials rather than war-surplus).[8] Francy was to see that the fleet 'stayed at the plank' for as little time as possible, because although it was powerful and well-armed, notice of its arrival in America must not be revealed to the enemy in time for them to try to intercept it on its return voyage. Beaumarchais now had a different slogan, and one that reflected the Americans' new requirements; 'Commerce first, war goods second.'

He had reckoned that the fleet would reach America in February at the earliest, as it was scheduled to make a detour to the French Islands, to provide the Americans with the supplies of flour and salt they so badly needed. The prospect of this coming in bills of exchange, drawn on *French* treasurers, before the fleet returned, would put him in a far better position to cope; but as it happened—due to the terrible disbursement that the outfitting had cost the company—it was soon realized that the fleet could not sail until the first days of January.

XX

Facing the Enemy

Throughout 1778 there was a heavy correspondence between Francy in America and his employer. Fourteen letters in triplicate were sent to Paris, by different channels, in the vague hope that at least one would reach its destination. Francy, experiencing a sense of isolation upon being exposed to a very different culture, reacted badly to American life, disparaging it at every level; but his most chilling comments were always reserved for Silas Deane, for the agent now believed that Deane was too 'cowardly' and self-centred to be counted upon. It must be acknowledged, however, that Francy based this assessment on letters sent by the commissioners in Paris to the Congress—which he had been permitted to read—and they were hardly likely to be unprejudiced since Lee quite clearly had a hand in their composition.

'You will get, by the *Proud Rodrigue*, all my accounts with Congress that are now in order,' Beaumarchais informed his agent, 'including the insurance, and with policies furnished, since I was my own insurer.' He also stressed that he wished Francy to inform Congress it was an accepted practice in European commerce for those running the insurance risks to be entitled to 'the payment thereof,' and he absolutely wished to benefit by this rule. This admittedly questionable custom caused great difficulties for Francy with people that he dealt with in America, since Beaumarchais, (as Hortalez), had stated in an earlier letter to Congress that the insurance risks must be borne by them; but, as that proposal had proved to be too onerous for the Americans, he had then asked simply for the insurance costs to be paid by them instead—with the only consequence being that Congress would not be asked to pay for the cargoes they did not receive, and 'which have been plucked on their way from Europe to America.'

In one letter to Francy, Beaumarchais included a copy of the statement he had already received from Congress, in which they had agreed to the terms he had set out—an agreement that still stood, 'notwithstanding the faithless Passy commissioners,' who had disputed each imported cargo. Beaumarchais was determined now to have nothing more to do with the commissioners as long as 'this rascal Lee' was one of them. He thought the Americans must have a poor grasp of their own interests to leave a man of such suspicious character in place (it seems never to have occurred to him at this juncture that Franklin might also distrust *him*).

Francy had asked Beaumarchais to obtain a commission for him as a sea captain; which, as he explained, would allow him to be freed faster should he ever be taken a prisoner at sea.[1] Beaumarchais had, in fact, already been promised this commission by the Minister of Marine, and he hoped to be able to send it by the *Proud Rodrigue*—'But don't count on it until you have it in your hand,' he advised. 'You know our country; it is so large that there is a long way from where something is given to the place where it is received!' … But it *had* been promised.

Casimir Pulaski[2]—a Polish aristocrat, and one of the 'volunteer officers' sent to America by Silas Deane—had started to complain about everything once he had arrived in the U.S.A., which Beaumarchais found particularly irritating, since, as he wrote to Francy, he had received no further money from Pulaski's account except for what the Pole had given him personally, 'on which I have just paid 100 *louis* on his behalf.' He would send Francy his account, to challenge the (now reluctant) officer, since Pulaski was supposed to have written to him settling his debt.

On the other hand, Beaumarchais fully approved of Francy's actions on behalf of the Marquis de La Fayette,[3] that 'brave young man.' This immensely rich adventurer had managed to sail for America, motivated by the romantic idea of the American revolt. He did so, despite opposition from his guardians, but with a written guarantee from Silas Deane that he would be commissioned a major general in the continental army. He had somehow fallen prey to loan sharks while in New York, and Francy had made the necessary financial arrangements to rescue him from them. In fact, Francy had advanced him the money he needed with the proviso that the interest would not start running until the 'major general' had ceased to fight for the Republic.

Beaumarchais approved entirely of Francy's unprompted actions; 'You serve me according to my heart when you oblige such men of character,' he told him. He had still not been paid for the advances that Francy had made to La Fayette, 'but I am not worried!'—and the same went for a Monsieur de la Rouerie,[4] also a 'brave young man.'

Beaumarchais planned to do much for Francy in gratitude; 'I esteem you and love you, and you will see proof of it before long.' He also sent his regards to the Baron von Steuben,[5] to whom he had also lent money on his departure for America. He could only congratulate himself, he wrote, on having given such a great officer to his friends, the 'free men;' and in a sense forced him to follow this noble career, for he had heard that Steuben was now a general inspector of American troops. 'Bravo! Tell him that his glory is the interest on my money, and I have no doubt that in that kind I will be more than repaid!'

He had by now received a letter from Silas Deane, written in English, and also one from Carmichael, who claimed to have forgotten his French already. 'We have as many intrigues and cabals here as you do [at Versailles],' Deane wrote cynically; 'And why not, since we are now the accredited friends of Louis XVI.'

Beaumarchais missed them both. They were 'brave Republicans' who had been as useful to him in their country's cause as the 'base schemer,' Lee, was still deadly. Both men believed that they would be returned to France, and they promised to see him soon in Paris.

In Paris, meanwhile, Beaumarchais kept up a steady pressure on the ministers. He advised Sartine, 'When the matter is very important and time is very precious, one can never recommend such an affair too much to the man who handles a lot of them, (and mishandles a few of them).' This was no way to talk to the Secretary of Naval Affairs, however close their acquaintance, but he boldly asked Sartine for:

I.   A new letter to M. de Marchais, [a harbour commissioner] who had declared that without a covering letter from the ministry he would not give one man to the *Proud Rodrigue*. '… Which will become the *Humble Rodrigue* as it cannot be proud except through your kindness, without which it is nailed to the harbour wall.'

II.   He wished to place an order to have fourteen cannons, with bombs, etc., delivered as a compensation for 'that hard word' *cash*. Beaumarchais was by now receiving numerous complaints from his creditors, who would no longer advance him ready money, and so he was asking to be paid for the advances he himself had made out of his own pocket, and also for supplies to be furnished by the navy.

Even more boldly, he complained of the ministers' treatment of him, speaking of him as though he was the 'puniest' corsair, when he was, in fact, *the most daring of them all*! He was even planning to cruise across the ocean in his own convoy, to attack and 'burn some moustaches,' and capture a few pirates himself; 'Because I have sixty cannons and 160 feet of keel, I should not see myself less welcome than those who do not get to our gasket!'[6]

Yet, returning to earth, he 'freely confessed' that he trusted in Sartine's sense of fairness to see him right in this present difficulty. Without the protection of the *Proud Rodrigue*, all his ventures were at risk, and all his talk hot air; for the great ship was fitted out for war and carried no cargo, while his other vessels would be emptied out and refilled. As their protector, his flagship would proudly cruise all over the American seas, for this was her true destiny. Could Monsieur Sartine ignore the fact that, while all the various projects connected to similar frigates were still in the air, the *Proud Rodrigue* was ready to plough the Atlantic as soon as the minister would let him have enough sailors to man her properly?

If the *Proud Rodrigue*, as a *privately owned* vessel, should prove unacceptable to the ministry, what was the alternative? Were he to ask the minister to build and outfit a vessel of such calibre, equally able to serve as a ship of the King's, 'anywhere I should choose to send it,' would Sartine still refuse him cannons and the rank of squadron leader for her captain, Brulet? Such meagre encouragement for such a great object must be nothing to a man such as the minister—so how could a ship be of less value to him, ready made, than if it remained to be built?

Beaumarchais believed that the 'multiplicity of the matters' the minister handled might have blinded him to the triple purpose of encouraging French commerce through the example that he had already set. He had single-handedly provided a French merchant fleet 'so far-reaching' that the new United States would be able to judge thereby France's desire to sustain her new trade relations with them once the present hostilities had ceased.

Sartine, though, had not the patience for this sort of trumpet blowing; for new hostilities between Great Britain and France had in fact started six months earlier, when a British fleet, under Admiral Keppel,[7] had stopped and searched a French ship, the *Belle Poule*, off the coast of Brittany on 18 June 1778. As a result, the first shots had been fired, but Beaumarchais, long expecting such an eventuality, now hoped that Sartine would find these 'great concerns worthy of the attention and protection of such an enlightened minister.'

Nevertheless, while trying to flatter the secretary for the navy, he complained to Vergennes that, for the lack of seamen, he now faced the necessity of cutting down—by perhaps as much as a half—a superbly fitted-out operation. He was even threatened with the possibility of having to cancel it completely, for he lacked even enough men to equip his finest ship. Of course, he understood Monsieur de Sartine's quandary completely, but he could only lament that commerce was 'encouraged in words only, while it is stalled in fact, and in sorry fact.' If the tradesmen in French ports were once again to see him unload his ships, after all he had promised them, 'there would ensue a disappointment akin to despair.'

Beaumarchais sent Vergennes a copy of his letter to Sartine, but he begged the more important minister to help him on his own authority, as he himself was already doing more than he could manage on his own. 'No subject of the

King deserves to be rewarded more than I do,' he entreated; 'You can well say that my zeal for my country devours me, and I feel that I would gladly pay with a gallon of my blood if it gave the slightest advantage to it.' The favour he asked was that Vergennes should recommend his shipping enterprise to Sartine as an affair of threefold usefulness.

In addition to this, he gave Vergennes the amazing news of another spectacular British defeat that he had received from America via Nantes the day before, and which he thought perhaps was worthy of inclusion in the *Courrier de l'Europe*, since such a snippet could only be helpful, 'and there would be no danger.' It would be helpful because, at the height of the British parliamentary debates, such news would be an extra cause of anxiety and could only increase the royal party's bitterness and would especially hurt their chances of obtaining further subsidies from parliament. 'A word will suffice, and you alone can give that word.'

But what could he do if he was denied the convoy for his fleet, and if they also refused him the means of convoying his own ships as well as others? His private outlay now amounted to more than six million *livres*, apportioned between his friends and himself; but the ships that would join his fleet would bring in above nine million, once he had been given the men to man them. In the same circumstances, he grumbled, the British would give to such an enterprise at least *four* convoy vessels, but the French—not a single frigate! So how should he and his colleagues manage? He relied upon the Comte de Vergennes.

Beaumarchais also now openly complained that Benjamin Franklin had shown him a 'disobliging aloofness,' apart from seeking to deprive him of what was rightfully his. Franklin, 'a man of the highest merit,' but who dined all the time in the houses of people who were indifferent to the aims of the new Republic, had never even been polite enough to set foot in the house of the 'best friend of that republic.' No, not once in the whole year that he had spent in France ... despite any number of invitations. Beaumarchais's backers had been outraged by Franklin's behaviour towards him, which had led them to conclude that Beaumarchais had drawn them into a 'bad business,' since those they were sustaining were, at best, ignoring their spokesman.

By way of explanation, when informed of Beaumarchais's complaint, Franklin had a very singular excuse. He did not want to meet Beaumarchais, he said, because he did not wish to look as if he was *criticizing* him, or disturbing the work that had been done before his arrival by his colleague Silas Deane. This was generally considered a poor reason, but Beaumarchais tried to overlook Franklin's discourtesy, attempting to distinguish between the commissioner and the nation that he represented.

But the fact remained that he had now waited for more than a year for the total of five millions that had been 'advanced' to him by the Committee of Commerce in America. Moreover, the commissioners at Passy had avoided, using every possible excuse, to remit one penny to him of the funds they had received; even John Adams,[8] the patriot statesman, who had replaced Silas Deane in April, had ignored him, Beaumarchais complained—had the newest commissioner been too preoccupied with seeing the sights of Paris and with keeping up his *social* engagements, along with the indefatigable Franklin, the darling of the Parisian elite?

Beaumarchais informed Congress in a letter of 20 December 1778 that, in view of their representative's extraordinary behaviour towards him, he now wished only to deal with the committee of commerce directly, for which purpose he had sent his agent to them. To stress the increasing difficulties of his position he included a copy of a letter he had sent to the American delegation in Paris some weeks before. This letter, of 8 September 1778, was acknowledged two days later by Lee, Franklin and Adams, who had then stated that they had been instructed to examine the accounts of Hortalez & Co. The occasion upon which, when asked for his opinion, Vergennes had given an 'ambiguous, diplomatic' answer, and when the commissioners had not 'deigned to honour' Beaumarchais himself with an answer. He asked members of Congress to believe that he was not saying one word in his complaint to them that overstated the truth.

His letter must have struck home with certain representatives, for a reply was sent to him within a month, with John Jay,[9] the 'President of Congress,' writing to him personally on 15 January 1779:

> The Congress of these United States of America is sensible of your exertions in our favour, and present you with their thanks and assure you of their regard.
>
> They lament the inconvenience you have suffered by the advances made in support of these United States. Circumstances have prevented a compliance with our wishes, but they will take the most effectual measures in our power to discharge our debt to you.[10]
>
> The liberal sentiments and extensive views which alone could dictate a conduct like yours, are conspicuous in your actions and adorn your character. While with great talent you served your Prince, you have gained the esteem of this infant Republic and will receive the merited applause of the New World.
>
> By order of Congress.

On receipt of this gratifying testimonial, Beaumarchais immediately contacted the commissioners at Passy, sending them a long letter in which he

attempted to explain to them why they were gravely insulting him by denying his right to the cargoes returning on the ships he had chartered. It was a
'sacred claim' because it involved the honour of both countries, as he saw it,
and it also involved a French policy for which he felt responsible.

He sent a copy of this letter to Vergennes on 10 February, and he apologized for appearing to set politics aside in it, but he would get back to that
'imperceptibly.' He also planned to send a copy of his letter to Congress, in
order to finish the painful job, first undertaken by Silas Deane, of removing
the wretched Arthur Lee, the 'most dangerous enemy of France,' from his
place as a commissioner in Paris! Lee, ever vainglorious, had earlier written
to his brother Richard Henry and to Samuel Adams[11] that he alone, by rights,
deserved to be made sole Minister to France!

Beaumarchais then received news from Philadelphia, which confirmed
his decision to take his complaints to the next session of Congress, since his
reputation was once more being denigrated. A sustained counter-attack from
himself in Europe and from his agent in America should finally succeed, he
told Vergennes; did the minister not agree? Congress appeared to think that
the war with their mother country was almost over, but this period of relative
calm was only giving certain members even more time for intrigues and cabals,
in which his good name was once more being bandied about. Francy was
deeply worried about the consequences of the feud between Lee and Deane,
and so he must not neglect any method of reinforcing the latter's cause, 'which
is ours.' 'That is what I have in mind at this time, when Congress counts on
the continuation of my shipments and services,' Beaumarchais advised.

Yet he believed, from what Francy told him, that Congress was convinced
they had no better friend in Europe than himself, and if this were true, it
would make them consider very carefully his opinion of Lee's character and
scheming. That would be his main 'theme' when dealing with them; but it
was up to his superiors to correct him if they thought him wrong. He would
only send the letter if M. de Vergennes approved of it.

The problems arising from the trade between France and her new ally,
Beaumarchais eventually decided, essentially lay in the rigid administrative
structure of the French bureaucracy. Crucially, the tobacco trade could never
be free in France, since it was shackled by the tax policies of the Farmers-
General; and it was as a result of this realization that Beaumarchais the
economist—although no Baron Necker—now attempted to reform the
French tax system![12]

In the meantime, he was still struggling with the American problem. He
wrote to the commissioners on 13 February about the continued quarrel over

the 'feeble load of rice and indigo' that had now arrived from Charleston, informing them of his intention to call Congress to account for making him such a puny remittance in return for the huge sums still owed him by the Republic—'… Whose word and whose *written* promise I have that they will discharge their obligations to me as soon as possible.'

He wanted, above all, he wrote, to avoid a legal action in a court of the Admiralty; for even though that court was held two hundred miles from Paris, any report of its proceedings, would—resonating throughout Europe, as it undoubtedly would—appear 'unseemly' between the noble delegates from America and the man known as the most zealous servant of the nation they represented. In the meantime, he acknowledged that the proceeds of the sale of the cargo of the *Thereze* had been remitted to him and should be credited against his claims (without prejudicing his rights for payment on all shipping expenses, etc.).

Beaumarchais included detailed information regarding the return cargoes on both the *Amphitrite* and the *Mercure*. The former had not yet been sold, and the latter had returned empty. '… This will allow you to update your accounts with Congress on this matter.' Zealous friends, he warned them, were taking measures to defend his honour and character in America, against the 'horrible intrigues' still being plotted against him in Europe. More pertinently, if the Passy commissioners did not immediately withdraw their summons to prosecute his correspondent in Nantes, 'for recovery of his cargo,' he would conclude that it was their intention to force him to go to law to fight off their discreditable attack upon him. This would be a grievous attempt, and one which would rebound on them when he came to present his defence, since *he* could well prove *his* case.

There followed the familiar outline of the events leading from Silas Deane's first contact with him up to the time of his departure from France. Beaumarchais felt he needed to continually remind the three Americans in Paris of the details of what he had come to see as a plot against him; and as always, he followed this up with a hint of intimidation. He could easily unmask the 'obscure speculators' that such an enterprise was bound to attract, he wrote; and who had, in fact, come together to deceive Congress on the nature and conditions of his shipments—falsehoods that he was now prepared to challenge in public, if need be.

Moreover, since he was now convinced that he no longer owed these double-dealing men his consideration, he would go further and name them. He had extracts of their letters in his possession, which showed they had sought to prevent Congress from discharging their debt to him, thus bringing about his ruin. Using these, he would show 'the honest people of my country' that the 'noble delegates of the Republic,' Deane excepted, had openly intrigued against him. How startling it would be for all of Europe to learn that these same 'honourable' men had sought to rob him of the puniest returns on the money he had expended. They had spread confusion, false information, and ruin on an affair that had become as deadly for himself as it had been beneficial to the new republic. He also threatened to have all the merchandise that the Americans had wrongfully accumulated in Europe seized and stopped in all French ports, their funds seized, and all their banking arrangements halted, with the deposits sealed.

It is difficult to imagine that Beaumarchais could really have believed that he possessed the sort of power to bring off any of these threats; even in France, where he still had some influence—but he quite obviously believed that he had the legal right to drag them before the courts, if only to force them to be fair with him. He knew, he said, with magnificent scorn, that he could never expect their *gratitude*.

Although he addressed the letter to the delegation collectively, since all three had signed the summons against him, his deepest resentment was naturally directed against Lee, 'the only author of the wrong I have suffered.' He would, he insisted, never have any further dealings with that 'ambitious agent;' nor could Franklin or Adams ever mediate between them. He had stated as much to Congress, and he had sent them copies of the ciphered correspondence that had earlier been exchanged between Lee and himself. 'It will clearly prove to Congress the hatefulness of his behaviour towards me, and the falsity of his subsequent slurs regarding the nature and conditions of my shipments to America.'

If Congress, 'deceived, seduced, or led by reasons unknown to me, should continue to entrust their interest to that politician, I know him too well to ever consent to have him enter in any way into my affairs.' (Beaumarchais's handwriting in this rambling letter shows how distraught his feelings were by the size and force of his pen strokes.) But having dealt with his refutation of Lee, he also warned the commissioners against the humiliation of giving Britain the 'pleasant spectacle of a public confrontation;' for such a failure would, he pointed out, deter French maritime merchants from taking on further American ventures 'than all the politics, and all the treaties in the world could do to persuade them.'

In a post-script he sent them copies of the invoices for the chartering of the first ships he had sent to America, and the agreement signed by Deane and himself as a caution for Congress—a deal that had certainly been settled by the commission on the charter for the sum of 351,400 *ecus*, of which Beaumarchais had paid 269,400 *ecus* in 1776. This long overdue money, he insisted, should be returned to him at the earliest opportunity.

As no verification was actually needed for the merchandise he had sent to America, in order to discharge such an advance made in France in French currency and based on a paid invoice, he was also asking—*for the twentieth time*—that they should repay his personal loan with interest—along with the expenses, etc., that had been due to him since October of 1776, and which he now very badly needed. Such, he felt it necessary to explain, was the reason that he called those ships he had chartered 'my own ships,' although otherwise they may belong to whomever the gentlemen of the commission pleased. That is, *after the sum he had expended on the chartering of these ships had been repaid to him by them*; for more than three years he had refrained from sending the bailiff to them, for this collection, and for many others. In view of this, was it still asking too much for them to stop the scandal of their bringing a summons against his correspondent; if only in gratitude for the 'mildness and honesty' of his behaviour towards them, and his long patience?

It was not only the Americans in Paris who were frustrating Beaumarchais; his compatriots in America were also undermining him. Francy, greatly alarmed, wrote to say that the French ambassador to the United States had come up with a plan to compensate the Americans financially for the French artillery supplied to the republican army. His solution being to match it with the sums due from the French government to the Americans for the articles that had been supplied by *them* to Admiral d'Estaing, as his ships patrolled the Caribbean! France, it had now been decided, owed the Congress considerable sums for the victuals the Americans had furnished to the French fleet. Now, Gerard had carelessly suggested that they be written off against the amount due to Messrs. Hortalez & Co, saying that the 'King would see to it that Hortalez would be satisfied!'

Beaumarchais was decidedly not 'charmed by the suggestion,' and he immediately applied to Vergennes for enlightenment on this unexpected new threat to his finances. Francy, in a panic, asked him to clear up the matter at source before Beaumarchais replied to him officially. It was only too certain, he wrote, that Gerard's unorthodox method of settling accounts could only complicate, and certainly delay, the response of Congress to their demands for payment.

Beaumarchais, having trod the line for so long, was now fast losing patience with his French masters. A question for Maurepas to ask himself, he told the minister, was: 'How useful is it for France to continue shipping to America all the stores they cannot do without?' The answer was 'Indispensable'. But as the merchants could only trade in America by a mutual exchange of goods, must not the Versailles administration do everything possible to facilitate the flow of the one merchandise of great value brought from America; that is, tobacco? He then turned the argument against the tax-farmers. Since there was only one buyer of tobacco in France, and since 'the flow of tobacco had become as necessary to French merchants as daily bread to the people,' must the government continue to allow a monopoly to exist in the kingdom, thus stopping the free issue of this commodity? Everything would be lost if the government did not completely free this valuable trade, and if it failed to treat the tax-farmer in the same manner as it did the humble baker; 'You sell at such a price, you will buy at such another.' By this bold statement, Beaumarchais was treading on exceedingly dangerous ground, because the tax-farmers were the King's men, and they gave back twenty-four million *livres* to his Majesty from that particular source alone.

He even managed to involve the Swiss banker Baron Necker, whose 'niggling manipulations' were a noted feature of the time. He wrote informing the baron that Paulze,[13] a farmer-general, whom Beaumarchais had approached 'in the name of all the French merchants trading with America,' had made him two offers, which the baron might consider:

I.   The tax farm consented to grant him the conveyance of his goods throughout the Kingdom; but to Beaumarchais alone, however, as a preference. Though he wished to assure the baron that he would never solicit such a favour purely in his own interest. 'For what would people say about me if, pleading for the common cause, I was satisfied to pluck the fruits for my private advantage?' Paulze, in fact, had found there was no great disadvantage in such a transit agreement being agreed for *all* merchants, but his colleagues were a long way from thinking as he did. All Paulze's associates opted for a literal interpretation of the text, which categorically denied this transit for commerce in favour of merchants. Baron Necker's celebrated firmness was needed if the merchants were to prevail on this capital point. Until the baron gave backing to French commercial interests in general, Beaumarchais would refuse the particular favour offered to him personally. (A hugely generous gesture on his part.)

II.   Paulze had undertaken to have his office agree to a price for tobacco at the highest figure the merchants could reasonably offer to the tax-farm. But he only engaged to do so if Beaumarchais could guarantee to get the administration to come to the aid of commerce, and consent to sustain the sacrifice of the tax loss sustained by the farm.

Here, all Beaumarchais's patriotic fervour was less influential than the importance of the matter itself, 'of which you and M. de Maurepas are aware,' he told Necker. He could only 'silently' desire to see this encouragement given to those merchants who had traded with America, at a time when it was to be feared that maritime traders would soon hear distressing news about their vessels which had left for the French Islands last December and January; but he was equally convinced that the tax-farm was more than able to make 'this small sacrifice' without having to lose much in consequence.

The transit—'first object of my prayers'—depended upon the financier alone. The question of the slight loss of revenue between the tax-farm and the King, or even of the entire tax sacrifice to be borne by the farm, was a point to be decided between Necker and Maurepas; but Beaumarchais knew that the success of any future trading between the merchants and America depended upon a complete restructuring of the present situation with regard to the importation of tobacco. To keep the two men up to the mark, he planned to see Maurepas on Monday; and Necker—if he agreed to it—on Tuesday morning.

Beaumarchais—'with my head and briefcase full!'—attempted to get Maurepas to encourage the tax-farm to agree to his proposals, through the mediation of Baron Necker. He took with him to both meetings written proof of a new tax scheme that threatened to charge 40,000 *livres* worth of duty on tobacco stored at a warehouse in Nantes, if the owner did not let it go at the price the tax-farmers demanded.

Maurepas listened to Beaumarchais 'kindly' and, after a long session of pleading, it was agreed that the setting up of an impartial and prompt examination should be granted. As ever, Beaumarchais's main argument was that, in such a grave affair, the discovery of even one error in the 'givens' was an important step towards the truth. Even if one supposed that the most meticulous official had been deceived in a few instructions, his subsequent conclusions might be so 'beautifully thorough and so methodical' in its construction that it would be generally accepted to be trustworthy, while remaining mistaken. As Beaumarchais pointed out, 'A deep knowledge of the laws relating to the revenues of the Kingdom are two points very rarely found together in the same subject.'

He begged for another secret meeting with Vergennes, 'for security's sake.' Time was supremely important, since he had promised that 'all the rest' would be common knowledge within three months, and until then he had been assured that everything would remain in *statu quo*. It seemed to him, he fawned, that the various errors made by others only served to increase Maurepas's trust in Vergennes, 'who does not make any!'—at least, none that any inferior would dare to point out to him. Therefore, Beaumarchais offered to spare Vergennes the 'unpleasant labour involved in pursuing this matter' by undertaking it himself, so that the minister would only have to verify the results by examining the documents.

Meanwhile, Beaumarchais had been forced to go to Rochefort, to recruit the sailors he would need.; he hoped to gather enough of them together, 'by dint of gold *Louis's* to send off ten ships. These had been loaded for the past three months, and could have ruined him by their delay in setting sail, for this might very easily have prevented the Commander of the French Islands from sending his return merchant ships without adequate escort. Such useless, useless, months; although the flour that he had loaded last October had left on time. 'I am sighing even as I write this,' he recorded.

XXI

Debts and Taxes

Because of the secrecy that he himself had imposed, Beaumarchais was always forced to copy his most dangerous letters himself, which delayed their receipt; but by now he felt that he could trust nobody, among them his own clerks.

The first report he tackled, writing it up laboriously, was the report from the tax-farm of Lorraine. This particular receipt, on what would be payable to the King, was, Beaumarchais thought, 'clean cut on "proofs," but of a disproportion even more ticklish than the duties on salt.' The farm of Paris came next. He assured Vergennes that, as had been expertly explained to him, the King would be handed forty million *livres* 'without any taxation or borrowing;' but Beaumarchais desired the 'reform plan' to be commenced by bringing about a *lit de justice*[1] at which it would be discussed. During the confrontation with his ministers that followed on from this suggestion, King Louis was, in fact, reclining comfortably on cushions!

Beaumarchais also asked Maurepas to postpone a discussion within the Council concerning certain manoeuvres of the discount bank, which would force merchants into a complete dependence on the bank administrators. At his interview with Baron Necker, Beaumarchais apologized for the fact that he had understood nothing of the banker's tortuous explanation of this point!—'... Although it may be my own fault,' the financier-playwright admitted ruefully.

The *Proud Rodrigue*, of sixty cannons, and the *Zephir* of twenty, were setting sail at the same time as two ships of forty-four cannon were almost due, since they could delay their departure no longer. Beaumarchais could only assume that the two returning vessels had set out too hurriedly from America and, as a consequence, their sails had been poorly trimmed, thus causing their delay. 'In this manner did unfortunate commerce pay for the mistakes of men;' and writing about this in his bath, he was still shaking with anger. To add to his anxieties there was a report in a London newspaper, which had listed the number of 'prizes'[2] the English had taken from the French merchant fleet.

Summoned by Vergennes to Versailles, the minister introduced Beaumarchais to a secret agent who had, he said, 'the complete confidence' of the Comte de Maurepas, who had specifically asked for the services of this man because 'in a matter of such importance you cannot multiply one's observations too much.' Maurepas had also called upon Vergennes to act as an independent witness to the meeting of the two men. Whatever was discussed at this meeting was too 'classified' to be recorded, and none of it has survived, although on 21 March Beaumarchais sent Vergennes a second account of this 'backstairs' meeting (in which he reported that—since he had received new information to add to what had passed between them—it had enabled him to make a new abstract).

It may have been that the subject of these secret talks was the Englishman Swinton, who had by now approached openly Beaumarchais 'on the great matter which had brought him to France.' At their subsequent meeting, Beaumarchais spoke sarcastically of his 'great esteem' for the spy, but advised him to give up any idea of more intrigue, which would 'prove expensive and not lead him anywhere'—which could also, he had added, with his usual air of menace when dealing with his rivals, result in harm being done to him while on French soil.

France, he told Swinton, had no ambition to increase her power in the Americas, and had no interest at all in fighting a war with Great Britain—which had no right to reproach France with making a commercial treaty with her former colony; even if this agreement had been the sole pretext for the recent outbreak of hostilities between the two countries. The French compact in no way precluded the British from entering into a similar one with their former colonists; Britain had only to fully accept the Americans as an independent power.

He firmly believed, he also told Swinton, that even though he was not a member of the administration, he knew the minds of the ministers well enough not to be mistaken in his conjectures. If Great Britain were to request, as a basis for peace, that France should abandon their interest in America, there would be no 'cowardly response from the French people,' and they would not back down, (which was also, he said, the firm opinion of the young King). But if Britain was seriously desirous of peace, and would put aside this unacceptable condition, they would not meet further obstacles on other conditions. The French were fighting them only through 'just resentment of the awful devices the English have used against us.'

The treaty with America, at first only of practical interest to certain merchants, had now become an 'affair of [national] honour'—but if Britain were to respect that treaty, they would find the French easier to deal with 'than they dared to hope.' If the British believed that this offer would be modified, then Beaumarchais would like to remind Swinton that Spain had now become a mediator between the two countries. In this capacity, Spain had the right to expect goodwill on the part of Britain, and her government was perhaps the only vehicle through which any 'peace overtures' could be made.

Swinton's mission to Paris, Beaumarchais informed him, appeared to be either absolutely impossible or extremely easy. Impossible if the rights of America were not safeguarded, but easy if the British ministry could find a way to save the honour of their Crown while letting America keep its well-earned independence; especially if Britain were to send France honourable propositions through the Court of Madrid—for France would now accept nothing from the British Court except through this diplomatic channel.[3]

Swinton would only know success if he took all this advice to heart. As a 'former' fellow secret agent, 'Figaro' advised him to go back to London 'without doing things that are as far from your principles as they are contrary to the good you want to procure for the two powers.'

In April, Vergennes also wrote about this 'English emissary' to Montmorin,[4] the French ambassador in Madrid. Swinton had come, he said, 'loaded with letters of recommendation to intriguers of both sexes, along with letters of credit with which to try to bribe them.' So far, he and Maurepas had managed to steer clear of him, but he had 'seen a person who works for me' (which must have been his 'Figaro').

The message that Swinton brought from London, Vergennes explained, was that the British were now prepared to give the French *anything* (for the moment) if they would detach themselves from the Americans; but 'this same person [Figaro?] had not hesitated to answer that this proposition would not be countenanced by King Louis XVI's government.' It was understood that Swinton had now written to Lord North for more specific instructions, and Vergennes could not begin to imagine what might result from 'this little game.' Whatever motions the British further proposed, he begged Montmorin to inform the Spanish Court that French ministers would not listen to any British propositions that were not transmitted to them through the channel of the King of Spain.

The 'emissary,' Vergennes wrote, was a man who 'passes for a gentleman,' but he had not been deceived by the proposal, and simply saw it as a way to try to dupe the French, for the channel was 'improper' and Lord North was not the man to start peace negotiations. On the contrary, he was 'understandably' trying to lead the French into doing something that would compromise them with their Spanish and American allies. Vergennes fully subscribed to the Spanish Prime Minister's expressed view that they would all only avoid the traps set by the English if they communicated with each other frankly 'and in good faith'—which was not a principle to be adhered to when dealing with one's servants, of course, however well they served you, since he calmly went on betraying his 'Figaro;' as his 'Figaro' knew quite well. 'No one knows better than you,' Beaumarchais wrote to him slyly, 'how crafty wicked people can be!' He was not writing on this occasion to ask the minister to right a wrong that had been done to him, 'because that is impossible,' although a wrong *had* been done him. He was only trying to protect himself from the consequences of a 'horrible incident' that would result in his disgrace if the King became aware of it, 'without his Majesty having been forewarned.'

The 'horrible incident' had come about because he had made an error of judgement, as he went on to explain, an error that was entirely due to his misplaced faith in good-fellowship. He had received an unsigned letter, but had found its contents worth answering, 'as I always do, according to how my heart and mind are affected.' An article on French prisoners of war—that had been sent to him by the editor of the *Courrier de l'Europe*—was the text with which the anonymous writer had chosen to concern himself. In it, the correspondent had listed a number of shortcomings in the way the French housed their own prisoners of war (taken in the recent sea battles), and he seemed to be waiting for any advice that Beaumarchais could give him before he could 'adjust his own opinion.'

In view of the harsh criticism that he heard everywhere spoken against the French navy and its ministers, Beaumarchais had returned a quick answer and sent it to the address shown. He sent Vergennes a copy of this reply, and hoped that he would be excused for its 'warmth,' and he also sent him the original letter that had given rise to his response. The result, he was unhappy to report, was that a 'so-called' letter from himself was now being circulated in many countries, 'disfigured, perverted, and full of cynical liberties.' The whole affair had, quite clearly, been a fraud, designed to 'set him up.'

He could now see that he had been entrapped, and he knew that 'some people' would certainly seek to harm him by sending his ill-advised reply to the King (in much the same way that rumours of things 'supposedly' said at Beaumarchais's dinner table were also being spread abroad). He begged the count to let the King and Maurepas see his 'true' letter, of which he had fortunately kept a copy. He could vouch for its authenticity, and he would challenge anyone to produce another actually signed by him.

He was, he knew, often indiscreet, and he frequently spoke out 'too loudly;' he always became 'twice as French' when he found people believing him to be otherwise, or acting so. In this case, however, he had simply replied to an anonymous correspondent who had appeared to him to be honest, and he earnestly begged the minister to help him avoid the repercussions. As always, Beaumarchais knew that he could not just rely upon the minister's goodwill, but must provide him with a 'tidbit,' so he then told Vergennes that he had important matters relative to America to impart, and he begged for a minute of the count's valuable time.

Beaumarchais's 'alleged' letter was, indeed, dangerous for him. It read:

I have received, Sir, the letter you honoured me with, your patriotism and your fears are right.

The British have pillaged our ships like highwaymen. But if our navy, instead of remaining idle in our ports, waiting for the decisions of ministers who cannot make up their minds, had only acted like a highway patrol, we would not have uselessly lost our commerce. The fact that part of this is insured in London does not detract from the gross mistakes our ministers have made in starting a war without taking preliminary precautions. It is true that we have taken more prisoners of war than the British have, but our mistake remains the same.

Admiral d'Estaing patrols the Caribbean aboard the best ship, while Admiral Byron[5] perishes in the cemetery that is St Lucia, without daring to emerge to do anything. Yet in spite of his cowardice the [British] government have failed to recall him. But if he remains in place, is it not as the result of our own ministers' indecision rather than that of their declared will?

Unless Beaumarchais could convince his masters that this letter was a complete humbug, he was in real danger of losing any remaining advantage he still enjoyed at Versailles; so not only did he send Vergennes a copy of the anonymous letter 'running around under my name,' he had also spoken to Le Noir, the chief of police, 'who was going to look into it.'

A manifesto from London, being distributed around Paris, had resulted in serious complaints from the new Spanish ambassador, Almadorar,[6] (who had received a copy from Spain). It certainly showed the Spaniards in a poor light, but Beaumarchais thought that their reaction to it was 'rather contorted.' Meanwhile, he was himself annoyed to receive no news of the departure of the Spanish fleet from Cadiz, and he thought that the Spanish were taking too long over coming to a conclusion as to whether or not to join forces with France.[7] 'I don't know why,' he wrote, 'but I always have a little bit of ice lodged in a corner of my brain labelled "Spain." No matter how I try, I can't get excited about them. May God grant that I am wrong.'

On the other hand he would have been greatly cheered by a letter written by John Jay to the French ambassador to America on 18 June 1779:

Enclosed are Acts of Congress of 5 and 18 inst. respecting Bills of Exchange, for two million, four hundred thousand *livres* principal and 432,000 *livres* interest,

drawn on you in favour of Monsieur Beaumarchais. These are payable in several
sums, and at the respective times specified in the enclosed schedule. Sensible as
we are of Monsieur de Beaumarchais's efforts to serve these United States, and
on the seasonable supplies he has from time to time furnished, Congress are
earnestly disposed to make him this payment. They would gladly have done it
in produce [as he had requested], but the state of our finances, and the hazardous navigation render it impracticable.

Jay believed the drafts could be discharged 'with punctuality,' but if difficulties arose he would have time to represent them to Congress, 'who will
exert the means in their power to prevent any loss or disappointment to
Monsieur de Beaumarchais.'

News of this would not reach him for some weeks, but on 12 July, he had
thrilling news from Admiral d'Estaing, on board the *Languedoc* moored at
Grenada Island. D'Estaing had been frustrated in his admittedly feeble attempt
to take St Lucia, but had succeeded in capturing St Vincent and Grenada.[8] The
admiral had time only to report that Beaumarchais's flagship *Proud Rodrigue*
had kept its post 'on the line' and that it had contributed to the success of the
King's forces in a recent naval battle. The ship had been conveying ten merchant
ships when it had been called upon to join the French forces of Grenada, and
he knew that Beaumarchais would forgive him for 'having used the ship so well,
as your interests will not suffer, rest assured of it.' The brave Captain Montaud
had unfortunately been killed in the action, and d'Estaing would soon forward
the *statement of graces* [acknowledgement of services rendered to the naval min-
ister] and he hoped that Beaumarchais would help him solicit the rewards and
medals that *his* navy had so richly deserved!

'It is noble of him,' Beaumarchais wrote to Sartine, 'to have thought at the
moment of his victory that a word from him would be appreciated by me.'
He took great pride in the note from the admiral, 'as a passionate lover of my
country, against the arrogant English,' and he sincerely mourned 'my brave
Montaud;' but he also took a childish joy in knowing that the English 'who
have been tearing me up in their papers for the past four years, will be able to
read there that one of *my* ships contributed to the taking of the most fertile of
their possessions.'

He was also overjoyed to realize that his home-grown enemies, and those of
the admiral and the ministers who had supported him, would now be 'gnaw-
ing their fingernails' at this splendid success.

Capitalizing on this triumph, he wrote to the King, who had by now been
informed of the fake letter, and who had accepted it as such. 'Sire, I do not ask

for compensation for my work,' Beaumarchais now pleaded. 'Your wise ministers know that I am supremely happy to be always useful to your Majesty ... '

Neither did he ask for compensation for his ship having been commandeered to take part in a naval campaign 'for which it was no longer fitted,' he went on; he was 'too much honoured already by its inclusion into a victorious squadron.' Yet he could not resist reminding King Louis that essentially 'war is a game for Kings, it crushes private individuals' and that the *Proud Rodrigue* had, when pressed into service, been escorting merchant vessels engaged in commercial operations, 'equally useful to the State in another way.'

One of his captains had died, and thirty-five men were no longer fit for service. One of his ships had been wrecked—with three cannon balls in its side and four at the 'floating' line, two of which had gone clear through; its sails were torn to pieces, the rigging all 'chopped up.' His merchant seamen were in a state of complete exhaustion by the time they arrived at Fort Royal,[9] for they had also been pressed into service with the squadron. He had been obliged to send new orders to the head of his little fleet; which, having lost eleven ships, would now be unable to leave under the protection of the *Proud Rodrigue* for at least three months. All this had ruined his company, whose debts were enormous, and which postponed returns should now have been on their way to him—and so he was forced to implore his Majesty for help, although the service he was requesting was of little importance.

It was simply that, having been advised from Grenada that *he* had been charged 90,000 *livres* for urgent repairs to the *Proud Rodrigue*, he could not meet this added expense. On the more than two millions that he had borrowed so far this year for his fleet, he had to pay out 100,000 *ecus*, half on the 25th of that month, and the rest by October. He begged his Majesty to please order the modest sum of 400,000 *livres*, to be *lent* to him, for a few months only, from the royal treasury; '... Count Maurepas knows from experience that I am faithful in my engagements.' When the considerable sums that he expected to receive from Martinique arrived (which was where his merchandise had been sold), he would reimburse the treasury, both capital and *interest*.

It could only be after he had carried out a full accounting, 'alas, impossible today,' that he would be able to submit a statement of his losses (in part due to his flagship having been commandeered by the navy) to the ministers—at which time he would call upon the King's justice for their reimbursement, but it was as a personal favour that he asked for a short-term loan. This loan was agreed to; and, astonishingly, the whole amount was then deducted from a million *livres* indemnity that had been earlier granted him, but which had not been paid for over a year.

This did not mean an end to his financial troubles, however. By November, he was ill again, and this could also have been nervous in origin, for Beaumarchais was now being 'hounded' for the sum of 33,000 *livres* in back-taxes; adding interest 'for twenty years of silence,' the 'devils' had decided to double the sum! Sixty-six thousand *livres*! Plus some 12,000 added for 'expenses,' and 'here I am, obliged to pay 80,000 *livres* to the people who, for twenty years, have owed *me* 40,000! And on the ground that, loathing suits as I do, I have not bothered them!'

He had asked them to make a new accounting, but this had been denied him, even though the judgement against him had been taken by default while he was away from Paris. 'Form, form, form, that awful bailiwick of the legal profession. It serves as a blanket for the iniquity of an atrocious request.' Consign and count, that was the object of his request, and to pay cash, 'if he owed anything,' was the favour he now begged of Maurepas. (The suit in question concerned the relatives of his first wife.)

Maurepas had apparently promised to help him, and Beaumarchais was 'counting on his kindness.' He knew that he could depend upon Monsieur Maurepas being straightforward with him, he grovelled; 'You help people without ceremony whenever you can. That's what I adore in you!'

He also enclosed a 'short' memorial on a petition, which would be reported on Saturday by the solicitor to the Council of Dispatches.[10] It concerned the publication in London of a 'Justificative Memorial' (a written defence) in which France had been harshly criticized. Beaumarchais had sent a similar paper to Monsieur Vergennes, 'very poorly written because I am so ill,' but which contained 'true facts,' capable of countering the many insidious accusations of the St James's Cabinet[11] about the 'alleged perfidies' of their much abused country.

Vergennes wrote to him on his sickbed, to say that he believed they could 'without inconvenience' publish a refutation of the allegations of the 'Justificative Memorial to the Court of London' [St James] regarding Beaumarchais's shipments to America; but he first wanted to see his comments before sending the article to the *Courrier de l'Europe*.

The 'observations' on the 'Justificative Memorial'—as rewritten by Beaumarchais—started with a sustained attack on a 'magnificent ambassador' [Lord Stormont], for misleading the people of his own country in his ministerial dispatches, purely 'in order to augment the misunderstanding between nations.' The memorial was based upon the faulty reports of Viscount Stormont, 'whom I name here without scruple, because he has seemed to invite me to do so, by freely making use of my name and my shipping operations to accuse France of *perfidy*.' It was through 'international fact,' known to all of Europe, that Beaumarchais could dismiss this charge, and he would throw it back upon its authors; which he then proceeded to do. Files at the French Admiralty were crammed with far more damning, and truthful, complaints against the English, 'who today accused us of perfidy.'

But what was their real motive in doing so? Were they trying to mislead the people of Europe, or simply divert their own countrymen's attention from their government's increasingly insane behaviour, while trying to inculpate the French?—even though French ministers had nothing to do with America's independence; 'Nothing.' The 'fire of discontent' that was now 'smouldering all over America,' had not been lit by any action of King Louis XVI's government. All that had happened from the time of the iniquitous Stamp Act of 1766 to the present day was the direct result of the multiple mistakes made by the English administration, the truly astonishing 'imprudence and blindness of the cabinet of St James.'[12]

France had remained strictly neutral throughout the 'intestine' quarrel of her 'unjust rival'—a neutrality that she had kept with each of the two nations until the time when reason, prudence and the force of circumstances, and above all concern for her own security, had obliged her to publicly change her conduct; if only out of the fear of becoming a victim herself.

Moreover, although the English looked upon recent French actions in their sphere of influence as a breach of faith and an infraction of existing treaties, they must also appreciate that the issue arousing her colonies was unique. It could never be likened to any other seditious movement that might emerge in other colonies of the New World. The fact was that the King of England's refusal to do justice to his subjects in America had been a total subversion of constitutional law. King George had forgotten that he wore his crown as a constitutional monarch and not that of an *absolute* ruler; a role that he had increasingly sought to play.

The fact was that the English nation was itself divided on the subject of freedom for the former colonists since, in a sense, it was relevant to their own civil rights. Even in Parliament, respected men on all sides were now questioning openly whether the English themselves were not more rebellious to the 'constitutional charter' than were the Americans. The fact was that a noble lord[13] had proposed 'in front of the whole house' that the opposition should withdraw from Parliament in protest at the actions of the King and his government. In a case of such abuse, the people had the right to recall powers so ill-administered, because such a decision as that of making war upon the Americans belonged to the people, in their capacity as the first founders of the English constitution.

The King of France, however, had remained superbly neutral throughout this quarrel between the two nations. Many academic 'logicians' had argued over the advisability of his Majesty respecting the commercial rights of a nation which did not respect the rights of anyone's commerce, or to prohibit his own merchants from sailing to North American ports, even though France was not at war with the inhabitants. It had been decided that, by the absolute right of his neutrality, the King owed both nations a scrupulously equal treatment. France could no more deny her merchants the freedom to do business with America than she could deny them the right to any country in Europe, or *England*.

At least that was, in the writer's opinion, the conduct that the King of France should have scrupulously followed; but he was forced to confess that this 'youthful and virtuous King,' while recognizing that the French merchants had grounds in asking for protection for the commerce they wanted to open with America, had listened to the diplomatic arguments of his ministers, whose conclusions had been otherwise—ministers who must today repent of their judgement, in the light of the arguments put forward by the 'honest writer' of the 'Justicative Memorial;' a man who now accuses them of 'perfidy,' despite their having done everything in their power to accommodate his English masters. The writer of this present article had been personally injured by the repressive authority of these ministers while trying to encourage the 'very active efforts' of the men of commerce who were more truly enlightened as to the true interests of France.

He could only conclude that it had been an excess of consideration for the enemies of French commerce that had made the ministers deaf to his entreaties; for which they had never received the slightest thanks from the other side of the Channel. If France had only imitated England's example, then France could have taken every advantage of their predicament. The French navy could have fallen upon the English fleet, or seized her possessions in the Caribbean—which, far from pushing France into war, would have condemned a powerless England into an eternal peace. Was it through the tenderness of conscience or honour that France had done none of these things?

It only remained for the writer to prove, in answer to the 'Justificative Memorial,' regarding the attacks upon French commerce, the writer's person and his views, as well as the alleged cooperation of the French ministry, that the Viscount Stormont had circulated false reports about all of these matters. He agreed 'frankly and straightforwardly' that French merchants, among whom he counted himself, *had* shipped arms and munitions to America; but they had done so in spite of the numerous obstructions placed in their way by their administration. The English writer of the 'Justificative Memorial' was, however, *wrong* to suggest that their efforts amounted to the criminal act of 'smuggling.' Did he not know that wares, whose exchange or sale is free in one kingdom, do not become contraband there just because its exportation to a certain destination may be detrimental to the interests of another foreign power?

In spite of Lord Stormont, who had tried to turn the French merchants into the vile instruments of their ministers' perfidy, the writer would argue that his commercial colleagues had done no more than balance the risks with the advantages involved in trading with America. Again, in spite of Lord Stormont, the British cabinet, and the manifesto writer, none of his fellow merchants had ever supposed that they owed an unjust England the courtesy of refraining from trading with a country that had become their enemy. They had all, on the contrary, deduced that the Americans—having more pressing needs as a result of their war with England—would set a higher price on the commodities they required. In this respect, French commerce operated in exactly the same way that any other country, *including Great Britain*, would perform.

After this, Beaumarchais taunts the British for their failures in America, exulting in the success of the Americans' efforts to free themselves. Being Beaumarchais, he also confessed to being elated by the fact that it had been his writings and his example that had first encouraged the French manufacturers and merchants to seek this new outlet in the new United States; but, being 'Figaro,' he cannot resist censuring his own government for allowing the British ambassador to influence them to the point of ruining the French merchants' enterprises by failing to give them the full protection they could have expected. Beaumarchais/Figaro's response, in fact, then became a catalogue of complaints against his own government, citing the many instances in which they had given in to Stormont's 'false' accusations.

He also brought up the subject of the many would-be soldiers—'most of them not being French'—who had volunteered their services to the Americans, and had again drawn upon King Louis's ministers the wrath of Lord Stormont, while those seeking to fight in the *British* ranks, against the Americans, had of course gained his permission to do so without any difficulties being raised. Had milord never considered that it was not the duty of a neutral power to interfere in the choices made by free men? What was it to the French upon whose side these brave adventurers exerted their courage?

Although politics is nothing but a sublime imposture anywhere, no ambassador has ever taken such liberties with the sublimity of his! France, the Viscount storms, was sending these troops to America! Were there many men who reasoned as he did in England? Was he not aware that Congress had used very few of the men who been sent to them, 'by their agents in Europe,' and had refused service to most of them? Would they have done this had they thought that these warriors had been expressly sent to aid them by a King whose friendship and assistance they

were so eagerly soliciting? And how did his Excellency think the King of France
would have viewed the insult of these officers being so summarily dismissed? Only
to imagine that the French administration had been supplying troops to America
was a further proof of the illogicality of his lordship's thinking.

His lordship had been very careful to omit any mitigating factors in his
reports to the Court of St James, but he could not deny them when challenged.
Indeed, the writer had left out a thousand other facts in this reply, equally
'distressing for our commerce,' but he hoped that this extract would suffice
to show the untrustworthiness of the allegations contained in the 'Justicative
Memorial.' Whenever the ambassador circulates some political lie or false news,
all detrimental to the Americans or the French, the proper response should
always be 'Don't you believe it, Sir—that is *pure* Stormont.' As, indeed, was
the 'Justificative Memorial;' it was pure Stormont. Except for the style perhaps,
which would not have lacked charm if its miserable author had managed to
overlook the fact that Lord Stormont had supplied the gist of the narrative.

There was more, and all along the same lines. As in an opera libretto,
Beaumarchais believed that important information should always be repeated at
least three times, and so throughout one hundred and four paragraphs, he railed
against the injustices done to France, to King Louis, his ministers—and himself—by the unjust English; who, by her 'usurpations, bad faith, arrogance and
despotism, stood in a class by herself, apart from all decent human societies.'

Beaumarchais's acute if highly theatrical observations on the pamphlet
known as the 'Justificative Memorial of the Court of London' were published
in November 1779; but the French administration, alarmed by its outspoken-
ness, took fright as usual, and the pamphlet was suppressed within a few days
of its appearance.

Printed Matter

Despite its quick suppression Beaumarchais's 'Observations' still managed to offend a number of highly placed people. The Duc de Praslin[1] wrote to Vergennes on 17 December, wishing to point out that there was an error on page 37, which was a slur upon the Treasury of 1763. The author had incorrectly stated that the government of the late King Louis XV had cravenly limited the number of French vessels to be retained in the peace treaty drawn up between Britain and France, solely to satisfy the British. If the offending pamphlet was the work of one individual, he was prepared to let it pass, as being the product of a man 'who had not troubled to read the treaty he had written about;' but if this work had been published under the authority of the government, as the public believed it had, then these so-called 'true statements' involved the duke's honour.

Vergennes of all people, protested Praslin, must surely know that there had been no clause fixing the number of ships that Great Britain 'deigned' to suffer France to keep, nor was one ever proposed. 'I assure you that peace would not have been made if our enemies had offered it at the price of dishonour.' The fleet had, in fact, in the years since 1763, been 'much restored,' and the British had seen this restoration with a 'worried and a jealous eye.' Praslin wished to have the article publicly refuted; King Louis XVI owed it to the honour of his grandfather and 'the nation that he governed.'

The Duc de Choiseul, too, wished to draw attention to a misstatement that had particularly outraged him. As he could not believe that Vergennes had authorized the pamphlet without reading the offending passages, and therefore approved of them, he now thought it imperative for the minister to properly inform both the King and the public of its lack of authenticity—particularly in the matter of 'limiting the number of ships that France was permitted to maintain.' This was a false and absurd allegation that Choiseul thoroughly denounced and such a statement could have very dangerous repercussions.

Both these eminent men agreed that the King must publicly deny the argument of this pernicious statement, for the good of the nation. It was far from him, said Praslin, to fear any reversal of the present state of hostilities between France and Great Britain, but who could answer for the events of another outright war? Should France lose this one as she had done the last, the British, who had not earlier thought of limiting the forces of France in 1763, could—inspired by this memorial, where it is set out as *fact*—advance a similar condition of peace, '… Without fear of contradiction from a government who imagined they had already suffered this indignity.'

Choiseul was of the opinion that the writer of the 'Observations,' by introducing such an invention into his treatise, had done the ministry an immense disservice by 'floating such a preposterous suggestion.'

Beaumarchais gave a lot of thought to what Vergennes revealed to him of the letters from the two veterans of the offending peace treaty; but he concluded that the solution the minister preferred—which was to follow the line indicated by the dukes—might have an equally 'terrible effect,' since an official denial would simply confirm the general opinion that there must be some truth in his accusation. It would be far better, Beaumarchais reasoned, to have an *erratum* inserted into the next issue of the *Courrier de l'Europe*, 'which would satisfy everybody.'

He would send this new correction to the ministers, and if they did not find it sufficient, they could suggest alterations; but he must point out that if they suppressed the *Courrier* entirely it would be impossible to have the amendment inserted, and so the situation would remain as it was. He hoped they would not deprive him of the chance to correct the offending sentences from the text, 'saying something very noble and appropriate'—for it would be much simpler for 'an honourable man to retrace his own steps' in such a frank manner than for the administration to blame a writer whose sole object had been to honour France and the King. Could the ministers not see to what use the English would put their suppression? Indeed, why crack down on a whole work for the sake of a few words that can be expertly removed? An error of fact was easy to retract.

He also wanted it made clear that he had already received 1,200 letters congratulating him for a piece of writing 'that uplifts the hearts of all good Frenchmen, the court excepted, where there was little patriotism.' The English would say that everything he had asserted was false, hence the complete suppression of the work, and the French would again be at a disadvantage against English rumour—while the reproach of perfidy against the two dukes would return with all its strength, simply because the record had not been set straight, but only smothered.

Beaumarchais had not long to wait for an answer, for on 19 December, a sentence of suppression was passed against the offending article, which meant that the issue in which it had appeared could no longer be put on sale. The pamphlet had, in any case, been published and circulated in violation of the 'regulations of the library,'² and it was forbidden for any publisher, printer, bookseller and others to print, sell, trade in or distribute any remaining copies—all of which should be surrendered to the Registrar of the Council within two weeks. This judgement was posted everywhere, and the Lieutenant General of Police in Paris was left to execute his Majesty's express orders.

Beaumarchais, outraged by the cabinet's actions, and ill with a fever, returned to his bed; but, always anxious to outwit his superiors, he wrote to the *Courrier* on the same day, asking the editors to publish his 'new' reflections in a supplement to be specially printed. It was, he said, all a question of a misprinted word on page 37. He had meant to write 'agencies' not 'vessels,' and this one word would have altered the entire meaning of the sentence, rendering it more accurate, 'Since it stated an unquestionable fact.'

Despite his fever, Beaumarchais also wrote to the ministers, complaining of their treatment of 'a warrior fighting for his country.' It was grossly unfair of the King to condemn a writer of his reputation to the ranks of 'the scum of scandalous libellers,' simply because he had fallen into error, and even though he had offered to correct it. Why had they not let him straighten out the matter in his own way? 'I have never blushed to admit publicly that I had made a mistake,' and what could be better all round than for an author to make an open and *free* denial, particularly one who could have it broadcast as rapidly as himself? Was it fitting to reward zeal, hard work and patriotism with the sort of dishonour meted out to pranksters? By the sarcastic tone of these letters it was obvious that Beaumarchais meant them to be circulated, or at least for them to be read aloud in the political salons of Paris and beyond, for he was 'writing for the gallery.'

Before dismissing him, he begged the ministers to read what he was about to send to the *Courrier* and to *The North Briton*,³ a radical English publication edited by John Wilkes, and famous for its scurrilous articles attacking the British government. He had suggested in his article for the *Courrier* that all those who sent back their 'faulty' copy would receive two new correct ones, although he did not say who would pay for them! To cancel 'the great principles of reply' would only further discredit his piece. He also wished to know if the Duc de Choiseul had dismissed it using words dictated by the ministers? If he had not, he found it very suspicious that the duke had employed an almost identical form of condemnation. The 'fact' he had presented may have, perhaps, been erroneous, but it was hardly *absurd*.

All that he required was permission to make amends, 'honourably and fruitfully' he pleaded, for how could his government have the cruelty to deliver his person and his work to the degradation of a stigma? Then followed a hint of blackmail; 'My friends at the *Courrier* would only have to publish

the 1,500 letters I have received in the past six days, in which good citizens
have poured out their hearts in thankful approval' to make the government's
position untenable. But it was not a good tactic to remind the ministers (and
his enemies) that his writing had been compared to that of Tacitus (a republican), Cardinal de Retz (an opponent of the royal prerogative), and Algernon
Sidney (who had been beheaded in 1683 for anti-royalist activities!).

He must have been surprised when Vergennes agreed to forward his
'Observations' wherever he wanted, although he warned him that it was too
late for them to have any real effect (which may explain why he was allowing
them to be made public). The count was sorry that Beaumarchais was taking
this matter 'so hard,' for there really was no reason for him to feel bad about
it. He had certainly committed an error, the more serious because he could
easily have checked it at source, but the manner in which Beaumarchais proposed to make amends was 'not obliging, either for those concerned or for the
nation itself;' for how could France maintain her dignity if she confessed that
she had suffered the humiliation that Beaumarchais had 'exposed'?

He was wrong to assume that the government had taken their judgement
from the Duc de Choiseul, since all men of the 'same mind' saw the problem in the same way. 'Check your comparison, see for yourself whether it
is not improper. You must learn, Sir, to accept what you cannot prevent.'
Beaumarchais would remember this rebuke, for these exact words are repeated
by the master to the manservant in *The Marriage of Figaro*.

The Duc de Praslin, too, had to be satisfied; and Vergennes wrote to him
saying the King and Council had been as shocked as he by the 'absurd and
mendacious statement,' but his Grace must understand that this was merely
a comment by a private individual, 'without any mission.' It was a careless
piece, and it had been thought advisable to destroy every trace of it. He
enclosed a copy of the judgement rendered by the King, and he hoped the
duke would find it satisfactory. Since Vergennes was a not-so-secret enemy of
Choiseul and Praslin—among many others—they might have thought that
he was behind the writing.

But the two dukes were not the only men to be outraged by the offending piece. Count Bulkley, Lord Clare, who had served for some years in the
French army, and who considered himself 'the most ardent Englishman who
ever suffered in the service of France,' (he was actually Irish), had also read
the 'Observations'—where he had been surprised to see himself slandered by
the suggestion that he had sought permission from the French government to
leave their service in order to bear arms against the Americans.[4] This 'punish-
able insolence' could not be allowed to pass unchecked!

Vergennes well knew, Clare raged, that when he had asked for permission to serve with the English army in America, he had done so only because he wished to acquire new knowledge of his chosen profession. At that time the quarrel was only between Great Britain and America, and the name he bore being an insurmountable obstacle for service with the latter, he did not have any choice in the matter; but from the time that the circumstances had changed, he had returned to France, and had since continually solicited the minister of war to be sent against the English, 'for whom I am suspected of so much partiality.' He could only hope that Vergennes would not fail to punish 'such false and insolent remarks' about an officer who had served France 'without reproach;' otherwise he must deal with this 'impudent libel' in his own way—which meant a duel. Beaumarchais was, alas, no swordsman.

Others, some of them previous victims of the writer's wit, were only too happy to join in a general lambasting of the author, for many signers to 'the last peace treaty' had also been outraged by it. Their complaints, filed with Vergennes's office, were duly reported to the Council. They were mostly concerned by the judgement that had suppressed the pamphlet but which had 'strangely' not inflicted any penalty on the infamous writer (which only confirmed the rumour that he could not have dared to publish such a libel without first communicating it to the ministers).

Another duke, Nivernais,[5] a plenipotentiary at the last peace treaty, had also joined in the controversy, and it was as a result of these three ducal requests that the Council's judgement of suppression had come about; yet even this judgement proved the inconsistency of the ministers' thinking. For what was most peculiar about this business was that the author of the 'Observations,' whose name appeared boldly on the title page, had broken the laws of the Library, an offence for which others had gone to prison, yet he remained free and unpunished—a circumstance that led many to believe that the 'Sieur de B' had been authorized to publish the piece after all. It was a 'slap given by the ministers on that villain's cheek,' according to a wit of the court—a jibe that Beaumarchais also repeats in *The Marriage of Figaro*. 'How did you like that slap you recently received?' the count asks the young page Cherubin; 'He received it on *my* cheek,' Figaro answers. '*That's* the way that lords do justice.'

Beaumarchais heard a rumour that Admiral d'Estaing was planning to write an 'apology for his military career'[6] and he wrote, earnestly begging him to 'chase away that idea.' He beseeched the admiral 'on behalf of all those who honour you,' but he was mostly writing in the interests of Maurepas, who wanted d'Estaing to keep silent with regard to the critical attacks that had been made against the minister during a recent campaign. Beaumarchais had hopes of the admiral taking office as one of the twenty Marshals of France, for in a sense he now saw Estaing as his particular protégé.

Estaing returned from capturing Grenada in July 1779, and was crowned with flowers by Queen Marie-Antoinette and her ladies, wearing white satin 'Grenada' hats. Royal attitudes towards the American revolutionaries were seen to be changing, with the Queen's hairdresser creating a special coiffure '*aux insurgents*' in honour of the rebels. A new ballet was performed in the autumn, with an American revolutionary hero, John Paul Jones, as a leading character. There were dances by American officers and their ladies and a display of military drill in the third act, (sensibly performed by professional soldiers). For Beaumarchais, however, this only proved that royal interest in the distant military struggles in which he was daily engaged 'had no more substance than the passing fashion.'[7]

He soon received news from America that was not so amusing. Francy had written twice from Williamsburg,[8] sending him fifty-six letters of exchange from Congress, and on 26 February 1780, Beaumarchais acknowledged receipt of these. The first message announced that neither the *Proud Rodrigue*, or the fleet that it escorted, had arrived at Chesapeake Bay, since they had been officially attached to a royal convoy in the Caribbean, and two million *livres* would not make up for the loss caused by this critical delay. In fact Beaumarchais was even more aggrieved than Francy about this, since he knew what his agent didn't—that he had agreed, as early as October 1778, to let his ships then sailing to Virginia take the long way round by the French Islands, to carry supplies needed for the troops there, and so become allied to the French fleet, then on manoeuvres. Beaumarchais knew, in spite of all the pledges his crew would not be touched, that his loaded ships had nonetheless been delayed from October 1778 to May 1779. He had shipped goods from one French harbour to another, some four or five times at the army's request, only to then have Admiral de la Mothe-Piquet[9] order his ships to follow him to Martinique, even though their papers were arranged for Santo Domingo.

Worse had followed, since once his unfortunate flotilla arrived at Martinique, Admiral d'Estaing had picked the cream of his crews and taken the *Proud Rodrigue* to Grenada, where its captain, Montaud, had been killed. Estaing had then returned too soon for Beaumarchais's ships to load new merchandise for the North American ports, and most had sailed away empty; even the possibility of loading up at Santo Domingo, where Estaing had put in briefly, had not helped at all.

But what neither Beaumarchais nor Francy knew was that the merchant flotilla had been led by the King's squadron from Santo Domingo to Savannah, where the *Proud Rodrigue*, then still in service under Estaing's orders, had been left at Charleston, South Carolina. Moreover, on the admiral's return to Europe on October 26, he had ordered his deputy, Grasse,[10] to convoy seven vessels to be refitted at Chesapeake Bay, and to take Beaumarchais's fleet along with them.

The *Proud Rodrigue*, 'running out of every supply and full of sick people,' had gone to join the French fleet at Charleston, but they had crossed without linking up. What was worse, Grasse preferred to return to Santo Domingo rather than to obey the order to make for the bay, so the merchant ships were left unprotected. Moreover, Grasse had also taken off with two of the captured English ships that Estaing had ceded to Beaumarchais as a prize, to partly compensate him for the losses he had sustained when the admiral appropriated his merchant fleet.

Beaumarchais now learned, from Francy's letters of 24 and 26 December, that many other ships of his had fallen into British hands, and the *Proud Rodrigue* had reached its destination only with great difficulty. 'What a mess this is! It is enough to make one lose one's head!' But he would try to bear with it, and go on working and spending money. As soon as the exact figures would allow him to compute his losses, he would ask the King and his ministers to compensate him.

Such recoveries, though, were based only on fixed losses and disregarded the advantages that would have resulted from a good trip. One year had been lost, and now, with more debts accruing and returns failing to arrive, the impossibility of resuming preparations for a new trip made him despair. 'But "courage and truth," you know that's my motto.'

Francy, too, was entertaining false hopes if he imagined that letters of exchange would be negotiable in Europe; even if he thought they were as secure as Beaumarchais believed them to be unsound; a delay of three years made them useless to him. After the length of time that he had already spent waiting—another three years almost—all he would receive for his pains was a partial remittance payable three years hence! What company could sustain such delays without going under? He would have to look for new resources in Europe, since so little was reaching him from America. Francy was the only one who could even guess at what frustrations he was enduring.

To make matters worse, Francy had further news for him—it would seem that their new ambassador to Congress, the Chevalier La Luzerne,[11] was reported to have taken 'against him.' This news certainly surprised Beaumarchais, as he was not acquainted with the second ambassador; moreover, he knew that Luzerne could not have received a bad account of him from the Comte de Vergennes, 'Who would be as surprised as I am, if he knew of it!' He advised Francy to treat the ambassador with all the courtesy that his position required, but to carry on his business steadfastly, without letting petty personal ill will bother him. If the chevalier carried matters to a point of harming their interests, Francy's duty was to take accurate note of it and to send Beaumarchais some proofs; it would then be up to him to seek justice at Versailles.

Francy was, despite their straightened circumstances, to continue as before, since most French shippers were now discouraged and refusing to fit out and load their ships for America. 'But if the French flag of convenience is never seen on any ship, the Americans will look on the treaty of commerce with France as being illusory. Then the necessity of getting from Europe that which they most need will drive them back to England, and we will be left holding the bag.' For that reason alone he would go on encouraging all those that he believed had enough spirit and courage to take advantage of it, or at least to serve the country. 'My desire for my country's success will leave me only with my last breath.'

He also sent Francy a copy of the 'Observations.'

XXIII

Patriot or Traitor?

Beaumarchais pleaded with Vergennes on behalf of Silas Deane; 'I cannot keep silent when I see an honest man suffer as the result of injustice'—or, rather, the ingratitude of a country 'which he has served with such zeal.'

Indeed American ingratitude had been extraordinary, as Francy reported in his letters to Beaumarchais. Almost from the first days of his arrival back in America, Deane had been involved in an acrimonious dispute with a faction in Congress that opposed any payment to Hortalez & Co, with the Lee and Adams families leading the opposition. Richard Henry Lee, Arthur's eldest brother, was deeply involved with the controversy surrounding Deane, intimating that Deane was an unscrupulous rascal who had continued to stand by Beaumarchais simply because the two men were raking in huge war profits together—and despite the fact that Beaumarchais had yet to receive the sums he demanded from Congress!

There was fierce hostility towards Deane, who was seen as being responsible for the unwelcome arrival in America of the French military party. The anti-Deane party (largely influenced by the Lee faction) also sought to destroy Benjamin Franklin's reputation, but they almost succeeded in hounding the life out of Silas Deane. James Lovell, in particular, as a member of the Committee for Foreign Affairs, detested him for his part in recruiting French volunteers. 'These Frenchman have used me up quite,' he complained, when having to interpret for the French officers. Never a diplomat, he was 'liberally gifted in intrigue and he loved mystery and mystification.'

Deane's problems had, in fact, started back in 1777 when Richard Henry Lee had used his newly acquired power on the Commercial Committee of Congress to have his brother William appointed as a commercial agent in Paris; for once there, along with his brother Arthur, he had started the cabal that was to end with Deane's recall. In this they had been joined by Thomas Morris, the younger half-brother of the 'financier of the Revolution,' who had also secured him the appointment as chief commercial agent in France.[1] It was Thomas's misconduct while acting in this capacity that would help to create such trouble for Robert Morris when Deane returned to America and exposed the activities of these conspirators, although Robert managed to stay out of the controversy until January 1779.

Deane's supporters, though, finally succeeded in getting an official state-ment from the Comte de Vergennes in support of their man. In it, Vergennes stated that Hortalez & Co was a private, commercial firm, but that some of its war stock had come from French arsenals (with the understanding that these depleted stocks should be replaced by the firm at a later date). But before this information—critical to his defence—reached Philadelphia, Deane had blown the entire matter into a public scandal by publishing a remark-able letter on 5 December 1778. In it, he not only denounced Arthur Lee's machinations at Paris but also accused Congress of neglect and of appalling ignorance of foreign affairs!

A direct result of this open letter was that Congress then split more vehe-mently into 'Pro-and Anti-Deanites.' Henry Laurens, definitely a member of the latter group, was thought to have been extremely unfair to Silas Deane in his public statements, having also charged Robert Morris with fraud.[2] This led to the failure of his motion to suspend hearings until Congress could hold a special investigation of the 'mysterious' operations of Hortalez & Co, and since Laurens felt that this showed a lack of faith in him, he resigned as the President of Congress on 9 December 1778. John Jay replaced Laurens; and Jay, the Chief Justice of New York, was a pro-Deanite.

Thomas Paine, the Secretary of the Committee of Foreign Affairs,[3] then entered the lists as a supporter of Arthur Lee, attacking both Deane and Robert Morris in the press. On 2 January 1779 he claimed publicly that he had written evidence that France had promised the supplies as a gift to the Americans even before Deane had reached Paris. The French ambassador[4] was forced to issue an official denial, followed up with a formal protest against Paine's indiscretion in revealing 'classified' information. Under pressure, Paine resigned within a week of making his statement, and by 15 January Beaumarchais had been given the written apology from Congress that had so delighted him. Morris was also exonerated of any sharp practice.[5]

The sordid controversy did have at least one positive result, although it came far too late for Beaumarchais. Arthur Lee, now *persona non grata* at Versailles, was recalled to America at Vergennes's request on 27 September 1779. William Lee and his fellow troublemaker, Ralph Izard, had earlier been dismissed in June. This now left 'the old doctor' as the sole commissioner in Paris, John Adams having embarked at Nantes on 22 March 1779, to sail home.

In 1780, after almost two years in America, Silas Deane returned to Europe, to draw a line under all the business that he had earlier undertaken for Congress, (at least according to him). After congressional hearings on his mission, Deane had declined the $10,500 in depreciated money that they had offered him in recompense for his services and expenses, although this is again according only to his account. He in fact returned to France as a private citizen, and had returned very possibly in order to pursue his undercover affairs with Edward Bancroft; for when he arrived in France for the second time on July 27 1780, he stayed briefly with Benjamin Franklin at his temporary home at Passy, and Dr Bancroft was then employed as a secretary for the commission.

In fact, of all the Americans surrounding Franklin, the New England physician was his most trusted aide, a friend even. An affable and unusually gifted man—writer, inventor, (he had made important discoveries in the field of textile dyes)—Bancroft proved an ideal companion for the old philosopher-scientist. Consistently hardworking and fluent in French, he had made himself even more indispensable to Franklin in Paris than he had in London; and, again, he presumably served as his spy.

Only John Adams had instinctively disliked Bancroft, since he regarded him as a gossip, and found his habitual mocking of Christianity offensive. He also thought him basically dishonest, and he rightly suspected him of using inside information, gained within the delegation and at Versailles, to profit on the London Stock Market. Indeed the mix of private and public business within the delegation was considerable, with not only Bancroft, but also their host, Le Ray de Chaumont, and possibly even Benjamin Franklin himself speculating on the secret French support for the American war, and the steady flow of information making this possible. If Deane had returned to Paris in order to take advantage through Bancroft, he was to be disappointed, for there was no room for him at the Hotel de Valentinois, and he was forced to seek other quarters.

Once again, Deane sought out Beaumarchais, who explained to Vergennes that Deane had expected to find enough money in Paris to live on until his return to America, where—according to Beaumarchais—the settlement of Deane's accounts would reimburse him for the advances he had made to the Americans; but, as he explained to Vergennes, 'either through the dishonesty or the negligence of his friends or agents, he now finds himself deprived of the strictest necessaries.' Deane had applied to Franklin for funds, only to be told there were no instructions from America to furnish him with money. Deane, having 'opened his heart' to him, Beaumarchais was now worried at the state of his mental stability; '… He displays a bitterness that borders on something more fatal.'

Beaumarchais was now himself in such dire financial straits that he could only offer Deane any real help 'in the future.' He was, however, of the opinion that it would be unwise to push a man such as Deane to despair, a man who had rendered great service to the State—'Which is what his wretched new-born republic is doing constantly to men of merit, men who have espoused its interests. I can already see defections so deadly to its cause that I cannot but shudder at such examples.'

He believed that Deane still belonged to the 'French party,' and his devotion in this regard accounted for nearly all his enemies in America. Could French policy ever do anything more generous and appropriate than what Beaumarchais dared to propose to the minister? One thousand *louis d'or* granted to this unfortunate man would 'uplift his heart to a sense of gratitude from which some day France may draw the greatest service. He has a beautiful soul and a sensitive heart.'

But Deane needed *prompt* assistance in whatever way Vergennes wished to offer it, Beaumarchais urged, either as a gift or as a loan; 'rest assured the money would bear the highest interest, if only in terms of one man's devotion to our cause.' Deane's passion when speaking to Beaumarchais about his present situation, and the ingratitude that was the cause of it, had affected the Frenchman deeply. He would never, as the minister surely knew, offer him a pointless or irresponsible suggestion, but he left this matter to 'monsieur's wisdom.'

Only a few days later, on 9 December, Deane wrote to thank Vergennes's secretary for the 'seasonal assistance offered to me.' He would, he said, have called at Versailles to thank the minister earlier had he not been confined to his chamber by a severe cold; but he wished to reassure the count that he hoped to have his accounts 'finally and fully stated within a few weeks, and my affairs so arranged, that I will be in a position to repay the sum lent me. But time will never efface his kindness from my mind.'

In April, Beaumarchais again reminded the President of Congress of their great debt to him; if the Congress kept records, they must be aware that he had already written to them to this effect. He had come to America's rescue and it was now their duty to come to his. A trick had been played upon them, but they were now in full possession of the truth and he expected them to act accordingly. Everything that had been sent to them was delivered according to specific arrangements made between himself and Silas Deane; *and Deane was the only person that he had ever dealt with.*

So far, Beaumarchais wrote, he had received some 2,400,000 *livres* worth of letters of exchange, *excluding interest*, which was all just worthless paper to him. The ruinous deals that he had been forced to make simply to keep afloat were, it would seem, to be his only reward for serving Congress—that is, apart from their commendation of 15 January 1789. It was the first gratifying word that he had received from America, but it confirmed to him that it was through error only that he had been deprived of answers to all his previous letters.

Silas Deane was now in France, and their unregulated accounts had now been finally verified and closed. Beaumarchais hoped that they would kindly check the statement submitted and remit more *realizable* funds to him in Europe.

It had also occurred to him, while going over the accounts, that Deane had spoken about the Congress allowing him a commission of 5% upon all purchases that he succeeded in securing in Europe. Although Deane had not pursued the subject, Beaumarchais suspected that he was at present somewhat anxious in regard to this promise being fulfilled, and it distressed him to see a man whose ability and exertions had rendered such service remaining uncompensated. He had therefore decided to offer Deane a commission of 2% on all remittances that he received from Congress, either in money or in merchandise, for the mass of the purchases made by them in Europe, and which were included in their accounts. This offer, however, was to apply only in the event that Deane's enemies prevailed in influencing Congress to withhold the promised commission from him.

The letter that he wrote to Deane on 11 September 1781 was to serve as Deane's 'title' on Beaumarchais, his heirs and assigns, for the 2% commission he offered him, supported only by an affidavit that Congress had done him an injustice in denying him his rightful commission. Beaumarchais regretted that this was a poor compensation for Deane's labours, but he could only deduct it from a commission of 10% allowed by Congress to himself; which as Deane well knew, was far from repairing the immense losses sustained over so many years. The commission, however paltry, was really no more than a token of the esteem and affection in which he held his former associate.

Francy had returned to France, but was now too ill to undertake the return voyage to America. Beaumarchais therefore had to postpone the closing and settling of his accounts with the Congress until his man was sufficiently recovered; he alone being capable of 'picking up the thread of this affair,' having done so very largely on his own initiative for the past three years.

Indeed, Beaumarchais was growing increasingly disenchanted with the slipshod and laborious processes of democracy; had he been dealing with professional merchants, matters would never have been so complicated. But doing business with the U.S. government was proving impossible, he thought, for the simple reason that they had entrusted the administration of their most valuable interests to an assembly of citizens, a Congress whose membership was continually changing before vital decisions could be reached. This meant that the new members were always liable to view earlier transactions, which might have already been investigated thoroughly, with the same uncertainty they would bring to the discussions of any 'new business.' Hence his utter dependence upon the one man, Francy, who could follow the situation from 'year's change to year's change.'

Meanwhile, Beaumarchais sent Robert Morris, then superintendent of finances,[6] an abstract of his accounts as settled by Deane, and he asked Morris to persuade Congress to assist him at the first opportunity; contradictorily asking him for bills of exchange, such as he had received in 1779.[7] He could, he wrote, no longer bear the weight of his unpaid claims on America, (which would suffice to enable him to pay off his debts in Europe). Neither Congress nor himself, he reasoned, should look too closely at the losses he would incur in 'negotiating' that paper, for he had come to see it as one of the unavoidable consequences resulting from the nature of 'the thing involved.' He would, however, be grateful simply for the remittance of at least a part of what he was owed, 'reserving any objection,' until his man was again well enough to travel to Philadelphia. His very embarrassing situation now forced him to receive what was his natural due 'as a favour' from the Congress, and he would be very obliged to Morris if he could now expedite matters.

For now, Beaumarchais continued to see Silas Deane as a victim. The 'misfortunes and malice with which his character … has been aspersed, have not changed the opinion that I had formed of him.' Even the complaints that he had heard voiced against certain of Deane's 'writings,' (which he had, in any case, not read), could not turn him against the American. He was only disillusioned to perceive that 'there are intrigues among Republicans as well as at the Courts of King's.'

Deane's 'writings,' the thirteen letters written by him to friends and family between May and September in 1781, had allegedly been intercepted by the British at sea, and afterwards published in the *Royal Gazette*.[8] They contained the American's highly disillusioned impression of the corruption that he believed to be already at work in his own country, at least in the way that it applied to his own situation, and the letters predictably raised a furore in Congress when they were published. Outraged, the congressmen branded Deane a traitor in addition to the older charges of profiteering and dishonest methods.

To complete his humiliation, in February 1782—after he had written a long letter to Benjamin Franklin, complaining of his treatment by his countrymen—instead of backing him, the wily old politician simply replied, 'It appears that your resentments and passions have overcome your reason and judgement'—a charge that could never have been levelled at Beaumarchais, whose complaints against *his* treatment by Congress were reiterated again and again, but with the same ingratiating diplomacy. By now he recognized that he would have to repeat the same message constantly as he was forever addressing a new audience. It was with increasing bitterness that he reminded them of the time when, 'crushed by war and England's persecution,' they had sent secret emissaries to all the powers of Europe. A time when he alone, 'for the good of mankind,' had worked unstintingly to find them friends in Europe, 'to excite hearts and minds in your favour.' Through his writings, he could even claim to be one of the first writers to influence all 'sensible people' throughout Europe in their favour, besides helping their secret agents—sometimes in peril of his life—as his correspondence in ciphers with one of the U.S. secret agents (then residing in England) would show when laid before them.

He had also 'scattered gold like straw' to remove the obstacles constantly placed in his way. Not to do so would have been to insult the nation he had elected to serve; 'From the Frenchman that I was, I became an American,' he boasted.

They were not to suppose that he exaggerated the facts in the petition that he now sent out to them; only the most righteous indignation had altered the style and character of his writing—but if they were only to compare this present letter with the one that he had written to them in *1776*, full of the ardent zeal which had made him espouse their cause, they would see how their bewildering and vexing treatment had brought about such alterations. He had spent the past three years in seeking for a solution to this incredible problem.

In all honesty he had been unaware that other people were trying to obtain credit from the gentlemen of Congress by using his name, 'deceiving them basely on my account.' If they were to believe the falsehoods of these 'honourable schemers,' then he was to be regarded only as an 'obscure phantom;' but even that still left the question open as to why Congress had always been satisfied to make use of his shipments without ever troubling to acknowledge receipt!

Francy remained too ill to travel to America and had been replaced by a less able mediator; an agent called Le Vaigneur. Beaumarchais now planned to send Silas Deane back to America, to give this letter to Congress, with new evidence of Deane's commitment to their cause—so not only did he expect 'honourable treatment' at last, but he also asked for a public mark of their esteem, and for them to distinguish him in some way.

Yet only 'Figaro' could have demanded recognition in one sentence and suggested blackmail in the next. If he could not obtain honourable justice, he would be 'outraged and mortally wounded,' so what could he do to redeem his reputation? Should he be forced to demand justice at the 'bar of Europe'? Would he be forced to publish an account of his manifold deeds on their behalf, 'suffered and kept secret to this day'? No, he was sure they would not reduce him 'to this horrible extremity;' not a people who were today noble and free; splendid rivals of the proudest sovereigns, and an ally of his King.

Apparently neither his appeal to their sense of justice nor the hint of blackmail had the desired effect. By July 1787, Beaumarchais would still be writing to the 'President of Congress,' repeating his old complaints. There was, in fact, no such executive by then, and the man to whom he addressed his letter, John Jay, had now been named minister to Spain.[9]

When Deane returned to France, he had come, he said, with no other mission but that of settling all the debts for which he had been responsible in generating in Europe. They were to be paid 'with the first monies available to the State,' and Beaumarchais believed Deane to be the only accredited agent of that state. Certainly no letter from the U.S., emanating from any authority, contested Deane's claim to be acting in their name. As a result of his misconception, all his letters were now in Deane's hands, as the American's were in his.

While Beaumarchais was unaware that Deane had no official status, he was also ignorant of the fact that, within weeks of returning to Paris, Deane was writing to his friends in America, telling them of his failing confidence in the cause of independence and advocating an accommodation with Britain. These were letters that he had sent through Bancroft, who showed them to the British authorities, who then pretended they had been intercepted, and later published them in *Rivington's Gazette*[10] (about the same time that Cornwallis had surrendered, on 19 October 1781, thus virtually ending the American Revolution).

With the account seemingly 'settled,' who could have doubted that a *partial* payment, at least, should have been made to Beaumarchais at the earliest opportunity, even if financial difficulties prevented the Congress from discharging the whole debt? Yet he was to wait in vain from 1781 to 1783, when the only answer he received was to see a new agent from Congress arrive in France, charged—Beaumarchais was told—with a mission to discuss, close and settle all the accounts of the important European suppliers. This man was Barclay,[11] (the American consul general in Paris).

Beaumarchais pointed out to him that his accounts had already been discussed and closed in 1781 by Deane, and that they only needed to be settled. Optimistic as ever, Beaumarchais had already closed and settled his own accounts with his major creditors in Europe; his optimism being based on Deane's statement that he was about to be paid in full. As a result, he was now even further in debt.

To his dismay, Barclay told him that he could not acknowledge Deane's actions, explaining that Deane was no longer an accredited servant of the state—that he was, in fact, now seen as an enemy of the American republic, accused of treason, and in virtual exile. For the first time, perhaps, Beaumarchais began to accept that he had misplaced his trust in a man who, on the evidence presented to him by the consul general, matched his own creation 'Figaro' as an arch conniver. He also now fully realized for the first time why Congress had regarded him with such suspicion; believing perhaps that he, too, had been a part of the double-dealing and speculation, the profiteering from their circumstances that Barclay so carefully explained to him.

It was therefore agreed between them that Beaumarchais would re-open his accounts, to allow the new man to re-check them. But to his utter dismay Barclay then decided that it would perhaps be better if they should after all be *destroyed*, since they had been agreed to by the discredited Deane, an untrustworthy auditor! Beaumarchais, shocked almost into a physical collapse at this outrageous response, protested that such a solution was impossible, and after a long debate Barclay allowed that they could send Congress a copy of the account, as closed by Deane—along with any relevant correspondence and with any documents of proof, properly authenticated, so that his superiors might judge the facts of the case. All of this Beaumarchais duly carried out, and once again he waited patiently for a reply from across the ocean.

Meanwhile, the creator of his current misfortunes, the now thoroughly discredited Silas Deane, had fled to 'neutral territory' in Ghent in northwest Belgium. Alarmed by the appearance in Paris of the American consul general, he had departed in such haste that he left many incriminating papers behind; papers that now showed the extent of his involvement with Edward Bancroft; with details of Deane's passing of American and French secrets to his friend, and of their attempts to make a fortune from the secret trade of purchasing supplies for Congress, along with a wealth of speculation and double-dealing.

Thomas Jefferson,[12] when he became U.S. ambassador in Paris, inherited the mess that Deane had left in his wake, and matters came to a head in 1788. A Frenchman named Foulloy had somehow come into possession of Deane's letter book for the year 1777, along with his ledgers for the years 1776 to 1780, claiming that he had taken them after the American had reneged on a debt of 120 guineas. Realizing that they could be used for blackmailing the new American government, Foulloy approached Jefferson at his new residence in the Hotel de Lageac and showed him the two books, saying that he was thinking of selling them to the English; but since the books contained passages that might injure the new nation, he was offering them to their ambassador first.

Jefferson played a cool hand, asking to keep the incriminating volumes for twenty-four hours, to study them in detail. Foolishly, Foulloy agreed, and Jefferson had the most important passages transcribed. These were not concerned with Deane, whose part in the 'John the Painter' act of terrorism was known, but more disturbingly seemed also to implicate Dr Franklin and Robert Morris in the affair. Jefferson was so alarmed by these incriminating sentences that he seriously considered paying Foulloy to have them excised.

Meanwhile, he fobbed off Foulloy by promising to write to Congress, requesting the funds with which to buy them. John Jay, the republic's Secretary for Foreign Affairs, immediately instructed him to complete the purchase without delay, even before seeking permission from Congress, seeing at once the embarrassment the sentences would create; but Jefferson, playing for time, delayed for so long that Foulloy, discouraged by Jefferson's procrastination, cut the price to just 20 guineas, which the ambassador accepted. He then turned over the books and they were destroyed.

Deane meanwhile, feeling insecure in Ghent, crossed over to England.

XXIV

Backlog

In *1785*, Barclay—still consul general—curtly informed Beaumarchais that Congress would agree to nothing, would send him nothing, and would pay him nothing until Barclay himself had closed the account.

It was only too apparent that Congress was once more trying to gain time, using any pretext to avoid paying. Under protest, and not consenting in any way to Barclay's renewed demand that Deane's old account should be destroyed by him, Beaumarchais handed him *copies* of the many documents that had accompanied the disputed records, in order to enable the American to prepare a conclusive statement for his superiors. As for destroying the original accounts?—What madness!—Why should he get rid of his only proofs? The American's suggestion was preposterous.

Eight months were then spent in accomplishing the monumental task of working their way through years of accounts. The insurance premiums that Beaumarchais had taken out for the safety of his ships were the principle point at issue, and both he and Barclay agreed to take advice concerning it from two maritime merchants of Bordeaux.[1] Their counsel, when delivered, was that in European business insurance costs were always due on all cargoes delivered incurring risks, whether the shipper had it insured by others or had insured it himself.

The articles concerning the commissions due to Beaumarchais were also submitted to the judgement of the Bordeaux merchants who, after taking into account the time spent at sea, the danger of the work involved, and especially the trust shown by the commercial house in making such courageous and risky advances in a time of war, decided that no European businessman would have taken less than 60% commission. Deane had set it at 10.

With that long process finished, Beaumarchais must have thought that, whatever the differences between Deane's accounts and Barclay's re-evaluation of them—and whether or not the man agreed with Deane's auditing—he would at least receive from Barclay the amount he had settled on. But the consul general then notified him that his mission had involved the *discussion* of these matters only, and far from being able to settle the outstanding claim, he did not even have the authority to close the account! He could only send his advice to Congress, and it would be necessary for his papers (and all of Beaumarchais's documents) to be taken to America and submitted to his principles.

Beaumarchais could not summon up the resources to cope with this breathtaking effrontery. After being deprived of his capital for almost ten years, he had still to submit to this new postponement, although Barclay assured him that he would not have to wait long for an answer. The packets left France in 1785, and were received and acknowledged in the same year by Congress. Yet by July 1787, neither man had received any sort of reply from America. 'Was there,' Beaumarchais stormed, 'in the annals of any nation on earth a more singular example of the denial of justice?' Was this extraordinary unreasonableness on the part of Congress anything to do with the insinuation that he had sent them defective armaments and substandard munitions? Beaumarchais informed John Jay[2] that he could prove he had stopped certain ships, believed to be carrying goods of poor quality, from leaving France, and it had been proved in reports filed by Americans assessors that all the merchandise was in excellent condition. Since these men were still living, these facts could be easily ascertained.

He asked Jay to further verify this in an original paper entitled 'In the Name of God,' which had been taken from a business journal that he had kept detailing the negotiations between himself and Silas Deane. Jay would find within its pages two letters from Deane and two replies from Beaumarchais, in which he had refuted that very same insult. He had thought to answer his detractors publicly when these innuendoes first began to appear, but he had refrained out of a fear of 'bringing a universal blame upon your country.' He had then believed that he should reserve his reply for more important occasions, or when his needs proved more 'pressing.'

Beaumarchais had, he said, been told by Jay's predecessor as Secretary for Foreign Affairs that he had been 'misinformed' by several members of Congress about the services Beaumarchais had rendered, and the integrity of his complaints; they had astonishingly found his letter of 1783 to be 'illiberal'! Yet earlier, these same men had been keen to drink his health at a public dinner given to Congress by the French ambassador, calling him 'the best friend America had in Europe.' Carmichael, then a member of Congress, who had been a guest at this dinner along with his agent Francy, had told him of this extraordinary compliment; '... But, alas, all that is changed today.'

He was still prepared to be accommodating. If the U.S. was not financially able to discharge their debt to him at present, was there any consideration to prevent them from fixing the balance due, and sending him a few partial remittances? If not, could they at least set the terms of his future reimbursements, and in the meantime send him the interest accrued on the outstanding sums? Surely they could see how wrong it was to force him to constantly solicit for the payment of 'a sacred debt'?

Their arguments, he asserted, enclosed him in an unbreakable circle, for what were they actually saying? 'We will reimburse nothing to M. de B. until his accounts have been regulated by us; but we will never regulate his accounts, so that we will not have to reimburse him ever!' Perhaps, he mused bitterly, a people who once having become independent and powerful can afterwards look upon gratitude as a 'private person's virtue,' and so beneath them; but nothing can dispense a State from acting justly, and especially from paying its debts.[3]

He hoped for an early official reply with regard to the decision that Congress would take on the matter—either to regulate and settle his accounts promptly, 'as an equitable sovereign should;' or to choose arbiters in Europe to judge the points at issue—insurance and commission, for example—as Barclay had proposed in 1785. If neither was to happen, they should tell him plainly that the new American 'sovereigns' refused to do him justice, and he would then inform them of what he would do to salvage his despised interests and his wounded honour.

Not all his time, though, throughout this frustrating decade, had been spent in pursuit of what was owed to him by the Americans. Since 1780, Beaumarchais had put his talents to many other uses.

In that year, he acquired the Baskerville style of type[4] to be used for an edition of Voltaire's complete works, and he had created a company for their publication in Kehl, Germany. In 1781, he organized the prospectus for the Paris Water Company, to provide water to the city on the London model (created by Beaumarchais in company with the Perrier brothers).[5] He had also been writing, trying to follow up the success of his first great satirical play with a sequel; but it had only taken a mere *reading* of his comedy *The Marriage of Figaro* at the Comedie-Francaise for a production to be at once forbidden by the King.

Despite his losses in North America, he had been phenomenally successful in his commercial interests elsewhere. Once the Franco-American alliance had been signed, the covert operations of Hortalez & Co had been dwarfed by the open shipment of supplies under the protection of the French navy; yet Beaumarchais had rallied from this serious blow. In the red, he had risen to the occasion with the genius for business that had characterized his entire life, and while continuing to send war supplies to the Americans on credit, he had afterwards brought his ships back from Martinique and Santo Domingo laden with products particular to that area, all of which he sold at a tremendous profit. Between 1776 and 1783, when Hortalez & Co was dissolved—there being no further reason for its existence—he had engaged in a business which generated over 42,000,000 *livres*, and even despite the U.S. debt, he achieved a profit. As a result of his enterprise, on behalf of the emergent American nation, Beaumarchais had been able to invest one million *livres* in French government bonds, and he had lent 700,000 *livres* to the Duc de Choiseul from his personal fortune.

He was also once again the talk of the finest Parisian salons, for readings of *The Marriage* in private homes was proving sensational; but, equally as important, between 1783 and 1790 the author of *Figaro* would oversee the publication of the 70-volume works of Voltaire. It was itself an irony, in that a banned playwright was thus legitimizing—even if he had to do it outside France—the entire canon of an old radical.

The scheduled performance of *The Marriage of Figaro* at Versailles had again been forbidden by the King, although it had been acted in a private performance on 26 September 1783, while yet to be approved by the censorship committee. A year later, however, on 27 April, the play had reached the professional stage, and was given 67 performances—a triumph! This deliciously seditious masterpiece was—like *The Barber of Seville*—lauded by the same aristocratic audience that it mocked, on this second occasion perhaps even more so. The Queen attended a performance, arriving late at the theatre due to the demands of a diplomatic visit; the first act had already been played, but an enthusiastic public demanded that it be given over again.

It was the latest 'artistic sensation' and French women now carried fans with verses from the play woven into them. Others wore bonnets 'a la Suzanne,' with garlands of white flowers as worn by the actress playing the female lead. The pressure for tickets was so great that duchesses found themselves jostling with prostitutes in the gallery. The King's instinctively hostile reaction was not based upon ignorance, but on a secret reading of the play, and one might interpret his hostility as prescient where this radical work was concerned. Fashionable audiences, by applauding the sentiments against their own order, were 'slapping their own cheeks.' The reading had been punctuated by cries of disgust from the King, and he had ended it by swearing that it would *never* be performed. But it had been, fast becoming all the rage, with everybody in society boasting of having attended at least one performance. Even the King gave way and allowed the Queen to see it; while a copy of the text was placed in the Trianon library, under its original title of *The Follies of a Day*.

In March 1785, perhaps anticipating the tremendous and horrifying events that would blow the *ancien regime* sky-high within the next four years, Beaumarchais had a house built for himself and his family in London. It was an extraordinary location to decide upon for a man who had played such a subversive role in recent events; yet, contrarily, it would seem that he was safer in England than in France. Returning to Paris in 1785, he had been jailed in the prison of St Lazare from 8 to 13 March, in punishment for a letter published in the *Journal de Paris,* which had offended the King.

On 8 May 1785, the Duc de Choiseul died, and Beaumarchais—as one of his main creditors—was named as a receiver of his estate. On 18 August, *The Marriage of Figaro* was played again, with even greater success, and on the following day *The Barber of Seville* was performed in an amateur production at the Trianon theatre at Versailles. It was an astonishing presentation, with Marie-Antoinette herself playing the principal female role of a servant, and the King's youngest brother, the Comte d'Artois, also in the cast. Louis XVI, although still disapproving, seemed unable to hinder its performance; but that his wife and brother should have it produced at his own court! The author was amused, and perhaps incredulous, for did such laxity stem from a failure to realize what was happening in the country?

The only attack upon Beaumarchais came not on account of the plays, but because of the opening in November of the new Paris Water Company. This drew the fire of the young demagogue, the Comte de Mirabeau,[6] who saw the introduction of running water into ordinary dwellings as being one more sign of the *enfeeblement* of society! Figaro countered his criticism with a witty satire, *Les Mirabelles* (a pun on his critic's name) that has not endured.

In 1786, he finally married Therese de Willmaulaz,[7] who had given him a daughter, his only child, ten years before. On 28 March, his opera *Tarare,* with music by the Italian composer Antonio Salieri,[8] passed the censorship committee; while in May, the musical version of *The Marriage* was premiered in Vienna, with music by Salieri's rival, Mozart.[9]

These were indisputably busy and productive years for Beaumarchais. The Congress must not believe that he was a man to bow down to misfortune.

The Americans were, in fact, experiencing their own disasters. As the new colonies coped with establishing a viable economy, despite the post-war depression, there was a sudden collapse of currency, which resulted in a public rejection to the imposition of new taxes. From August 1786 to February 1787, the authorities were faced with an armed revolt in western and central Massachusetts, under the leadership of Captain Daniel Shays.[10] It occurred to Beaumarchais that the shortage of money available to ease the lives of the newly independent Americans might well be the excuse for the non-payment of his own debts.

Besides which, there were other financial matters to occupy him in France, due to the monetary crisis of mid-1787. On two occasions—once under Turgot and once under Calonne[11]—free trade in grain had been proclaimed, which meant the suppression of all internal customs dues and all taxes on the marketing of wheat. Each time, the *parlements*—recently recalled by the King (as Beaumarchais had once suggested in a memorial) and generally in a hostile move towards any reforms—were loud in their protest. Other interested parties followed their lead, and provincial millers, fearing a food shortage, kept a tight hold on their flour. The people dreaded a period of expensive bread, and so, when Calonne was dismissed, the banker Necker, recalled to power, re-established crop control.

But what could be done to put an end to the privileges of the entrenched nobility, which, by reducing the revenue, led to an unbalanced budget? The aid to the American war had added enormously to the State deficit, just as Turgot had predicted. Even Marie-Antoinette's personal extravagance, then beginning to alienate her subjects, paled into insignificance when compared to the money spent on this vast American adventure. Calonne, with great courage, had proposed to abolish all fiscal immunities and to impose a 'territorial subsidy' payable by *all* landed proprietors irrespective of their social position. Only by some such innovation could the country be saved, yet the largest landowners were the nobles, prelates, and members of the *parlement*, and were they likely to bring in a law that would impoverish them? Absolutely not, and in the Assembly of Notables,[12] convened for the purpose of dealing with this situation, they formed a coalition to oppose the project—to which the King yielded, making this attempt at fiscal reform just one more failure among many.

Beaumarchais, however, had other things on his mind. He was having difficulties with the Perrier brothers, who were claiming that he had taken too controlling an interest in the running of the water company, and too large a share of the profits—a claim that might even have been true, since it was clearly in his nature to take command. Even so, free of financial problems for the first time in years, he purchased a large lot of land near to the Bastille on 26 June, where he would build a mansion.[13]

Silas Deane died in 1789, at the age of fifty-two. He had lived wretchedly in London for several years, sick in body and distressed in mind, 'with a total loss of his powers,' according to his friend Bancroft, who visited him occasionally. Strangely ignored by the English government, despite his intrigues against them, they made no attempt to try him for treason, nor did they seek to deport him; but, unable to earn a decent living, he fell into debt and started to drink heavily. He had been living for the past few years with a prostitute who had in some way persuaded him to take out a lease on a house and sign it over to her. Later, when he was arrested for debts and also suffered a stroke, the woman threatened to have him thrown out … 'and left to his fate.' It did not happen, but it would have been a sordid ending to an increasingly squalid life. In the estimation of his former colleague and conspirator, Deane suffered from 'dropsy, palsy, and idiotism,' by which Bancroft probably meant that Deane was by then suffering a form of senile dementia.

He seems, however, to have made a partial recovery, and—again in Bancroft's words—having 'no means of subsistence in this country [England], nor any connection which could enable him to obtain it,' he decided to leave for Canada in 1789—this being the nearest place to his homeland where he could not fear prosecution for his actions against his own people. He died just as the ship was entering the English Channel on 23 September 1789, his body being taken ashore without ceremony, to be buried in Deal. His mean burial was, perhaps, apt for a man who believed his soul 'to be no more than the blaze of a candle and his body a piece of manure.'

Beaumarchais was stricken by the news of Deane's death; and not only because he had lost the chief American witness to his dealings—even if the man's word could no longer be relied on. On 6 April 1781, Deane had submitted an official document showing that, based on his own records, Congress owed Beaumarchais 3,600,000 *livres*. Some part of Beaumarchais's magnanimous nature continued to believe that Deane had always been a dedicated patriot, but a hero who had fallen victim to bad luck and the intrigues of evil men.

By 1789, French revenue had reached a total of 475 million *livres*, but expenditure was 600 million, half of which was accounted for by interest payments on loans. How was the balance to be found?—for the privileged would not hear of any economy or any tax that might fall upon them. The only answer seemed to be for the King to raise the money he needed by a variety of previously discredited financial expedients; either by issuing notes or by devaluing the *livre*, in the manner of so many of his predecessors.

But Louis XVI was still too honest for his unique position; it would never have occurred to him to manipulate the currency. What did come to him was an expedient long fallen into disuse, and which would prove far worse in the near future than a mere devaluation; he convoked the Estates General. In other words he would ask his chief taxpayers to give their consent to the sacrifices they would be forced to make, and it was at this meeting—when King Louis spoke on the subject of financial crisis and state debt—that he attributed some of it to the expenses of 'an exorbitant but honourable war;' that of American independence.

By calling the Estates General, King Louis had made a great mistake, for almost at once the delegates forgot they had been summoned to resolve a financial problem, and instead discussed politics and turned themselves into a constituent assembly, to which the King gave way. It came about, then, that on the one occasion when Louis XVI made a positive decision, that decision actually amounted to a capitulation to his enemies. It was the finishing stroke for the 'relative' monarchy and the stormy prelude to an absolute republic. The old regime was on its deathbed, an inability to reform itself had condemned it, and it had died of weakness at the very moment when it was being accused of despotism; a fact that bitterly amused Beaumarchais, who had for so long been the victim of these incompetents.

A vague desire was certainly at work among the people of France; a desire to change their world. Though what they were to change, and how they were to change it, they did not, as yet, know. Strangely France, by reason of her agricultural production and her trading, was actually now the foremost country in Europe, and militarily, she led also, because of her reconstituted armed forces; Gribeauval's modernised artillery and Sartine's improved navy making her the most formidably armed nation on the continent. This meant that, at present, everything was poised for future victories, but these collective advantages were not sufficient to make up for empty coffers.

The inescapable truth was that France was about to change. Fear of famine was becoming a thing of the past, and the Industrial Revolution that had galvanized Great Britain was also on its way across the Channel; new sources of motive-power—coal, steam, gas—were there for the using. Ironically, the whole of the material side of life was in the process of being transformed at the very moment when, because of the presence of a King who had not learned his job, the monarchy was bogged down in the slothful past.

Beaumarchais had in many ways prejudged this situation, and his satirical plays had shone a light into the squalid and scandalous world of his 'betters,' thus creating a mood for change even among those who would be most damaged by it. For a time he stood back to see how this real-life drama would develop; was it to be a heroic tragedy or a tragic comedy? As it was, he found something of everything in it—sublimity and absurdity, epic and farce. The fact that he welcomed the possibility of transformation, however dangerous, as eagerly as he had once welcomed the move for independence in America is shown by how swiftly he adapted to the emergence of the political clubs, all working to lay the foundations of a republic. He was elected president of the district where he lived, the *Blancs Manteaux*.[14]

In the early months of 1789, however, feelings in Paris were at boiling point. Already, in April, dearer bread and lower wages had led to the looting of paper mills, and by mid-July the fever had grown more acute. Gangs of rioters, seizing weapons from the Invalides, then besieged the Bastille, releasing four forgers, two madmen and a pervert, and slaughtering the governor of this ancient fortress. In the space of a few hours a legend was born, and Beaumarchais watched it, in the company of the mistress of the Duke of Orleans, and the duke's children, from the roof of his new mansion near the prison.

There was a strong desire to wipe the slate clean and start again, but the people had no programme, and neither had King Louis XVI. Only a handful of the leaders, declared or hidden, knew what they were after; but they were not, all of them, after the same thing. Did Beaumarchais, a disciple of the 'philosophers,' hope for a government of enlightened thinkers, or did he hope for something more radical? It is hard to say, since he appears to have exhausted his satirical vein, and throughout 1790 Beaumarchais drafted *The Guilty Mother*, which although subtitled *The Other Tartuffe*,[15] was actually a return to his more sentimental comedies. It would be performed two years later by a minor group, at the height of the Revolution; but despite the reference to Moliere's immortal hypocrite, there is no hint of 'Figaro's' genius for ridiculing the excesses of his aristocratic targets in this gushing drama. In fact, he seems almost to have lost his keen appreciation of the comic disparities to be found in the society he had twice so acutely analyzed.

His opera *Tarare,* however, triumphed when it was performed on 3 August 1790.

It would seem that the more powerless the King became the better his mind worked. He had called upon the Comte de Mirabeau for help, but he had done so too late. Having been imprisoned in the palace of the Tuileries, he decided on flight from France, but again he was too late.[16] Once he was forcibly detained in Paris he knew that the royalist cause was lost; but weak as he had always been in his duties as a monarch, he stood firm as a rock in adversity. For this reason, if no other, Beaumarchais admired him; insults left King Louis unmoved and he faced imprisonment without complaint.

This particular year, 1791, was one of ironic significance for Beaumarchais, for on 3 September the French declared the new Constitution and the Declaration of the Rights of Man (the failure of which, he could perhaps have cynically regarded as a foregone conclusion). This last was based on Thomas Paine's[17] book of the same name, a justification for the revolution then taking place; published in France in that same year. At the same time, across the Atlantic Ocean, Alexander Hamilton was hard at work organizing the Bank of the United States, perhaps the foundation of the capitalist system in the New World. While France was heading towards total revolution the late revolutionaries in America were now heading for conservatism; divided in opinion as to whether the 'right of revolution' could be exercised any time citizens objected to governmental authority.

Almost everybody considered King Louis XVI to be an embarrassment; for now that he was a captive in the hands of the revolutionaries, what could the next step possibly be? Handing over the legislative power to a 'sovereign' assembly, while leaving only the shadow of executive power in the hands of a ministry responsible to that same body, had done nothing to resolve the conflicts that would inevitably arise between the two powers concerned.

All true authority in the State for the moment lay with the elected municipalities and their elected officials (of whom Beaumarchais was now one); power was no longer exercised from above but from below. No matter how many oaths of loyalty were made to this bastard constitution, it was foredoomed to failure. Furthermore, the numerous 'clubs' did not want it, and it was in these circles that the Revolution was developing, not in the official assemblies. The clubs had the political machinery in place, and they could bring pressure to bear—the Sections, the Communes and the Tribunes, with their petitions and newspapers. Whenever the King or the assembly resisted their will, they simply staged a 'day,' bringing the capital to a standstill. The instruments of their will were the working people of Paris, who carried pikes, wore red caps and short jackets called 'Carmagnoles,' their breeches held up by shoulder straps, of which they were so proud they called themselves *sans-culottes*.

Beaumarchais was once again to be involved in 'war-work,' if not to match that he had done in the cause of the Americans; for at the beginning of March 1792 he was caught up in what became known as 'The Affair of the Guns.' These armaments were to be brought from Holland, and Beaumarchais had planned to purchase them for the new army. Whether or not he had succeeded in doing so by the time the French declared war on Austria on April 20th, he had been accused of hoarding arms by 4 June, and on 11 August the *sans-culottes* invaded his new mansion, looking for the weapons. Arrested and imprisoned in the Abbaye, along with those who were destined for the newly erected guillotine in the former Place Louis V, he was freed only by the goodwill of the commune prosecutor, Pierre Manuel.[18]

On 22 September, Beaumarchais took the opportunity offered to him by this same friend and left for Holland, ostensibly to 'settle the affair of the guns;' while in France his new enemies attacked him at the national convention. Strangely, he went to the Low Countries via England, and he appeared to be in no hurry to leave a country that was still dangerous for him, since he would remain in England until the end of February 1793.

XXV

Open Letters

While staying in England, Beaumarchais wrote an article in the form of a last appeal to America; pleading for the justice so long denied him, and the article was published in the *Courrier de l'Europe* on 11 December 1792. Perhaps by design, but possibly also due to his own emotional deterioration, it was written in the style of one of his most maudlin plays:

My poor wife, and you, my darling daughter; I don't know where you are or where to write to you, and I know of no one who can give me any news. I have learned that the seals have been affixed for the third time on my house in Paris,[1] and that I am under accusation for the wretched affair of the 'guns from Holland.' (And for a so-called abomination of a more serious kind, added thereto to do away with me faster!) I ask all honest people who read the foreign gazettes to have the humanity of letting you know of my whereabouts. My dear ones, it is from London, from this hospitable and generous land, where all people who are persecuted in their own countries may find shelter, that I beg you not to worry about me. I see all four of you grieve, and my daughter's tears fall on my heart and break it. But that is the only thing I cannot bear.

The National Convention,[2] deceived by the cruellest tissue of nonsense ever to have come out of an informer's mouth, has—on the faith of the Le Cointre deposition—issued a decree of accusation against me. [Le Cointre was a deputy at the National Convention, who had been used by Beaumarchais's enemies to betray him.] But those who have misinformed him, aware that such a contemptible accusation would not stand up to a two-minute inquiry, have plotted to smear me in such a way as would condemn me regardless. They have denounced me as one that has written to Louis XVI, listing me among those who are conspiring against French liberty. But this charge, more serious even than the first, is groundless. Please, my dear wife and sisters; don't worry about me. Dry your tears, dear daughter, they disturb your father's serenity, who needs composure in which to clarify with the National Convention the serious matters they need to apprehend, so as to throw those abject calumnies back into the hell-mouth out of which they came.

I have never written to Louis XVI on any subject concerning the Revolution, either for or against, and if I had, I would be the first to proclaim it. We are no longer in that time when men of courage needed to belittle themselves when they wrote to powerful people. Had I been in contact with the King, equal to the task, I would have imparted to him such truths as might well have prevented his present misfortunes and those that now tear apart our unfortunate France.

I am far from betraying my country, for whose liberty I have long wished and indeed have sacrificed a great deal. All those vile accusations brought up against me at the National Convention would be the most abject abominations were they not also the most arrant nonsense.

The Senate, which was taken aback, is made up of just people, and yet I have not been heard—and my enemies hope undoubtedly that I never will be. By arresting me abroad [in Holland, where the National Convention had ordered him to obtain the 60,000 guns that he had contracted for on their behalf], they flattered themselves that I would be taken back home under the odious suspicion of treason. And where their hired assassins would have repeated on me the scenes of 2 September. [This refers to the massacre of that day in 1792, carried out by the *sans-culottes* largely upon those confined in the Abbaye de Saint-Germain des Pres, where he had been a prisoner.]

'Moderate thinking' was now considered a crime in Revolutionary Paris, those who were guilty of it were to be eliminated, and Beaumarchais was seen as one of the foremost of these. The creator of 'Figaro'—one of the most outspoken critics of his day—was now regarded as 'faint-hearted,' or at least 'half-hearted.' On his previous return to Paris, he barely escaped from the house of Pierre Manuel, when men came to arrest him again. The killers, having missed him the previous night, were out looking for him, and he had walked around Paris for hours before making his escape from the city, at last finding shelter with some 'good country folk.'[3]

It was also hoped that the infuriated populace would have executed me on the way, before it was possible to undeceive them, [he went on]. It was the fifth time in four months that they attempted to have me killed, which would certainly have come about without the generous intervention of a magistrate of the Commune, whom I shall name in my memorial with gratitude. He fetched me out of the Abbaye only six hours before all exits were locked, and without his intervention, I should certainly have suffered the same fate as so many innocent victims.[4] If I do not prove unquestionably, to the satisfaction of my poor country and of all Europe, that this shameful plot against me is but a vile villainy, concocted to achieve my downfall, then I am a lesser man than I believe. If there is one line written by me directly to Louis XVI in the past eighteen years, I say woe unto me, anathema on my property, and I will voluntarily place myself under the sword of justice.

This is a remarkable piece of self-deception on his part, since records were still kept at Versailles. How could he hope to deny that he had written *directly* to the king on many occasions?

> I am writing a petition to the National Convention to beg them to make a distinction between the ridiculous affair of the guns and the serious accusation of my engaging in a correspondence with the dishonoured King. Before clearing myself on the first charge I must be obviously 'washed clean' regarding the second. I must defend myself or die.
>
> But, in the name of God, my dear wife, if you wish me to keep my wits, try to keep our dear daughter from crying.

King Louis XVI was executed on 21 January 1793. With the King gone and a republic firmly proclaimed, it was necessary to draw up a supplementary constitution, and a new National Assembly—the third in four years—undertook the task. This was the National Convention that Beaumarchais intended to approach, but there were three more urgent matters to occupy it in its first year: war; the safety of the nation; and finance, the lifeblood of the State. Above all, the Convention was concerned with its own survival, and that of each of its members, who lived under the rising tide of danger. The 'Reign of Terror'—the period of Jacobin rule under which hundreds of people were executed for so-called treason—had begun a few months earlier, in October 1793. Beaumarchais had made his escape from France only shortly before this date, and the 'Terror' would last until July 1794; but he could, indeed, have been one of its most illustrious victims, remembered as they were for their 'historic last words.'

It would be a mistake, however, to think that the 'Terror' was the work only of bloodthirsty fanatics. Those responsible for it held the opinion that 'purges' were necessary for the health of a true republic, although a still stronger reason was that they killed in order to avoid being killed; having 'purged,' they went in terror of being purged in their turn. They also feared the reprisals that would come from a possible reaction no less than the violence of the enthusiasts they encouraged. Robespierre,[5] even at the height of his power, had to take measures to protect himself from the Right and the Left alike.

In 1792, war had been declared against Austria amid scenes of wild enthusiasm, for the Revolution was now on the march to free *all* oppressed peoples, and its aim was to cast down all tyrants from their seats. The natural consequence of this was that France faced a coalition of all the outraged monarchies; England and most of the European nations declared war on

France, while the newly formed United States of America—far distant from this conflict—remained neutral.

Beaumarchais, too, remained as aloof as he could from a situation that he had actually helped materialize, even as his persona triumphed on the Paris stage. On 20 March 1793, *Le Nozze de Figaro* was performed in the operatic version of the *Austrian* composer Mozart, and the artful servant's clever thwarting of his despotic master was proving greatly to the taste of the newly liberated Parisians.

But what was the real-life Figaro's exact role at that time? In June 1793, he left the 'haven' of England for the insecurity of Holland and Germany, to once again 'settle the affair of the guns,' and to settle it in favour of the new masters in France. Was he still seeking the approval of his enemies there, and did he plan to return to Paris, a city where he could still face the public executioner? He did, in fact, begin writing his self-defence, '*Mes Six Époques.*'[6]

On 14 March 1794, Beaumarchais was listed among the *Émigrés*, which meant that his property was at the mercy of the State under the new law proclaiming all political emigrants to have sacrificed their rights. Although the State did not abolish private ownership, it seized all hoarded wealth, especially of those who had turned their back upon the Revolution. Beaumarchais was seen by his enemies to have done this, despite the fact that his presence abroad was, according to him, 'solely in the interests of France.' His newly built house in the Marais had already been raided, and on 4 July 1793 his family was arrested. The law condemning the *Emigres* forced his wife to divorce him, simply to hold on to what was left of his property.

He could not return to France just yet, regardless of the fact that the Revolution was soon to reach another, less terrifying, stage. After July 1794, with Robespierre guillotined and his coterie disbanded, new theorists were to try their hand at putting together yet another Constitution, on the basis of five Directors and two Chambers. No great advance upon its predecessor, it would simply replace the rule of doctrinaires with that of shady speculators. But it was still unsafe for Beaumarchais to return to his old haunts.

One might have thought that he would have functioned as well as any man in the company of the new speculators, for Beaumarchais the businessman would have felt thoroughly at home in the new society. Yet even after the prison gates were opened, and 400,000 men and women detained under the 'Terror' had streamed through them, and even though the assassins of yesterday were now being assassinated or deported in their turn, France was still not safe for him. For the time being, he remained in exile in Hamburg, Germany, where he suffered his first heart attack.

He also made a new appeal to the 'whole of the American people' on 10 April 1795, calling it a 'Request for Justice, after Twenty Years of Suffering.' In it, he could only repeat the tedious recital of his persecution, but with the added particulars of his banishment from his native country, which now kept him in exile (although he had, in fact, since been vindicated). He also added a new detail; for at the time of his deepest involvement with their cause, he wrote, he had thought of being admitted to the 'high rank' of citizenship in their country. He would not weary them with his recent troubles, for in view of the distress now experienced by many of his countrymen it would seem contemptible to dwell on them; but he was old and sick, perhaps so ill that he could not hope to live long enough to see the end of this incomplete business, and this would be the last time he could address them in the form in which he was now presenting his case: 'May these last efforts of a banished man, dying in squalor somewhere in Europe, be of some benefit to my most unfortunate daughter, the only child I leave behind, without fortune or protectors.'

He set before the Americans 'the great issue' in as incisive a way as he could, with 'all the evidence needed for a legal discussion,' boldly stating that the American people had been in his debt for almost twenty years. He knew that he could no longer rely upon the men that he had spent so much time in appealing to for almost two decades, but it was their successors who were now his debtors. Though he was no longer sure of the best kind of procedure to be followed in a matter of this kind.

He could only again present them with the facts of the case: of his struggle to involve the French government; his success in creating of 'Hortalez & Co;' the secret shipments he had arranged; and his many setbacks. He made clear the long enmity of the malevolent Arthur Lee, who had died in 1792, writing with irony of the decision made by Congress to appoint Lee to examine the Hortalez accounts in 1787, when he had renewed his claims. Lee, of all people, his most ardent foe! Was it any wonder his old adversary had concluded that it was *he*, Beaumarchais, who owed the Congress 1,800,000 *livres* and therefore any debt between them was to be cancelled?

He dwelt at length upon his relationship with Deane, in whose honesty he had implicitly trusted, however naively. 'Percentage dealers' might laugh at the blind faith which had made him neglect to take the correct precautionary measures, but he had been motivated by larger feelings than the making of money. Had he followed their advice, no stores from France would ever have reached America, since he had met with one hundred obstacles for each possibility.

He intended to have his correspondence with Silas Deane printed and published, 'so that each one of you can read it,' for it would reveal important particulars that were crucial to the judgement they must bear upon him, and he stressed again the long catalogue of the American leadership's failures to meet their word, as recorded in many unsatisfactory petitions to Congress.

In May 1793, he reminded them, Alexander Hamilton,[7] first Secretary to the Treasury, and the 'probe assistants' that helped him carry out his financial duties, had—after 17 years—examined Beaumarchais's accounts 'in an equitable fashion,' even though it was full of errors, naturally to Beaumarchais's disadvantage. Yet Congress had earlier admitted to Deane that they acknowledged the services Beaumarchais had rendered in secret, and they had regretted their conduct towards him, and had been noble enough to attempt to make up for it. Beaumarchais included a copy of the letter from the Congress in which they had admitted their fault, and which they had addressed to Benjamin Franklin, then head of the American delegation in Paris in 1779.

There followed more on the subject of the useless bills of exchange and, out of respect for this, he referred to the only letter from Congress that he had received in almost twenty years—'Twenty Years!'—but which had then encouraged him to multiply his services.

Beaumarchais asserted that he had obtained favours from King Louis XVI that had saved America more than a million on the debt they owed to the French government, a debt that had been entered into *his* accounts. By confessing to this, Beaumarchais placed himself at risk with the present French administration, for anybody who was connected with the royal government during that period 'deserved a ticket to the guillotine.' A year earlier, he would not have dared to make such a statement, 'not for all the fortune that you are keeping from me,' since such a declaration would have imperilled his wife and sisters. '… Fortunately this terrible period is now at an end,' for France was sick of violence and sacrifices.

Perhaps the Americans considered him a deserter to their cause after he had ceased shipments in 1778; but he had explained at the time that officials had redirected the cargoes he had assigned for America to the French Islands. His man Francy had told as much to Congress, 'who found it difficult to believe,' even though these same doubters then asked him to resume his shipments! It was only in hindsight he realized that financial arrangements should have been settled *before* his ships left France, and not years later, when all his risks and losses had materialized. Although his affairs in France were presently in disorder, he would find the papers of that time which would clarify everything.

He wished the people he now addressed to know that he had no *present* intention of seeking justice in a European court of law, he only appealed to their sense of equity, and they alone would be his judges (although Beaumarchais made it clear that he was reserving some juicy details for his political memoirs should he be forced to reveal them). They would be regretful if he was pushed to this extremity, he threatened, for as they well knew, 'one does not stir the cesspool of politics to create some new stench.' He was not, in any case, charging a whole nation with the wrongs he had suffered, but only a few corrupt individuals who had intrigued against him.

Should he, however, be pushed to the extremity of seeking a legal settlement in a European court of law, he would willingly submit to an American referee for the political section. If, that is, they would consent to allow him an attorney for the legal part and a businessman for the commercial side. He had already proposed this solution before and he would have submitted to their findings then—without appeal against the judgement of such arbitrators—provided he could have fully informed them of the circumstances.

He had begged the states of Virginia and South Carolina to adopt the same solution for all the money that they owed him, even if they wished to appoint different arbiters. Apart from money, he also wished (without renouncing his French nationality) to be accepted as a *good citizen of America*; although he would have considered losing his French citizenship in the latter years until he received letters informing him that the 'Reign of Terror' had been replaced with a 'Reign of Justice.' For over a year now his fellow Frenchman had ceased cutting off people's heads without first hearing them out.

He had still not lost all hope, and he begged the Americans anew to give him the arbitrators that he had asked for earlier. He also begged them to give him a public writ, which could serve as the basis for negotiations for his daughter or her successors, when he was dead. His petition of January 1791 would be the best legal document to show that Hamilton and his assistants had recognized, in the name of the American people, that they were his debtors for a sum assessed by them of 2,280,331 *livres*, 17 *sols*, 8 *deniers tournois*—not that he could ever recognize this faulty evaluation of their future settlements as being the exact payment for what was truly owed to him. But he would accept it, if he must, as a minimum of the debt at last recognized by them, and *below which he could not be brought*.

The affidavit he requested was only a precaution in the event of his imminent death. If he recovered his health, and if America granted the arbitration he requested, he agreed to prove that not one of the objections that had prevented him from being paid in twenty years could have been sustained in *normal* business practice. Most of all he would prove that the late King Louis XVI had never charged Beaumarchais with making this colossal sum a gift on his behalf.

On 21 June 1794, Gouveneur Morris,[8] the U.S. ambassador to France, had been given a receipt by the French Foreign Minister, Buchot, which was the proof of purchase signed by Beaumarchais on 10 June 1776—proof the

Comte de Vergennes had refused to give to Monsieur Grand, banker for the U.S. in 1786.[9] Beaumarchais now wanted to show that this last undertaking, which had cost him three years' losses, was so 'strange in law, in politics, in commercial usage,' that he had been much too intimidated to agitate publicly about the problem. Even now, he was trying to keep everything respectfully legal, and as formal as he could, ailing as he was, and so many thousand miles away from them, surviving in a garret in northern Germany in 1795.

There were eight separate paragraphs, each dealing with some fact, all of which he had wearily trotted out in other declarations. The most important, since he strenuously underlined it, was the seventh paragraph, in which he again stressed that he had never received from King Louis XVI the one million *livres* to offer the Americans as a gift. All the gold that had been used by him had been painstakingly collected, both in his capacity as a merchant and on the basis of an equitable commerce. He had collected this money not only in France but also in other European states, as loans or as cash flow. But, alas, his creditors had not exercised the patience that he had shown with his American debtors, and he had been forced to dig into his own reserves in order to repay them. Some of his debts had, in fact, not yet been cleared—but that, he hastened to add, did not concern the Americans as his debtors. It was simply one more reason for them to play their part in enabling him to pay off such debts by fulfilling their own obligations towards him.

'Figaro' here again briefly shows his face, when Beaumarchais states that, before offering his petition to the American public, he planned to leave certified copies of this incriminating intelligence with a number of public men in various European cities, so that in the event of his death, his daughter and her heirs would be able to recover the necessary documents, to continue his cause. This would enable them to find the 'judges of my judges,' should he still not obtain the satisfaction he was entitled to.

An 'accident' that he had sustained the night before he wrote this paragraph had caused him to change his plans into something more fitting with his present condition, he wrote. Some biographers have alleged that this mysterious 'accident' was very possibly an attempt at suicide; he was certainly at his lowest ebb. As a result of this accident, Beaumarchais now sought a change of direction. He would no longer seek to prove his rights, despite his anguish at leaving his only child without support; but he ardently prayed that by appealing to the sense of justice of the American people, they would at least have pity on his orphaned daughter.

By his final paragraph, he was reduced to pleading that, if they should once more reject his rights, they should at least give *alms* to their friend, 'whose accumulated services have had no other reward!'

XXVI

'America's Best Friend'

On 12 June 1796, Beaumarchais wrote to his friend and former associate, Chevalier, who had settled on Long Island, New York:

> After three years of banishment from France, entailing incalculable losses, I have just received my re-entry diploma, 'as valid as can be.' [It was dated 2 June, and was signed by a member of the Directory, the Executive branch of the French Republic.][1] I have received it in Hamburg, and in three days I will be in Paris!

He wrote elatedly, but he felt that he would feel estranged from all that had happened there since he had fled for England.

He had been surprised not to hear from Chevalier for almost a year. 'Is the entire world involved in a conspiracy to intercept my correspondence with my dearest friends?'—or was it simply that Chevalier had nothing to tell him, or that he was simply tired of dealing with a man so constantly crushed? 'Put an end, I beg you, to this depressing silence …'

He returned to Paris on 5 July 1796, finding it a very changed place—but changed in ways he had not anticipated. The previous year, the theorists had tried their hands at putting together yet another Constitution, on the basis of five Directors and two chambers, which was so far proving no great advance upon its predecessors. The clubs were still organizing 'days,' and the few neo-royalists that were left tried to do the same; but the Revolution had been officially terminated with the creation of the Directory.

However, religious freedom had been restored only in theory, and devout Catholics would be persecuted for a long time to come. Dance halls (the whole city was dancing mad) now flourished in ex-monastic houses and churches. The Directory had invented a new faith, 'Theophilanthropy,' to which it made over the principal churches of Paris, and which it subsidized from its secret funds; although the people remained obstinately addicted to their 'superstitions.'

There could be no doubt that the egalitarian revolution had miscarried, and in place of feudal privileges—round which the original argument had raged—it had substituted the privileges of parvenu wealth. The Republic had indeed declared war on the rich, but only on the rich of the old regime, not that of the brash new entrepreneurs. It pained Beaumarchais to see the new men making fortunes out of army contracts without having to endure any of the complications that had plagued him. Under the Directory, it was the rapacious that ruled the roost.

Money, for Beaumarchais—then in dire need of it—had become a joke. As early as 1789, Pétion[2] had launched the idea of issuing a paper currency, backed by the sale of confiscated land, believing his scheme would provide the state with new resources, and the new purchasers of national property with the means of paying for what they had bought. The new notes had been called 'assignats,'[3] and their circulation was controlled only by the supply of the correct paper and the speed with which the printing presses could work. In 1796, the 'plates' were to be destroyed, but only to have recourse to others less discredited, and the 'mandat'[4] replaced the assignat. Both were far more effective than dogmas and speeches, and could be said to have been the foundation on which the Republic was built; and by 1797, Beaumarchais was in dire need of them.

To some extent, he did 'rise again,' as he had promised Chevalier he would. His play *The Guilty Mother* was produced in May 1797, triumphing at the Comedie-Francaise. Throughout that year, he would produce a considerable amount of writing on various subjects, although his main dramatic work had long since been concluded. *The Guilty Mother* was a pale reflection of his talent, totally lacking the 'Indecent Merriment and Gross Immorality, mixed however with Satire' that had so disturbed the English Mrs Thrale when attending one of the first productions of *The Marriage of Figaro*.[5]

He wrote to Chevalier in New York again on 1 September 1798. He had been at his old tricks, he said, pulling strings, and it had been decided that the French Republic owed him twelve or thirteen million *livres*, having just referred him to the umpteenth commission, which was going to review his accounts—and all this at a time when he had thought to leave France, to settle all of his debts 'in the fatal continent where you live!' He was now tied down with the new business that had just been imposed upon him, but Chevalier could rely upon one thing: once this 'new shackle' was removed from him, he would not remain above fifteen days in Paris, whether or not the present government entrusted any kind of business to him. He was soliciting an appointment as an *ambassador* to America, and what a coup that would be! Congress would not find it so easy to shrug off the accredited representative of a vital ally.

He would bring enough funds 'necessary to my trip,' and he teasingly hoped that the two countries would not be at war with each other by then, and 'that it will not be simply enough to be a Frenchman in America to be denied justice.'[6] He still had no real means of support while he waited for the commission's decision, and he was, for the moment, living on loans. 'As they are due in four or five months from now, you may judge how I feel about your being slow in sending me my *viaticum*!' Apparently, he expected Chevalier to send him a travel allowance for his voyage.

While in exile in Germany, Beaumarchais had met up with the wily former aristocrat, the ex-Bishop of Autun, Charles de Talleyrand-Perigord,[7] a magnificent turncoat, and a survivor who could match his own skills. After having joined the ranks of the revolutionaries, the irreligious churchman had earlier also 'consecrated' the new occupants of Episcopal sees in the name of the godless republic, making them little more than civil servants—a joke that Beaumarchais may well have appreciated, since the depth of his religious orthodoxy (despite his habitual use of pious platitudes) was probably always in doubt. Talleyrand, the great opportunist, had been made the foreign affairs minister for the new government in 1797, a position that he would hold for another ten years.

The two men met occasionally in Paris, as Beaumarchais gradually crept back into favour and began to mix with the new elite:

> … I was smiling to myself last night at the magnificent compliment you paid me when you said that I was everyone's dupe, [Beaumarchais wrote to him in one of his final letters]. Being duped by those one has obliged, from the sceptre to the shepherd's crook, is to be a victim but not a dupe. Even if I could have kept at that price all that base ingratitude has taken from me, I never wished to have done otherwise; that's my profession of faith. I don't mind what I lose myself, but what affects my country's reputation or happiness wears out all my sensibilities. When we make a mistake, I become angry like a child, and although I am neither 'fit for' nor employed 'for anything,' every night I repair in my mind the errors of the day. That is perhaps what makes my friends say I am a dupe, with everyone else being supposedly concerned only with himself. What a detestable country we would live in if this was true of everybody; but I am sure, very sure, of the contrary.
>
> When will you see my little 'dupe's deal?' [A paper he had written concerning the current 'difficulties' that had arisen between France and the U.S.A.] You will not find it devoid of interest, and you will find resources there for the past, the present and the future. The future, the only time that exists for us, the other two having passed away while we talk about them!

It must have bitterly amused Beaumarchais to see that when the war between Britain and France started up again (not that it had, strictly speaking, ever stopped), the Americans insisted upon keeping a strict neutrality and non-involvement in the new French struggle. The conservative federalists who controlled the American government from 1789 to 1801 were in fact profoundly suspicious of all the Jacobinism emanating from France. The administration of John Adams would pass various acts similar to those in Britain to counteract subversion by the 'contaminated' French revolutionaries; but then, the New England Yankee had never liked France or the French, as Adams had made plain during his stay in Paris.

Beaumarchais, then approaching his sixty-seventh year, yet ever the eternal optimist, still believed that a future existed for him; but there was, in fact, very little future left. The years of constant anxiety and poverty in exile, as in the case of Silas Deane, had proved a great burden on his physical strength, if not his mental powers. He had never really recovered his health, and on the night of the 17th or the morning of 18th May 1799, he 'passed away,' quite literally, very quietly in his sleep. One of the most dynamic characters of the late 18th century, only his creation Figaro, herald of the Revolution, remained to keep his name alive; the enormous efforts he had made, as 'America's Best Friend' would be partially buried with him.

Again, it is an irony he would surely have appreciated that, despite the enduring distinction of his two great plays, it has been argued that his playwriting was almost in the category of a hobby.[8] Yet this is partially true; for studies of his financial and commercial activities firmly show that politics had always been his real interest, and commerce had been his most successful enterprise—as witness the fact that, despite his interminable problems, Hortalez & Co (the least successful of his commercial ventures) had managed to close its activities without a loss; a triumph in the circumstances.[9]

It had been during his stormy directorship of this company that the second of his great comedies was produced. *The Marriage of Figaro*, publicly staged in 1784, was an even greater sensation than *The Barber* of ten years before, and it was even more subversive. In the intervening years, public criticism of the 'old regime' had become increasingly stronger, and the American War of Independence had created further dissatisfaction. French volunteers, returning from that war, soon informed their families and friends about the social equality and political rights they had found in America and these reports stirred up greater discontent. People were now seriously questioning why a small but extremely powerful elite, a group that had not earned such privileges, should rule their country. As Figaro/Beaumarchais had said to his employer in *The Marriage of Figaro*, 'Because you are a great lord, you believe yourself to be a great genius! Yet you took the trouble to be born, and no more.' As Napoleon pointed out at a later date, the public performances of this last play were the 'revolution already in action.'

This raises a crucial question about his true disposition; for how much of a genuine revolutionary was Beaumarchais, and how much did he actually contribute, not only to the American rebellion, but also to the cataclysm that would overwhelm his own country within a decade of the American triumph? There is little doubt that France's main motives for eventually offering help to the Americans was to bring about the abasement of Great Britain, and if possible to regain some of the American lands lost to that country in 1763. There is equally no doubt that the fiercely patriotic Beaumarchais shared in these aims, but that he was drawn to the ideal of a republic was also a contributing factor, although conventional evaluation finds that he saw the American War of Independence as no more than a profit-making venture. In the opinion of John Richard Alden,[10] 'It is not certain even today whether the subsidies which he handled were entirely gifts, although they were so in the main. The validity of the claims may well be questioned, especially since the firm of Rodrigue Hortalez & Company closed with a small net profit.' But of course it did, and for very little of that profit could Beaumarchais thank the Americans; any money he actually made out of this strange enterprise had been due entirely to his genius for commerce!

It would not be until 1835, in fact, when Beaumarchais had been in his grave for thirty-six years, that Congress would fully acknowledge its debt to him; but even then the negotiations were to be further protracted. The complete sum was never admitted, and his heirs were forced to settle for a mere 800,000 francs, when Deane had clearly shown that Congress owed Beaumarchais millions of *livres*. Of course, Deane's evidence was considered to be 'perjured,' and the scandal that wrecked him had likewise hurt his friend, and would continue to damage Beaumarchais for as long as it was convenient for Congress to believe in the word of Arthur Lee. The morbidly suspicious and cantankerous Lee, a useless member of the Continental Congress when elected in 1782 for a period of three years, proved himself to be no more capable of constructive effort as a politician than he had done while acting as a commissioner. Another victim of his constant troublemaking, Benjamin Franklin, needed only one word to describe him: 'insane.'

Yet Lee died without ever providing any manner of proof, either against Franklin or Silas Deane. Deane could certainly be attacked with some reason for showing poor judgement, but how corrupt was he, in fact? Beaumarchais believed him to be innocent but perhaps naïve, and until recent years the consensus of historians has been that Deane was a dedicated patriot but one not entirely suited for the role he played in Paris, although that verdict has now been drastically revised. It is suggested that he fell into the hands of a 'kindly teacher of treason,' and that teacher was Beaumarchais, although it was more likely to have been his old friend Edward Bancroft, who had become a spy for the British in December 1776, assuming the name of Edwards. He had spied on the American commissioners in Paris to the last, unsuspected by his 'countrymen'—with the exception of Arthur Lee, of course; although Lee could never have convinced anybody of his distrust for the man because he was known to suspect everybody!

But the waters were murky from the start; for even Congress had decreed that Deane and Bancroft should only ever meet in secret, and intrigue came naturally to Bancroft, whose diplomatic career can only be described as sinister. Bancroft's treachery would not come to light for nearly seventy years after his death in 1820 and he had continued to be a British subject long after the Revolution had succeeded. The British cabinet knew of every confidence that he shared with Deane, and of every instruction received from Congress inside a matter of days. Deane's French and American secrets were passed over to a contact at the British embassy, and sent from there to London. Bancroft's dispatches, written in invisible ink—he was a keen experimenter with inks and dyes—were placed in a sealed bottle and then concealed in the bole of a tree on the south terrace of the Tuileries Gardens.[11] They were placed there every Tuesday evening after 9.30; and the routine, however unsophisticated, worked to perfection. From the start of Deane's activities in France, his mission was an open secret to the British.

With Bancroft, though, his treachery had always come at a price, and perhaps his sole motive was largely mercenary; an initial payment to him of 400*l* was eventually increased to 1,000*l* a year by his satisfied British masters. Yet Deane died a poor man; treachery could not be said to have been a profitable game for him, if he had followed Bancroft's lead.

And 'Figaro'? Of the three men, Beaumarchais, for all his losses, was the greatest gambler; although his speculations, so far as it is known, never descended to the sordid levels of the Americans. In fact, at the nadir of his fortunes, when seriously in the red, he had risen above his circumstances as only Beaumarchais could. Finally realizing that the Americans had no intention of replacing his shipments to them with goods that he could make a profit from, he had simply diversified, bringing back goods from the Caribbean instead. With his genius for commerce, he had no need to sink to the level of Deane or Bancroft.

What is without question, however—regardless of motives, no matter how ambiguous—is the fact that the American revolutionaries owed him a debt that would far exceed that of mere financial profit. It has been said nine tenths of the military supplies that made the American victory at Saratoga possible came from France, or through foreign merchants the French government secretly encouraged, and who had orchestrated this enterprise? Beaumarchais, very largely. Again, General Washington's victories at Trenton and Princeton were, perhaps, only made possible by the supplies furnished by the French or through their instigation; and again, it was Beaumarchais who had provided these materials.

Yet even in France, Beaumarchais is largely remembered today only as the author of two comic plays that ridicule and question the established way of doing things, and which certainly influenced political events. If not an accredited member of the French Enlightenment, he was at least associated with their ideas, and these ideas spread to America, where they would influence revolutionary writers such as Thomas Paine, the 'champion of liberty.' In his book *The Rights of Man*, Paine said that he saw 'a dawn of reason rising on the world;' and the playwright Beaumarchais had certainly played a part in opening a window on this daybreak.

Perhaps 1776–1783 was the most intense period of Beaumarchais's life; the time in which he felt that he was doing most to further the 'dawn of reason' by helping to give birth to the first truly modern nation. There is never any doubt that, to the end of his life, he felt his work on behalf of the colonists had played a vital part in their success; yet there is little evidence that the Americans have ever fully appreciated his efforts on their behalf.

It has been said of Napoleon I that his presence alone on the battlefield made the difference of 40,000 men; but it might equally be argued that the secret activities of 'Figaro' throughout the length of the War of Independence had made an even more crucial difference to the fortunes of the Americans. Certainly, without the help of the French, they would have taken longer to win their independence from Britain, and Beaumarchais was a supremely important—if not *the*—prime mover in their eventual triumph.

Americans, however, have a tendency to overlook their deep historical relationship with France, even while acknowledging the profound philosophical influence of that country on their thinking; primarily, perhaps, because they share a language with the British—a language that they did not share with their French 'best friend.' Beaumarchais remains astonishingly neglected by successive American historians in their versions of the great revolution that so clearly defined their future.

Notes

I

1. Beaumarchais (1732–99).
2. 'Honorary' titles were unpaid positions, but could not be bought by anyone. In some way Beaumarchais earned the right to purchase them.
3. The property is in the department of the Loire.
4. Carlos III (reigned 1759–88).
5. Choiseul, Etienne Francois, Comte de Stainville (1719–85).
6. Chaulnes, Marie Joseph Louis, Duc de (1741–1793).
7. Sartine, Charles Marie-Antoine de, Comte d'Albi (1729–1801).
8. Paris-Duverny (see La Blache).
9. Goezman, Louis Valentine (1730–1794). He wrote a number of memoirs against Beaumarchais.
10. La Blache, a '*grand seigneur*.' Like his uncle, Paris-Duverny, he was a member of a great family of the *Dauphine*.
11. Maupeou, Rene Charles de (1714–92). Of an old family 'of the robe.'
12. Du Barry, Comtesse (1743–93).
13. *Parlements*. Any of several high courts of justice in which royal decrees were registered.
14. Marie-Antoinette (1755–93).
15. Artois, Charles, Comte d' (1757–1836) King of France as Charles X (1824–30).
16. It must have been singularly awful weather for Beaumarchais to have taken so long to cross the Channel, and to have been driven so far off course, unless he purposely avoided arriving in Dover.
17. Jean de Vignoles was also a former agent of Louis XV, then living in exile in London.
18. George III (1738–1820).
19. John Stuart Bute, third Earl of Bute. (1713–92). The king's choice as Prime Minister (1762–63).
20. Éon, Charles de Beaumont, Chevalier d' (1728–1810).
21. Elizabeth Petrovna, Empress of Russia (1741–62). Daughter of Peter the Great.
22. Guérchy, Claude Francois, Comte de (1715–1767).
23. 'True Bill'—formerly in Great Britain, now only in the U.S. The endorsement made on a bill of indictment by a grand jury certifying it to be supported by sufficient evidence to warrant committing the accused to trial.
24. '*Nolle Prosequi*'—literally 'do not prosecute.'
25. Broglie, Charles-Francois, Comte de (1718–1814).
26. Vergennes, Charles Gravier, Comte de (1719–87).
27. Conti, Princes of. (1717–1776) and (1734–1814).

II

1. *Sous francs*, a French coin of the lowest denomination.
2. Beaumarchais, *Letters*.
3. Guines, Adrien Louis de Bonnieres, Comte de (1738–1806).

4. Chatham, William Pitt (the Elder), First Earl of Chatham. (1708–78).
5. The Seven Years War had greatly undermined the solvency and authority of the Crown.
6. Beaumarchais, *Letters*.
7. *Ibid.*
8. The academy was in Carlisle Street, run by an Italian master of arms. The chevalier often assisted with fencing lessons, ready to take on all comers.
9. D'Éon must have enjoyed remarkably good health, for he seems never to have been examined by a doctor; or, if he had been, they were bribed or threatened to keep his secret.
10. The Freemasons were first established in London in 1717.
11. John Wilkes (1727–97). Expelled from the House of Commons and later outlawed.
12. The 'Friends of America' were a not too secret society.
13. Ferrars, first baron (1755–1811). Beaumarchais misreported his rank; the baron was in the army not the navy and he was a captain not an admiral, at only 20 years of age! But he had openly declared that he would oppose any measures of the court with regard to the American patriots.
14. Arthur Lee (1740–92).
15. 'Junius' was the pen name of the anonymous writer of a series of letters (1769–72) attacking the ministries of George III.
16. Beaumarchais, *Letters*.
17. La Maitre, *Beaumarchais*, pp.177–78.
18. King Joseph I (reigned 1750–77).
19. The Second Continental Congress had convened at Philadelphia on May 10, 1775. It established the Continental Army.

III

1. Beaumarchais, *Letters*.
2. Although Beaumarchais also admired and envied the more democratic British political system.
3. Choiseul, Duc de (1719–1785).
4. The 'Peace of Paris' was a treaty of 1763, signed by Britain, France and Spain, in which the victorious British made excessive demands on the defeated countries.
5. Turgot, Anne-Robert Jacques (1727–81). Controller of Finances 1774–76. His attempt to abolish feudal privilege incurred the hostility of the aristocracy.
6. J.R. Alden, *American Revolution*, p.180.
7. Few of Vergennes's letters to Beaumarchais survive.
8. The French ambassador to the Court of St James, the Comte de Guines.
9. Vergennes, *Correspondence*.
10. Beaumarchais, *Letters*.
11. *Ibid.*
12. *Ibid.*
13. Laureguais, Louis Leon Félicité, Comte, later Duc de (1733–1824). He was exiled five times. A friend and protector of men of letters and scientists.
14. Beaumarchais, *Letters*.
15. *Ibid.*
16. *Ibid.*
17. Rochford, Nassau van Zuylestein, 4th Earl. The first English-born son of an ennobled Dutch family.
18. North, Sir Frederick (1732–1792). Known as 'Lord' North until the death of his father in 1790, when he became the Second Earl of Guildford. As Prime Minister from 1770–82, he has been held responsible for the loss of the American colonies.

IV

1. Beaumarchais was asked to submit a plan to Vergennes some time in May 1776.
2. Montesquieu (1689–1755). French political philosopher. His work had a profound influence upon political thought in Europe and America.
3. King Louis XIV (1638–1715). His various attempts to wage wars throughout his reign ultimately failed.
4. Doniél, Henri. Author, writing between 1884–92.
5. Stormont, David Murray, Viscount (1727–1796).
6. Beaumarchais, *Letters*.
7. Maurepas, Jean-Fredéric, Comte de (1701–81). Chief Minister.

V

1. Kalb, Johan (1721–1780). Known as 'Baron de Kalb' in America.
2. Achard de Bonvouloir, Julien (1749–83). Of an ancient family of the *Dauphine*.
3. The French Cape is on the northern coast of the island of Hispaniola, now divided politically into Haiti and Dominica.
4. Canada remained loyal to George III, even though it was then predominantly French in population.
5. Franklin, Benjamin (1706–1790).
6. Adams, John (1735–1826).
7. Deane, Silas (1737–1789).
8. Boyd, Julian. Writing in the *William & Mary Quarterly*, XVI, (1959).

VI

1. The Farmers-General (*Fermiers Generaux*) was a privileged group, the summit of the financial hierarchy, that was allowed to collect certain taxes on behalf of the Crown. Constituted in 1726, the number of members varied between 40–80 during the eighteenth century, with each member personally chosen by the king.
2. *Moidores*. A former Portuguese gold coin, from *moeda de ouro*. Why Americans should have put their trust in this money is hard to understand, for the Portuguese were a strong ally of Great Britain.
3. *Livres*. A unit of money, formerly equal to one pound of silver. The *livre tournois* (of Tours) was worth about 19 cents or 9.4d when replaced in 1795 by the franc. In round figures, during the period of the American Revolution, 25 *livres* made a British pound.
4. The *livre* was divided into 20 *sous* of 12 *deniers* each.
5. *Quintals*. A unit of weight that was roughly equal to 100 pounds.
6. San Domingo, more properly 'Santo Domingo,' on the southern coast of Hispaniola.
7. Germain, George Sackville, Lord (1716–1785).
8. 'Navigation Acts'—acts of Parliament dating back to 1381, attempting to allow English ships alone the right to carry goods from and to England and its colonies.
9. Shelbourne, William, Earl of (1737–1805).

VII

1. Duchess of Kingston, née Elizabeth Chudleigh (1720–1788).
2. The Viceroyalty of Ireland dates back to medieval times.
3. Spying at Versailles was a popular pastime among courtiers with too much time on their hands.
4. Pliarne & Penet. Merchants that shared one company.
5. Duflos, Claude Augustin (1701–1785). An engraver.
6. The Dutch were, at this time, the bankers and traders of continental Europe. They had no political interest in the idea of revolution, their only interest being to profit by the breaking of the British 'Navigation Acts' and to sell supplies to belligerent countries. (Benis, *Diplomatic History of the U.S.*).
7. German mercenaries, but incorrectly known as 'Hessians,' perhaps because three successive commander-in-chiefs were Hessians. They quickly acquired a reputation for cruelty.
8. King's Guard. Not to be confused with the King's Regiment of Foot, which was raised in New York.
9. Why the court hearing should take place away from Paris is uncertain.
10. Miromésnil, Armand Thomas (1723–1796).
11. When house-to-house fighting failed to dislodge the militia, it was decided to set fire to Charlestown, Massachusetts (17 June 1775).
12. The colony had already raised six provincial regiments.
13. Vergennes, *Correspondence*.
14. The man remains unknown.
15. Vergennes, *Correspondence*.
16. Spain's objection to the American Revolution was that an independent America would push into her possessions in Louisiana and Mexico, and dangerous ideas of independence would spread to her other colonies.
17. Fox, Charles James (1749–1806). Third son of the first Lord Holland.
18. Brest, in Brittany, was the chief naval station, planned by Richelieu in 1631 and fortified by Vauban.
19. Lee, General Charles (1731–1782).
20. Washington, General George (1732–1799).
21. This port no longer exists.
22. The 'Confiscations Act' allowed the British government in America to seize the property of seditious persons by way of a penalty.
23. The normal British regiment/battalion had 10 companies, eight of which were called 'battalion companies,' and two of which were 'flank companies,' these latter made up of the best soldiers in the battalion.
24. Arnold, Benedict. General and traitor (1741–1801).
25. Montgomery, Richard. Continental general (1738–1775).
26. Carleton, Guy. British general (1724–1808).
27. Howe, Richard, Viscount (1726–1799).
28. Howe, Sir William (1729–1814).
29. Carlisle, Frederick Howard, 5th Earl of (1737–1788).
30. Grantham, Lord (1695–1770).
31. Manchester, George Montagu, 4th Duke of (1737–1788).
32. Chatham, former royal naval dockyard on the River Medway.
33. Sweden was in conflict with Russia, and the British had at that time a treaty with the Russians, whereby each would come to the aid of the other.

VIII

1. Montaudoin is not sufficiently important to be recorded.
2. Grimaldi, Spanish foreign minister, a Marquess.
3. Which suggests that he distrusted Beaumarchais's mercantile abilities.
4. Castle William was blown up at 9pm on 17 March 1776, by the 64th regiment of the British army. The convoy remained in Nantasket Roads, five miles south of the city, before setting sail for Halifax rather than New York, as the Americans had expected.
5. Yet the army that besieged the British was, perhaps, almost in a worse case. By January 1776, only 8,212 of the 20,370 men authorized by Congress to be enlisted were in place, and only 5,582 of them were present and fit for duty.
6. Lee had been detached from the Siege of Boston in January 1776 and directed to raise volunteers in Connecticut for the defence of New York. He arrived there on 4 February, having been delayed by problems with gout.
7. Dartmouth, William Legge, 2nd Earl of (1731–1801).
8. Antigua, one of the Leeward Islands.
9. The 'King's Inner Council' was a private council of the king's, but not composed of the same people who made up his more political 'Privy Council.'
10. Ellis, George, Chevalier (1753–1815).
11. Barré, Colonel, Isaac (1726–1802).
12. Burke, Edmund (1729–1797).
13. Sandwich, John Montagu, 4th Earl of (1718–1792).
14. The British, though, had taken three ships, three brigs and eight smaller craft, along with 48 cannon and 25 mortars.
15. Hopkins, Ezekial (1718–1802). First commander-in-chief of the Continental Navy, from 22 December 1775.
16. Turgot, previously a successful Intendant, was now swiftly incurring the enmity of the reactionaries at Versailles.
17. The Salon Guemenee was one of the most politicized of Parisian gatherings.
18. Breteuil, Louis August le Tounelier, Baron de (1730–1807).
19. The Comte de Cligny appears not to have taken up this role.

IX

1. Many black servants were imported from the French colonies.
2. Du Vergier, of a noble house in Brittany.
3. Maurepas (1701–1781).
4. Martinique, in the Windward Isle of the Lesser Antilles.
5. Levis's memoirs do not match those of St Simon in an earlier reign.
6. Malesherbes, Lamoignon de. A friend of the French philosophers.
7. Germaine, Claude Louis, Comte de (1707–1778).
8. Miron probably lived in the same house.
9. Barbeu-Dubourg, Dr Jaques (1709–79).
10. Bancroft, Edward (1744–1820).
11. Chaumont, Jaques-Donatien, Comte Le Ray de (1725–1803).

X

1. Presumably Arthur Lee.
2. Lee again.
3. Wentworth, Paul (d. 1793). A double spy who was motivated by a genuine belief that many of the American 'patriots' were activated by the wrong incentives.
4. Gerard, a clerk.
5. Blaye was a minor royal arsenal.
6. The royal armouries were created in 1690 for the *Compagnie des Indes*. They were taken over by the government in 1769.
7. The engraving of the royal arms on French military ware was to separate them from their original owners (see above).
8. The Keeper of the Seals had a different function to the 'Keeper of the Seal' in England. In France he was authorised to protect secret documents.
9. The Scotsman, John Law, founded the first bank in France in 1716. But since his scheme for the development of Louisiana a year later had resulted in widespread ruin, financial speculation was still distrusted in France.
10. Carmichael, William, (d. 1795). An American agent previously based in Holland.
11. Tronson de Coudray, Philippe (1738–1777).
12. It is not known how many people eventually worked for Beaumarchais, but all of them must have been committed to secrecy.

XI

1. Francy, J.B. Theveneau de. Beaumarchais's right-hand man.
2. Beaumarchais, *Letters*.
3. Gribauval, Jean Baptiste de (1715–1789). French general, and a great name in artillery development.
4. *Courrier de l'Europe*. Beaumarchais was heavily involved in its production.
5. Printed matter, on entry into France, was invariably read and censored at the point of ingress.
6. Swinton. The name is most likely a coincidence; there is no evidence to show that Swinton the publisher acted as a spy.
7. Including his secret communications.
8. Pullecourt, Baron. Chief of Paris Police (1774–?)
9. Presumably because the count was in the confidence of his distinguished guest.
10. Penet. Presumably still acting in concert with his partner.
11. Nantucket, an island off southeast Massachusetts.
12. Ticonderoga, a fort constructed by the French; it served as an outpost for Fort St Frederick (Crownpoint) in New York State.
13. Admiral Howe furnished naval support for the New York campaign.
14. The *English Gazette* was not primarily a political journal, but one that often spoke for the government.
15. Monthieu, an armaments manufacturer.
16. Aranda, Pedro, Comte de (1718–1799). Spanish Prime Minister from 1766.

XII

1. 29–30 August 1776.
2. There is no proof of the identity of this correspondent, but the detail about the press-gangs was correct. This manner of forcing unfortunate civilians to serve in the armed forces would last until the next century.
3. Lorge, Duc de. The dukedom founded by a Marshal of France—Guy Aldonse de Durfort.
4. Was Vergennes providing Beaumarchais's ship with an armed escort, or was Beaumarchais taking advantage of the safety of a fleet heading for the Caribbean?
5. Again, the correspondent is unknown.
6. From his days of espionage there, presumably.
7. Le Noir, Jean Charles Pierre (1732–1897).
8. Unknown.
9. His identity is unknown, but he appears to have been an independent supplier of ships.
10. General Howe was very dissatisfied with the lack of backing from London, and by the government's inaction.
11. Throughout his career, Beaumarchais invested money outside France, both in London and Amsterdam.
12. Lorient, a port on the Bay of Biscay, in Brittany. Created as a port for the *Compagnie des Indes* in 1666, hence the name.
13. De Coudray's brother Alexandre was Queen Marie-Antoinette's avocat, who had also tutored The Comte d'Artois in the arts of war. Having been technical adviser to several secretaries of war, the whole family was well placed to make trouble for Beaumarchais at Versailles.

XIII

1. Barberini, of the Barbarins, Counts of Reignac.
2. Flessinges is possibly Vlissingen in the SW Netherlands.
3. Hopkins. Possibly related to Ezekial, or even one of his sons.
4. *Improbo labore*—literally, 'with persistent labour.'
5. Chevre was an old associate of d'Éon's who passed easily between England and France.
6. It is not known how many agents were directly employed by Beaumarchais throughout the French West Indies.
7. Chinon is in NW Central France.
8. Frenaye was obviously an important person within the department.
9. De Coudray ignored the fact that Beaumarchais could easily prove himself, through his long correspondence, as being the (French) originator of the scheme, and therefore their true benefactor.
10. Robin, Monsieur. Through his dealings with the various ministries, Beaumarchais always ensured that he kept in touch with his own contacts, kept apart from his official connections.
11. Taboureau, as a servant of Turgot, would have been distrustful of the scheme.
12. See Chapter XIV, note 6.
13. Linguet, Simon Nicolas Henri (1736–1824). Advocate.

XIV

1. Sandwich was notorious for being both corrupt and incompetent, and the sponsorship of such an article is typical of the way he managed political affairs.
2. Having earlier offended King Louis XV and been thrown out of office.
3. At least by his own account (Beaumarchais, *Letters*).
4. The *Westminster Gazette* was a parliamentary periodical.
5. Paine, Thomas (1737–1809). Revolutionary writer.
6. 'Schmitz'? If he is Smith, he could be Lord Germain's secretary.
7. Floridablanca. Took over from Grimaldi in 1777.
8. Ossun, French ambassador to Spain.
9. *Punctum vitae*—literally, 'a portion of life.'
10. In which Beaumarchais read the Spanish position correctly. In a memorandum dated 17 October 1777 Floridablanca reviewed the reasons why Spain opposed open war against Britain: (a) Charles III did not wish to appear to be dominated by his nephew Louis XVI; (b) A peaceful settlement had just been reached with Portugal and war with Britain would overturn that; (c) Spain's vast holdings in the New World would be jeopardized; (d) *The Spanish gentry liked England and were generally antipathetic to the French!*
11. As today, most embassies around the world employed men like Parker Forth as semi-professional spies.
12. Mansfield, David Murray, 7th Earl of (1727–1796).
13. Painboeuf, on the NW coast of France

XV

1. Unspecified.
2. Back in the U.S. the Secret Committee had become the Committee of Commerce; Tom Paine had become private secretary to the Committee of Foreign Affairs, formerly the Committee of Secret Correspondence, and this was the body that directed American diplomacy.
3. *The Marriage of Figaro* would be completed in 1778.
4. Hodge, William Junior. American privateers took about 600 British vessels during the years 1775–83. Prize money was estimated at $18,000,000.
5. Vaillant was obviously Beaumarchais's principle private secretary.
6. Beaumarchais was marginally involved with privateering, particularly in his involvement with Bermuda.
7. Vergennes, *Correspondence*.
8. D'Ostalis of Dunkirk was a shipping agent.
9. De Bonill, Martinique (the island had been French from 1635).
10. General Howe was waiting for the reinforcements he had requested from Britain.
11. Lovell, James (1737–1814). 'As … interpreter he combined a cold perfection in speaking the language with a distaste for the people and customs.' (Lynn Montross, *The Reluctant Rebels*).
12. Morris, Robert (1734–1806). The biggest contracts usually went to his company, Willing & Morris.
13. Chevalier bought the boat at an auction in Rochefort.
14. Throughout 1777 armed actions in the south were limited; the only exception being an attack by Indians on Fort Henry at Wheeling, West Virginia in September.

XVI

1. Presumably on their way to the Gulf of Mexico (see below).
2. There is no record of action in the Gulf at this period. Admiral Howe was still furnishing naval support for the campaign in New York.
3. Samuel Johnson (1709–84). Beaumarchais incorrectly identifies the source of Franklin's grief, since Johnson was still alive then. The relationship was often difficult, for although Johnson set a high value upon the friendship of a few Americans, particularly Franklin, he had a low opinion of Americans generally, seeing them as 'rascals, robbers and pirates.'
4. In 1775 the British had 131 ships of the line and 139 craft of other classes. By 1783 this total had swelled to 468, of which about 100 were committed to America. In quality, however, the British navy was in a very bad state, some little more than 'floating coffins.' (Rankin, *The American Revolution*).
5. Skenesboro, New York State, now Whitehall.
6. Johnson, Sir John (1742–1830). Loyalist leader.
7. Burgoyne, General John (1722–1792).
8. Arnold, Benedict (1741–1801). Continental general and traitor.
9. Morris, Robert. On 30 January 1776, he had also been appointed to the other Secret Committee. He was a practical man of business experienced in foreign trade, but his manipulation of the committee (to his financial benefit) led to an outcry.
10. Through Stormont's efficient net of informers, he now had knowledge (if not certain proof) of the covert operations, and he repeatedly lodged objections.
11. Captain Fantrell served several weeks in gaol.
12. Grand, Monsieur. A business rival of Beaumarchais.
13. Berard Brothers, shipping agents.
14. Dorsius, John. It is clear that Beaumarchais was not dealing directly with this agent.
15. Langton of Boston. Dealing directly with Beaumarchais. He was possibly John Langdon of New Hampshire, a patriot merchant.
16. Temple, Richard Grenville, 2nd Earl Temple (1711–1779).
17. Marlborough, 4th Duke of (1739–1817).
18. Queen Charlotte (1744–1818).
19. Sayer, James. Son of a printmaker.
20. Frederick II, King of Prussia (1712–1786). It was rather that Frederick had no desire for war with Britain (who had given him an annual subsidy in the last conflict). But his wish to injure Britain led to the curious idea that he had formed a sentimental friendship for the Americans.
21. He may even have been Joseph Hazen, a relative of Moses Hazen, a Continental officer.

XVII

1. Beaumarchais, *Letters*.
2. Almost 30,000 German mercenaries fought against the Americans, taking part in every major campaign north of the Floridas. They were well disciplined in the tradition of Frederick the Great, but quickly gained a reputation for cruelty and abuse of civilians.
3. There is no recorded battle at Augusta, Georgia, at this period.
4. Nicholson, Captain. A murky figure, of whom nothing more is known.
5. Eden, William. First Baron Aukland (1744–1814).
6. Although Vergennes would later use it to accelerate the French Alliance with the U.S. by pointing out to the kings of France and Spain that the Americans might now make peace

with Great Britain. Louis XVI consented to the French-American treaty the day after
Wentworth met Franklin.

7. Prince Ferdinand of Prussia, Duke of Brunswick-Luneburg (1721–1792).
8. Rutledge, John (1739–1800).
9. 'Battle of Pennsylvania,' non-recorded at this period.
10. A shallop, formerly a two-masted gaff-rigged vessel, was used primarily in shallow waters.

XVIII

1. A distant relation of Sir William Pulteney.
2. Secretary of State for the American Colonies from November 1775 until the end of the war,
   Germain has been charged with most of the British errors of strategy during the Revolution.
3. Clinton, Sir Henry. British commander-in-chief from 1778–82.
4. Necker, Jacques, Baron (1732–1804). Swiss born.
5. He had been visiting his brother, presumably in some capacity as a merchant.
6. This treaty of 1778 gave the U.S. a free hand to conquer Canada and Bermuda, while
   France was to take the British West Indies.
7. Provence, Comte de (1755–1824). Later Louis XVIII.
8. When informed that Howe had taken Philadelphia, Benjamin Franklin replied, 'No,
   Philadelphia has taken Howe,' and it is true that occupation of the Quaker City
   weakened Howe's army.

XIX

1. Laurens, Henry (1724–1792). Congressional President.
2. Lee brothers. Richard Henry (1732–1794), congressman; Francis Lightfoot Lee
   (1734–1797), congressman; Charles (1758–1815), naval officer; William (1739–1795),
   merchant, the most troublesome of the family, with the exception of Arthur.
3. Estaing, Charles, Comte d' (1729–1994).
4. Gerard, Conrad Alexandre (1729–1790).
5. Chevalier, a merchant at Rochefort, was one of Beaumarchais's most important agents.
6. Livingston, Robert R. (1746–1813). An important committeeman.
7. A brilliant commercial strategy from which Beaumarchais at last made an immense
   profit.
8. Or had been asked to provide since America was now short of these goods.

XX

1. In that his position would be clear.
2. Pulaski, Casimir (c.1748–1799).
3. La Fayette, Marquis d' (1757–1834).
4. A member of the minor nobility.
5. Steuben, Friedrich von (or de) (1730–1794).
6. 'Gasket'—a piece of line used as a sail stop, in the sense of a rope lashing a furled sail.
7. Keppel, Viscount, Admiral (1725–1786).
8. John Adams (1735–1826). Having been a member of Congress, Adams had been chosen
   to succeed Deane on 28 November 1777. Unlike Franklin, he was very unhappy with the
   post, since he did not like the French or their country.

9. Jay, John (1745–1829).
10. Beaumarchais was not alone in being ignored by Congress. Oliver Pollock (1737–1823), a patriot agent, had to mortgage his own property to raise the funds to furnish vital supplies to the continental army; but after the war, Congress was so slow in reimbursing him that he spent 18 months in custody for failure to pay his creditors.
11. Adams, Samuel (1722–1803). Political agitator.
12. There is no record of the nature of this attempt.
13. Presumably he also spoke for his fellow tax-farmers.

XXI

1. An informal hearing at which the king acts as judge.
2. Prize money was awarded to the men who captured a ship in accordance with a scale based on rank.
3. Floridablanca, the Spanish Prime Minister, hoped to use Spain's neutrality as a means of winning certain diplomatic goals.
4. Montmorin, French ambassador to Spain.
5. Byron, John (1723–1786). British admiral, 'Foul-Weather Jack.'
6. Almadorar, Spanish ambassador to France.
7. Spain allied herself with France by the Convention of Aranjuez on 12 April 1779; but the Spanish navy at this time made a bad showing. A French officer reported that 'they can neither overtake an enemy nor escape from one.' (*American Heritage Book of the Revolution*).
8. Admiral Byron withdrew from an effort to relieve Grenada, in a drawn battle on 6 July 1779.
9. Fort Royal, Martinique.
10. The Council of Dispatches was a diplomatic board.
11. The St James's Cabinet was an inner circle of George III's political dependents.
12. Here, Beaumarchais deliberately singles out King George III.
13. He doesn't go so far as to name him, but he had the choice of many.

XXII

1. Praslin, Cesar Gabriel, Duc de (1712–1785).
2. 'The Library' was a Censorship department.
3. *North Briton*—a periodical founded by the radical John Wilkes and the poet Charles Churchill (1731–64) as an organ of opposition.
4. The count must have meant that the Americans would have objected to him as an Anglo-Irish aristocrat. It was not unusual for British men to volunteer for action with foreign armies, usually involving some conflict of interest.
5. Nivernais, Louis Jules Mancini-Mazarini, Duc de (1716–98). Minister of State in Necker's cabinet of 1787.
6. Or, more particularly, to explain away the many failures of his fleet in the encounters along the Atlantic coast of North America and in the West Indies.
7. Antonia Fraser, *Marie-Antoinette*.
8. The old capital of Virginia.
9. Mothe-Piquet, Toussaint-Guillaume, Comte de (1720–1791). Admiral.
10. Grasse, Frederick-Joseph-Paul, Comte de Grasse-Tully (1722–1788).
11. Luzerne, Chevalier Anne-Cesar de la (1741–91).

XXIII

1. William Lee's formal appointment had, in fact, been sent to Thomas Morris, who was by then making such a killing in prizes at Nantes, that he withheld the document.
2. He might possibly have extended his accusations to other members of the Secret Committee of Congress, for not only Willings and Morris awarded their companies with large contracts. Relatives and friends of Silas Deane, John Alsop, William Livingston and Francis Lewis also prospered.
3. The impecunious pamphleteer had been rewarded with this post in order to give him a regular means of support. He had held the post since April 1777.
4. There is some confusion of identities here. Gerard, the first French ambassador to the U.S. remained in this post until October 1779, yet Francy had spoken of his successor earlier, and La Luzerne did not present his credentials until 4 November 1779.
5. Though public opinion would turn against Robert Morris, and he was defeated in the polls of November 1779.
6. Made so over the objections of many. The finances of the new republic were in a state of collapse, and Morris's office had been established to salvage what then appeared to be a total loss.
7. Which even in America were now regarded as worthless, with the collapse of continental currency. Beaumarchais must have been aware of this.
8. The *Royal Gazette* was a periodical with court associations.
9. Where Jay would remain for two years.
10. *Rivington's Gazette* was named for its publisher.
11. Barclay, American consul.
12. Jefferson, Thomas (1743–1826).

XXIV

1. Beaux & Taxier, Bordeaux. Merchant adventurers.
2. Then Secretary of Foreign Affairs. A post he would hold until 1790.
3. Commercial probity is one of the main themes in most of Beaumarchais's early dramas.
4. Named after John Baskerville (1706-1775). English printer.
5. Perrier Brothers, whose family owned the spring, the *Source Perrier* at Vergeze.
6. Mirabeau, Comte de (1749–91). Revolutionary politician.
7. Therese was related to Jean-Baptiste, Count Willmaulaz, a celebrated mariner.
8. Salieri, Antonio (1750–1825). Italian composer and conductor.
9. Despite the opposition of the Austrian court censors.
10. Shays, Daniel (1747?–1825).
11. Calonne, Charles Alexandre, Comte de (1734–1802). His 'reforms' irredeemably condemned the 'Old Regime.'
12. 'Assembly of Notables'—that is of 'distinguished persons.'
13. At 47 rue de Vielle du Temple. It is now a shop, though one can still perceive its elegant eighteenth-century outlines.
14. In what is now the district of the Marais. Named after the monastery of the '*Blancs Manteiux*;' their white habits.
15. A person who pretends to be pious.
16. The royal family's flight to Varennes in 1791 came too late to save them, and once King Louis was forcibly detained he knew that he was lost.
17. Paine, Thomas (1737–1809). Revolutionary writer.

18. Manuel, Louis Pierre (1751–93). Revolutionary, and a writer of mediocre talent. Accused of treachery, he was arrested in August 1793, and was the oldest of the Communards to be guillotined.

XXV

1. That is, his house had been officially closed up, leaving his property intact but now the possession of the State, pending a further inquiry. Madame Beaumarchais, his daughter and sister-in-law, were forced to seek shelter elsewhere.
2. The longest of the Revolutionary assemblies, from 1792–1795.
3. It was not easy to escape from Paris since the city was still largely walled at this period.
4. This was presumably Pierre Manuel.
5. Robespierre, Maximilien (1758–94).
6. In which Beaumarchais muses upon the great changes in his life.
7. Hamilton, Alexander (1757?–1804).
8. Morris, Gouverneur (1752–1816).
9. Why was Grand a banker for the U.S. (?)

XXVI

1. This body of five men would remain in power from 1795 until overthrown by Napoleon in 1799.
2. Pétion de Villeneuve was a lawyer and revolutionary advocate.
3. 'Assignats'—currency notes, backed not by specie but by the financial value of the new state lands.
4. 'Mandat'—money order.
5. Thrale, Hester Lynch (1741–1821). Writer, and friend of Dr Johnson.
6. Hostilities had broken out between America and Britain in 1797.
7. Talleyrand-Perigord, Charles Maurice de (1754–1838).
8. By almost every biographer.
9. Lemaitre, Georges. Author, citing earlier writers.
10. Alden, J.R., *The American Revolution*.
11. Bancroft may even have invented the 'drop' system used by modern espionage agents.

Bibliography

Adams, J.T. (ed.), *Dictionary of American History*, (5 vols), New York, (1942)

Adams, J.T. (ed.), *Atlas of American History*, (5 vols), New York, (1943)

Alden, John Richard, *The American Revolution*, New York, (1954)

American Heritage Publishing Co., Inc., *The American Heritage Book of the Revolution*, New York, (1958)

American Philosophical Society of Philadelphia, *Manuscripts of Arthur Lee*, (5 vols), Philadelphia, (1906–08)

Auger, Helen, *The Secret War of Independence*, New York, (1955)

Balch, Thomas, *The French in America during the War of Independence*, Philadelphia, (1891)

Bemis, Samuel Flagg (ed.), 'British Secret Service, and the French-American Alliance', *American Historical Review*, XXIX (1923–24), pp.474–95

Boyd, Julian P., *The William & Mary Quarterly*, *William and Mary College*, Vol. VXI, (1959)

Corwin, E.S., *French Policy and the American Alliance of 1778*, Princeton, (1916)

Dewey, Davis Rich, *Financial History of the United States*, New York, (1931)

Dictionary of National Biography, London (1885–1901)

Doniol, Henry, *Histoire de la participation de la France a l'establissement des Etats-Unis d'Amerique*, Paris (1884–92)

Einstein, Lewis, *Divided Loyalties: Americans in England during the War of Independence*, Boston, (1933)

Fay, Bernard, *The Revolutionary Spirit in France and America … at the End of the Eighteenth Century*, New York, (1927)

Fraser, Antonia, *Marie Antoinette, the Journey*, Weidenfeld and Nicholson, London, (2001)

Lasseray, Andre, *Les Francais sous les trois etoiles 1775–1783*, (2 vols), Paris, (1935)

Lemaitre, Georges, *Beaumarchais*, Paris, (1920)

Lokke, Carl L., *France and the Colonial Question*, New York, (1932)

Montross, Lynn, *The Reluctant Rebels*, New York, (1950)

Perkins, James B., *France in the American Revolution*, Boston, (1911)

Rankin, Hugh F., *The American Revolution*, New York, (1964)

Sachse, William L., *The Colonial American in Britain*, Madison, Wis., (1956)

Sawyer, Charles W., *Firearms in American History, 1600–1800*, Boston, (1910)

Wallace, Willard M., *Appeal to Arms: A Military History of the American Revolution*, New York, (1951)

Warner, Jessica, *John The Painter*, New York, (2004)

Index